BLOOMSBURY CURRICULUM BASICS

Teaching Primary Geography

Other titles in the Bloomsbury Curriculum Basics series:

BLOOMSBURY CURRICULUM BASICS

Teaching Primary Geography

By
Stephen Scoffham and Paula Owens

BLOOMSBURY EDUCATION

LONDON OXFORD NEW YORK NEW DELHI SYDNEY

BLOOMSBURY EDUCATION
Bloomsbury Publishing Plc
50 Bedford Square, London, WC1B 3DP, UK
29 Earlsfort Terrace, Dublin 2, Ireland

First published in Great Britain, 2017 by Bloomsbury Publishing Plc

This edition published in Great Britain, 2024 by Bloomsbury Publishing Plc

Quotations from National Curriculum documents used in this publication are approved under an
Open Government Licence v3.0: www.nationalarchives.gov.uk/doc/open-government-licence/version/3/

A catalogue record for this book is available from the British Library

ISBN: PB: 978-1-8019-9-3982; ePDF: 978-1-8019-9401-9; ePub: 978-1-8019-9-3999

2 4 6 8 10 9 7 5 3 1 (paperback)

Text design by Marcus Duck

Typeset by Newgen KnowledgeWorks Pvt. Ltd., Chennai, India
Printed and bound in the UK by CPI Group (UK) Ltd., Croydon, CR0 4YY

To find out more about our authors and books visit www.bloomsbury.com
and sign up for our newsletters

Contents

Introduction

National Curriculum geography

The stated purpose of the geography National Curriculum is to 'inspire in pupils a curiosity and fascination about the world and its people that will remain with them for the rest of their lives' (DfE, 2013, p. 1). The programme of study outlines the subject content for Key Stage 1 and Key Stage 2 under four headings:

- locational knowledge
- place knowledge
- human and physical geography
- geographical skills and fieldwork.

The subject content is not differentiated by year group and there is no guidance on progression, except to state what should be taught within each key stage. There is a single attainment target relating to matters, skills and processes.

The programmes of study have a strong focus on knowledge. Children are required to learn about the United Kingdom throughout the primary years and to develop their knowledge of major geographical features in other parts of the world. Seasonal and daily weather patterns are featured in Key Stage 1. Key lines of latitude and longitude are highlighted in Key Stage 2.

There are also clear specifications concerning place studies. In Key Stage 1, children are required to undertake studies of:

- a small area of the United Kingdom
- a small area in a contrasting non-European country.

In Key Stage 2, pupils are required to undertake studies of the human and physical geography of:

- a region of the United Kingdom
- a region in a European country
- a region within North or South America.

As regards skills, there are statements relating to reading and making simple maps at Key Stage 1. More-formal map-work activities are specified at Key Stage 2, including the use of Ordnance Survey (OS) maps and four- and six-figure grid references. Fieldwork and first-hand observation are identified as an element of the curriculum throughout the primary years.

The programme of study makes it clear that the curriculum aims to 'equip pupils with knowledge about diverse places, people, resources and natural and human environments, together with a deep understanding of the Earth's key physical and human processes' (DfE, 2013, p. 1). This suggests an integrative and holistic approach that draws on sustainability perspectives. Realising these requirements through creative and stimulating lessons forms the focus of this book.

About this book

This book provides both generalist and specialist teachers with the support that they need to teach geography in Key Stage 1 and Key Stage 2. It has two distinctive and defining elements:

- background knowledge and information outlining the potential of key geographical themes and topics
- lesson-plan ideas that explore how to teach these themes in lively and engaging ways.

The text is structured around the requirements of the latest version of the National Curriculum for England. By providing a succinct and accessible overview, it seeks to meet the needs of practitioners across the country and to provide a single reference point for informed and creative teaching.

How this book is organised

The introduction provides an overview of primary geography, identifying features of good practice, outlining the importance of geography as a subject and offering guidance on progression and assessment. This then leads into the main text, where the specific curriculum requirements are examined in detail through 30 areas of study. These are divided equally, with ten areas of study for Key Stage 1, lower Key Stage 2 and upper Key Stage 2 respectively.

At the start of each area of study, the relevant section from the National Curriculum for primary geography is quoted under the heading 'What does the curriculum say?'. These extracts are taken from the Department for Education's 'Geography programmes of study: key stages 1 and 2' (2013).

Each area of study then explores background knowledge, misconceptions and research, interesting facts and key questions. Following this, there are three lessons, offering a range of ideas for children of different ages and abilities. There then follows a final section containing further ideas and activities for fieldwork and investigation, along with cross-curricular links and themes, a paragraph on progression and assessment, and references to useful books and websites.

There are a number of points to highlight:

1. All the lessons begin with an enquiry question.
2. The lessons and areas of study are presented as a loose sequence but do not need to be followed in any particular order.
3. Wherever possible, map reading and other geographical skills are taught in context, although each section is foregrounded with some thinking and examples about the types of map skills that are appropriate for this phase.
4. Suggestions for fieldwork and practical enquiries are integrated throughout.
5. The opportunities to consider important aspects of the curriculum, such as values, sustainability and decolonisation, are highlighted in the themes at the end of each area of study.

It is worth noting that you can link different areas of study according to the needs of your school curriculum to form more-substantial units of work. This is entirely in line with the geography programme of study, which focuses on similarities and differences and supports comparisons. There are also plentiful opportunities to make meaningful links to other curriculum subjects. Not only is this intellectually valid, but it may also be a way of securing more time for geography in the face of competing demands.

Teaching National Curriculum geography requires teachers who are confident about what they are doing, experienced in communication and able to respond to new ideas. This book shows how to meet these requirements in ways that are appropriate for children in the middle years of childhood. If geography is to capture the imagination of the younger generation, it needs to be presented in ways that are creative and appealing. There is a wealth of material here that you can follow or adapt, according to your circumstances, which will not only develop children's knowledge and understanding but also fire their enthusiasm and interests, empowering their capacity as informed geographers.

Why geography matters

Geographical perspectives offer a uniquely powerful way of seeing the world. Since at least the time of the Ancient Greeks, geographers have attempted to put the local in a global context by writing down and recording their observations so that they can share them more widely. These endeavours have been motivated by a desire to understand and navigate the planet that is both our home and the source of the materials that we need in order to survive. Unless we can grasp how the world works and how we fit into it, we leave ourselves exposed to unnecessary uncertainty and risk. We also share spaces and places with others as we live our lives, making meaning as we go and leaving a mark on the world in various ways – through patterns of consumption, development, conservation or appreciation. Geography helps us to explore our identity and how we relate to others. It is a fundamental part of our psyche.

A rapidly changing world

Our Earth is changing rapidly – faster than at any other time in recorded history – and this is another reason why geography matters. Perhaps more than ever before, we are educating our children at a time when there is great uncertainty about what the future holds. However, geography is a subject with enduring purpose and a range of skills and knowledge, which both draws on and unites other disciplines. Through its contemporary relevance and synergy, geographers are particularly well placed to understand the holistic nature of the big issues of the day and their possible solutions. Unsurprisingly, UK students who study geography have a consistently high employment rate.

Learning about places

Geographers ask and explore questions about place. Today, even Earth's wildest places are affected by human influences, and this impact needs mediation in order to be positive and sustainable. The built environment is full of examples of creative endeavour. The questions that stimulate creative thinking about places are simple and fundamental: Where exactly is this place? What characterises it? What are its links to other places? How is it changing? How can we protect it or improve it now and in the future? How can I contribute? These and other similar questions have occupied geographers' minds for centuries and are best addressed by creative, collaborative thought and action. The future of every place on this planet is therefore the central concern of geography education.

Shared values

Geography education can help to show children how they can contribute to building a better world – a world in which cooperation, fairness, sensitivity and kindness to each other and the environments that sustain us become our guiding values. In *Sustainability Education: A Classroom Guide* (2022), Scoffham and Rawlinson argue that the overwhelming evidence of damaging ecological, environmental and social stresses make this an agenda that simply cannot be ignored. Establishing shared human values is an essential base on which to support, build and sustain a preferred future that will enable us to live within planetary limits.

Geographical thinking

When planning geography lessons, it is important to acknowledge the deeper structure of geography and its distinctive character as a discipline. Disciplinary knowledge is described by Ofsted (2023) as 'the knowledge of how geographical knowledge is formed, debated and contested' and is identified as one of the weaker areas of curriculum development. Teaching children to 'think like a geographer' as they question and explain the world can be better built into planning through an understanding of key geographical concepts as, when these underpin the geography curriculum, it has a greater sense of purpose.

Four concepts that stand out as fundamental to geographical thinking are place, environment, space and scale:

- place – a dynamic space given meaning and shaped by human and physical processes
- environment – the living and non-living world around us, and conditions arising from their interactions
- space – location and relationships
- scale – changes in perspective from the local to the global.

These concepts overlap. Place is essentially a human construct – a space or setting given meaning – while environment reflects the systemic interplay of the living and physical world. Both exist at different scales: we might identify a special place in our garden, village, town, city or region, for example.

Using these basic concepts to pose questions helps to access geographical thinking and uncovers other secondary concepts. For example, asking what places are like delves into thinking about diversity (and biodiversity). Enquiring about what happens in a place introduces thinking about human and physical processes and systems. Meanwhile, posing questions about how and why places are changing introduces the concept of time. Exploring concepts such as these and the connections between them is an essentially geographical endeavour.

Teachers can construct lessons that engage children with the modes of thinking that geographers themselves employ by linking key concepts to enquiry questions (see **Figure 1**). A conceptual approach also helps to indicate ways in which any individual topic can be extended and developed. Recognising the potential in children's own questions draws them

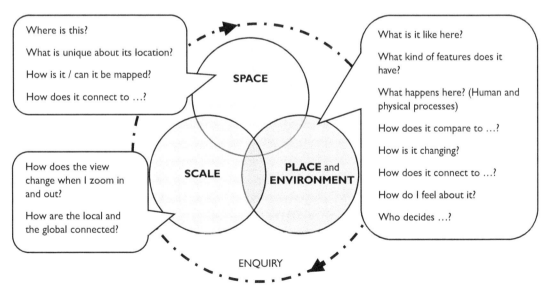

Figure 1: Place, environment, space and scale are concepts that stand at the heart of geography and that provide fundamental organising principles

into geography in ways that relate to their understanding and that they find meaningful and engaging.

Good practice in primary geography

If the purpose of geography is to introduce children to a lifelong conversation about being at home on planet Earth (Geographical Association, 2009), then it is a subject that needs not only to ignite fascination and foster passion but also to provide children with what Bonnett (2008) calls the twin pillars of modern geography: environmental and international knowledge. Good practice will ensure that children develop essential and relevant knowledge that is foregrounded by an enquiry approach, supplemented by geographical imagination, creativity and purpose, and safeguarded by the application of critical thinking skills. As Ofsted (2011) contends, children need to develop both core knowledge and a sense of place.

Teachers as curriculum-makers

Creative approaches to teaching geography could be seen as simply interpreting the prescribed curriculum in an imaginative way. However, in *Teaching Geography Creatively* (2017), Scoffham argues that a powerful and imaginative geography curriculum goes much further than this. In particular, it:

- blends core and personal knowledge, recognising how values affect the ways in which we use and change the world around us
- recognises that knowledge is constantly changing and needs to be continually reconstructed
- presents different narratives and ways of thinking about the world
- engages children with issues and questions that they themselves think are important and worthwhile
- acknowledges that learning involves spiritual and emotional as well as cognitive dimensions
- builds children's capacity to anticipate and respond to future challenges, both locally and globally
- addresses controversial issues and problems as part of a flexible contemporary curriculum
- respects the integrity of children and gives them a meaningful voice in structuring their learning according to their needs
- helps children to build their identity and see meaning in their lives as they find out about themselves and their surroundings
- places learning in the context of universal and inclusive values, in which children come to care about the world and its future.

Selecting curriculum content is a complex process. Theories of learning, philosophies of education, personal beliefs, and social and cultural values are all involved. Curriculum-making happens when teachers draw on their knowledge of geography, their knowledge of pupils and their understanding of the curriculum in order to devise meaningful learning experiences for the pupils whom they teach.

The Primary Geography Quality Mark (PGQM)

The Geographical Association has devised a self-evaluation framework to help subject leaders to develop strategies for improving geography teaching in their school. There are three levels of accreditation:

- The 'bronze' level recognises that lively and enjoyable geography is happening in the school.
- The 'silver' level recognises excellence across the school.
- The 'gold' level recognises excellence that is embedded and shared with the community beyond the school.

You may want to become involved with the Quality Mark, as it provides a flexible framework that supports curriculum innovation through a self-evaluation process designed to help subject leaders to develop strategies for improving the geography in their school (Owens, 2015). For further information, go to: https://geography.org.uk/quality-marks

Planning quality lessons

As you present the lessons outlined in this book, you may find that it helps you to be flexible if you keep a range of possibilities in mind. The following questions are offered as prompts to stimulate ideas. Have you:

- given the children a range of entry points that build on their previous learning and understanding?
- planned with assessment criteria in mind?
- used strategies and scaffolding to ensure all can access learning?
- thought about using games as a teaching device?
- considered opportunities for practical activities?
- thought about whether you are challenging rather than reinforcing stereotypes?
- taken note of any relevant research on children's misconceptions that may influence your teaching?
- made use of ICT to research information, record findings or analyse information?
- made links to other subjects where they overlap naturally?
- considered whether to make links at a range of scales, from the local to the global?

- taken advantage of the opportunities for presentations and classroom displays?
- given the children opportunities to respond creatively and use their own ideas to direct their studies?
- supplemented learning with appropriate story books and other media?
- checked the quality and date of teaching resources?
- explored the possibilities for fieldwork?
- asked children for their views about the content and learning?
- checked that you are balancing rigorous core geographical knowledge with personal feelings and interpretations of place?

Quality lessons can take many different forms. It is important to have the confidence to experiment and to test out new ways of working. Fieldwork and new technologies both have the potential to enthuse pupils and provide a sense of immediacy and relevance. Inspection reports note that a focus on problems and controversial issues often yields outstanding results. In its inspections, Ofsted looks for evidence of carefully planned strategies that are having a positive impact on the quality of teaching. Being aware of the features of good practice, building professional networks and finding out about current research are powerful ways in which to enhance your teaching.

Journals

At the time of writing, *Primary Geography* is the only journal that specifically focuses on primary geography teaching. Produced three times a year by the Geographical Association, it explores current developments, shares examples of good practice and alerts readers to new publications and projects.

Fieldwork

Exploration is the essential part of geography's heritage (Lambert and Owens, 2013). Fieldwork is a statutory part of the geography National Curriculum and should ideally be undertaken on a regular basis. The best practice regularly engages children with the outside world and develops skills in meaningful and current contexts. Geography fieldwork is distinguished from simply 'learning outside the classroom' by having the conceptual touchstones of place, environment, space and scale at the heart of enquiry and planning (see **Figure 2**).

Why do fieldwork?

A good deal of research testifies to the importance of going outside for both the mind and the body. First-hand experience touches us in ways that other learning does not, and is cemented into experience through strong emotional as well as cognitive connections. Real-world experiences are powerful and create lasting memories. Even just going into the

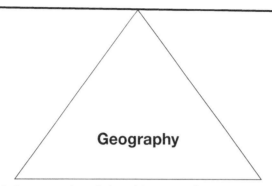

Core knowledge
Facts, location, names, vocabulary

Sense of place
Senses, emotions, values, opinions

Geography

Figure 2: Geography fieldwork balances core knowledge with a sense of place and gives it a spatial context

school grounds can offer children experiences that stimulate their sense of awe and wonder, whether it's through a glimpse of clouds, a spider's web or reflections in a puddle. Fieldwork also offers a reality check with the messy real world and challenges learning at every turn. Children need to manage risk, navigate real landscapes, use all their senses and gather data in the field, using a range of approaches and techniques. Many geographers argue that fieldwork is the crown jewel of geography and that it is best learned through the soles of your feet.

Health and safety

You will need to carry out a suitable risk assessment and ensure that any visits comply with health and safety policies, both in your school and according to national directives. It is good practice to engage pupils with a risk assessment before a visit and get them to write up their own assessment of risks and suitable actions to take. Use applications such as Google Maps to carry out a virtual risk assessment from the classroom, or even just use the photographs taken during your own risk assessment. Get children to write their report, identifying hazards and appropriate actions to take to stay safe.

Cross-curricular and whole-school dimensions

Geography has a central and, we would argue, crucial role in a broad and balanced curriculum. There are times when it makes sense to teach geography as a discrete subject, because ideas from other disciplines can dilute and obscure the thinking that stands at its core. On the other hand, involving other subjects can create synergies and draw attention to different perspectives, which can invigorate geography teaching. What is crucial is that, however geography is taught, whether alone or combined with other subjects, it retains its identity and rigour.

There are a number of different ways of combining geography with other subjects:

- **Hierarchical approach:** Here, one subject provides the main focus and other subjects offer support or enhancement. A good example would be a topic on volcanoes, in which information about eruptions from different times in the past provides additional information to enrich a study about volcanic processes and their impact on people, plants and creatures. In this instance, geography dominates and history has an ancillary role.
- **Theme-based approach:** Here, two or more subjects contribute equally in exploring a topic or theme. Work on the weather and seasons, for example, requires both a scientific and a geographical perspective. The key point here is that the combination of knowledge and skills from different disciplines yields deeper levels of interpretation and analysis.
- **Integrative approach:** In this model, a single focus or powerful learning experience prompts children to enhance their learning in various subject areas. Finding out about Shackleton's journey to the Antarctic, for example, may lead children to write their own accounts of what happened (English), learn more about the route and journey that he took (geography), investigate the design of the ship and the clothes worn by the team (design and technology), and calculate the quantities of food, the weight of the sledges and the number of dogs needed to pull them (mathematics). The focus is on discrete learning in a number of disparate areas.

We can think holistically and adopt cross-curricular approaches without losing the knowledge and understanding that stand at the heart of geography. Indeed, one of the defining features of geography is its interdisciplinary character – it bridges the sciences and humanities and brings them together in a unique combination. Recognising links and associations honours what are essentially geographical modes of thinking.

There is one area of learning where it seems particularly important to combine different subjects and perspectives. Questions to do with global learning, environment and sustainability can only really be understood in cross-curricular terms and/or whole-school dimensions. Global climate change, for example, raises geographical questions about the impact on different places, scientific questions about the processes involved and moral questions about our responsibility to other people and cultures. It challenges us to articulate our fundamental beliefs and to construct a vision of the future that draws on our understanding of the past.

Progression, differentiation and assessment

Progression

'A clearly mapped journey starting in the early years and developing through the curriculum is critical if pupils are to move towards becoming experts in the subject.' (Ofsted, 2021) Progression in geography can be evidenced in the increasingly complex array of information that children can remember and understand, the breadth and especially the depth of their knowledge and the extent of their understanding, especially through their ability to apply it and make synoptic connections.

As children begin to think geographically, their understanding of key concepts such as place, environment, space and scale will mature and develop. At the same time, children need to become increasingly proficient in using and applying geographical skills. Ofsted (2023) remarks in its subject inspection report that 'Procedural knowledge (the knowledge of how to use geographical skills) was rarely planned for in the same way as substantive knowledge (established facts about the world).' It is important to plan carefully when to teach particular aspects of procedural knowledge and consider when and how pupils will have the opportunity to practise and apply it.

Sequencing

Building a progression of geographical knowledge and understanding is complex, and requires careful thinking about prior knowledge to aid understanding within geographical topics, as well as between topics. We have given attention to thinking about how key aspects of knowledge might be introduced in this book to build conceptual understanding, and where there might be opportunities to revisit and consolidate knowledge. For example, in Key Stage 1, pupils need to learn about weather and seasons. It makes sense to learn about the components of weather first, ideally experiencing and recording this throughout the year and during the seasons, before formally introducing seasons and understanding how they are associated with particular types of weather.

In Key Stage 2, introducing climate zones early on builds on learning about weather and seasons and helps to explain later concepts of food, farming and trade. Learning about the water cycle links with this and introduces rivers and their dynamic roles, and it enables pupils to have the essential knowledge that they need to undertake a regional study of the Lake District. Revisiting concepts in ever-more-complex contexts helps pupils to think synoptically and make vital connections.

Breadth and depth

Progression has both breadth and depth, combining a range of experiences with increasing depth of understanding and application. Children's progression is not linear but is more like a spiral that allows for revisiting and consolidation. This is something that happens at different scales: children may make progress within a lesson, over the course of an area of study or over the course of a school year. As teachers, we support this process by listening, observing and intervening with appropriate feedback, so that we can help children to bridge the gaps in learning connections and stretch and strengthen those ones already made.

Assessment and differentiation

Effective planning pitches lessons appropriately to support all learners in making the progress of which they are capable. Standards of attainment can be used to gauge outcomes at strategic points within the curriculum in the primary years. The National Curriculum requirements are that pupils should be able to know, understand and apply the programmes of study at the end of each key stage. Working with a pathway of progression allows pitch and differentiation to happen; the latter may be in the form of additional targeted support or scaffolding. The key to understanding differentiation is through formative assessment, where you can gauge the next steps that a pupil needs in order to reach an identified target or outcome. Classrooms with strategies such as 'talk for learning' and peer- and self-assessment foster this approach best.

A progression framework

There are various progression frameworks that can be used to help you to plan and assess pupil knowledge, skills and understanding (see below). A progression framework can help to provide a structure for lesson planning and suggest opportunities for differentiation. It may also establish a baseline for reporting to parents on pupils' achievements.

Progression frameworks

The Ordnance Survey schools' mapping program, Digimap for Schools, has guidance about mapping progression that is very detailed and that supports progress from Year 1 to Year 6. Search for 'Digimap progression in mapping' or go to:

https://digimapforschools.edina.ac.uk/learning-resources/resource/progression-mapping.html

Guidance on progression in fieldwork is provided in a *Primary Geography* article by Julia Tanner. This includes a helpful audit sheet that identifies fieldwork possibilities on your doorstep: https://portal.geography.org.uk/downloads/journals/PG_SPR_2021_TANNER.pdf

---

Resources

There are a number of resources that are essential in order to teach primary geography effectively.

- **The internet:** There is a wealth of information available on the internet that will allow both you and the children to learn about the world beyond the classroom in a dynamic and stimulating way. There are references to appropriate websites throughout this book.
- **GIS mapping and data:** There is a wide range of online resources available, including Google Maps, Bing Maps, NASA Images and Digimap for Schools, all of which offer an introduction to GIS (geographic information systems).

- **Globes and atlases:** Building a framework that enables pupils to make sense of all the information that is available electronically is not always easy. Globes and atlases have a key role to play in placing new geographical knowledge in a meaningful context. In referring to them on a regular basis, pupils will develop increasingly secure locational framework.

- **Ordnance Survey maps:** Paper and digital Ordnance Survey maps at different scales will also be important when it comes to more-detailed map work. The curriculum specifically refers to their use, and children will need opportunities to read and use them at first hand if they are to become competent map readers.

- **Local street plans:** Plans of the school building and surrounding streets are further invaluable resources. Local fieldwork and investigations are ideal ways in which to develop pupils' spatial awareness. Encouraging children to use and construct maps and plans of the places that they have visited introduces them to geographical perspectives.

- **Fieldwork equipment:** Cameras, recorders, magnetic compasses, tape measures and other more-specific equipment will be required for certain lessons and investigations. There is a list of 'what you will need' at the start of each lesson.

Globes

Both fixed and inflatable globes are readily available from educational suppliers such as Wildgoose Education Ltd. for relatively modest sums. Just Globes have a particularly extensive range. Globes can also be ordered from Amazon.

Atlases

The main publishers of school atlases are Collins, Oxford and Philip's. All three companies, along with the TTS Group, produce atlases that are specifically designed for primary schools and that are supported by additional teaching resources.

References

Bonnett, A. (2008), *What is Geography?* London: Sage.

Department for Education (DfE) (2013), 'Geography programmes of study: key stages 1 and 2', https://assets.pub lishing.service.gov.uk/government/uploads/system/uploads/attachment_data/file/239044/PRIMARY_national_ curriculum_-_Geography.pdf

Geographical Association (2009), 'A different view: a manifesto by the Geographical Association', https://geogra phy.org.uk/wp-content/uploads/2023/01/GA_ADVBookletFULL.pdf

Lambert, D. and Owens, P. (2013), 'Geography', in R. Jones and D. Wyse (eds), *Creativity in the Primary Curriculum*. London: David Fulton.

Ofsted (2011), 'Geography: learning to make a world of difference', www.gov.uk/government/publications/geography-learning-to-make-a-world-of-difference

Ofsted (2021), 'Research review series: geography', www.gov.uk/government/publications/research-review-series-geography

Ofsted (2023) 'Getting our bearings: geography subject report', www.gov.uk/government/publications/subject-report-series-geography/getting-our-bearings-geography-subject-report

Owens, P. (2015), 'More than just core knowledge: a framework for effective and high-quality geography', in S. Catling (ed), *Research and Debate in Primary Geography*. London: Routledge.

Owens, P. (2020), 'Teaching map skills to inspire a sense of place and adventure', www.ordnancesurvey.co.uk/documents/resources/teaching-map-skills-primary.pdf

Owens, P. (2022), 'Teaching map skills to inspire a sense of place and adventure in the early years', www.ordnancesurvey.co.uk/documents/resources/maps-and-mapping-in-the-early-years.pdf

Scoffham, S. (ed) (2017), *Teaching Geography Creatively*. London: Routledge.

Scoffham, S. and Rawlinson, S. (2022), *Sustainability Education: A Classroom Guide*. London: Bloomsbury Academic.

Part 1
Key Stage 1

1 Developing map skills

What does the curriculum say?

Pupils should be taught to:

- *use simple compass directions (North, South, East and West) and locational and directional language [for example, near and far; left and right], to describe the location of features and routes on a map*

- *use aerial photographs and plan perspectives to recognise landmarks and basic human and physical features; a simple map; and use and construct basic symbols in a key.*

What do I need to know?

Maps show the spatial relationships between places. Geography is the only subject that focuses explicitly on maps, and map work is a defining feature of the discipline. Along with literacy and numeracy, spatial awareness is a key skill that children will need in one form or another throughout their lives. It is also one of the first types of understanding that children develop in infancy.

There are two main types of map. 'Formal' maps, such as Ordnance Survey maps, portray the world in a systematic way. They are devised to a standardised system, which means that anyone can understand them once they have been introduced to the underlying rules. 'Personal' or 'cognitive' maps, on the other hand, are the maps that we carry in our heads and are much more subjective. While these may not be strictly accurate and are difficult to communicate, they are extremely valuable in helping us to navigate and find our way around on a daily basis. Both types of map contribute to our understanding of the world.

This area of study introduces the principles that underpin formal maps. There are a number of basic conventions to consider:

- **Plan view**: Formal maps are constructed from an overhead perspective.
- **Symbols**: Features such as roads, buildings and landmarks are shown using stylised drawings or symbols. Contour lines and the symbolic use of colour, e.g. blue for water and red for main roads, are other examples.
- **Map key:** The map key enables the user to find out what each symbol means.
- **Direction:** The north point is usually at the top of the map and is often indicated by a compass drawing.
- **Grid:** A system of grid squares enables the user to both locate places accurately and estimate distance.

- **Scale:** The scale bar (and/or representative fraction) shows how distances on the map need to match reality. The smaller the scale of the map, the greater the area that it can cover.
- **Title:** Many maps have a title saying what they show or the area that they depict.

Children should be exposed to maps from the earliest age and are often fascinated by them. It is also widely acknowledged that practical experience in the real world can considerably enhance their understanding of map work. As they progress through the primary years, children should become increasingly familiar with basic map conventions. This area of study highlights plan view, symbols and directions in particular.

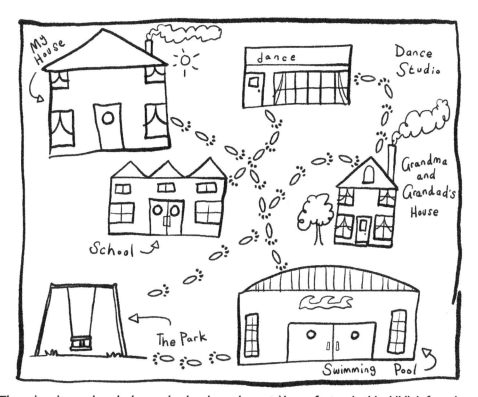

Figure 3: The swimming pool, park, dance school and grandparents' house feature in this child's informal map

Misconceptions and research

There has been considerable debate about whether boys are innately more cartographically competent than girls. This even led to a suggestion in the first version of the National Curriculum that girls should be given special support in map work. More recent research highlights the role of socialisation and the way in which girls focus on different features of the environment, which places this recommendation in a subtler cultural context.

Interesting facts

- The earliest known maps of the world date to classical antiquity and were created in Greece and the Middle East in around the sixth and fifth century BC.
- The first comprehensive maps of Great Britain were compiled by the Ordnance Survey.
- Maps and spatial information are important in many internet searches.

Key questions

1. Is there any difference between a map and a drawing?
2. When do you use maps and where do you see them?
3. Are some types of map better than others?

Lesson 1 Plan view

Why are plan views useful?

You will need
- access to the internet
- blank sheets of paper and light card
- a selection of everyday classroom objects
- toy vehicles, farm animals and other play equipment
- examples of different maps for a display
- a scarf or other material to make a blindfold and tail.

Key vocabulary
- aerial photograph
- direction
- far
- left
- near
- overhead view
- plan

- right
- side view
- shape

Getting started

Working either individually or in groups, let the children make some simple structures using building blocks. Once they have finished, get them to look at what they have made from different angles. Compare the side view (elevation) with the overhead view (plan). Explain to them that maps show what places look like from above.

Class activities

Shape game: Put a selection of everyday classroom items, such as a ruler, pencil case, cup and simple craft materials, in a tray. Ask the children to make a plan of each item on light card by drawing around its outline. Once they have done this, get them to put their work out on a display table. Can other children match each object to its plan shape? You could repeat this activity using different objects that the children have selected for themselves.

Signpost map: Ask the children to put a cross in the middle of a blank sheet of paper to indicate where they are sitting. Now talk about the different things that they can see around them, such as the windows, doors, cupboards, sink and teacher's desk. Create a signpost map by drawing arrows and simple pictures, showing the approximate direction and distance of each of these things from where they are sitting.

Aerial photographs: Using Google Maps, project an overhead photograph of your school building and playground onto the whiteboard. Help the children to orientate themselves by identifying different features, such as the school entrance, different play areas and the position of their classroom. Now switch to the plan view. How is it different? What is missing? Zoom out to a smaller scale to get a wider view of the area around the school. The children will be keen to find the places where they live and play. This is also a natural opportunity to talk about the routes that they take from one place to another, using vocabulary such as 'left' and 'right', and 'near' and 'far' in context.

Blindfold donkey game: Play the blindfold donkey game, either with groups of children or with the whole class. You will need to select one child to be the donkey, who is then blindfolded and given a tail. Other children call out directions for the donkey to follow, specifying the number of paces and the direction to take, using words such as 'left', 'right', 'forward', 'sideways', 'near' and 'far'. You can do this as a time-filler at the end of a lesson.

Small worlds: Give the children the chance to set up some imaginary scenes using toy vehicles, farm animals and other play equipment. Now tell the children that before they clear up, they need to make a plan of the scene that they have created, so that they can rebuild it at another time. Talk about how to do this and the advantage of using an overhead or plan perspective. Alternatively, you could photograph the scenes from different angles and talk about how the plan view shows the layout much more accurately than the view from the side.

Looking down: The idea of floating in the sky and looking down on the world from above is used quite widely in children's stories. Get the children to imagine what a bird might see as it flies over their area or what they would see from a hot air balloon. To develop this idea, show the children a video version of *Zoom* by Istyan Banyai, which starts in a farmyard and ends up looking down on the Earth from space.

Plenary
Set up a map display to broaden the children's interest and ideas. The display could include a map of the local area, a plan of the school, a street map, maps in magazines and brochures, maps from atlases at different scales and so forth. Encourage the children to contribute examples of their own. Why are maps so important in our lives?

Lesson 2 Symbols and map keys

How do maps use symbols and keys?

You will need
- access to the internet
- old magazines, newspapers and glue
- sheets of card and scissors.

Key vocabulary
- logo
- Ordnance Survey
- symbol

Getting started
As a class, discuss symbols that the children see around the school and the immediate environment. Examples might include safety symbols and signs on doors and classroom walls, logos on packets and advertisements, and traffic signs in nearby streets. Discuss why we use symbols. Why are they useful?

Class activities
Logos: Working from old magazines or newspapers, ask pupils to cut out some different company logos to glue onto a new page in their geography books. What company does each logo represent? Ask them to write a sentence saying which one they think is best at communicating information visually. Which one is worst?

Road signs: Look at images of road signs on the internet. Ask pupils to select six different signs and to make careful drawings of them. They should write what each one means underneath.

Symbol Pelmanism: Working in groups of four or five, ask pupils to cut out 30 blank cards, 5 cm by 3 cm in size. They should now select 15 common Ordnance Survey map symbols and make two identical drawings of each symbol on the cards. They place the cards face down on the floor and take turns to turn cards over in matching pairs to make tricks, or put them back in the same place if the symbols they have chosen are different.

School and classroom symbols: Ask pupils to make some symbols of their own for the school or classroom. They might focus on rules, e.g. no running, or identify areas, e.g. reading corner.

Ordnance Survey map symbols: Look at an Ordnance Survey map of your area. Divide the class into small groups and challenge them to find some different symbols in a specific grid square. Identify what they mean from the key. Make a class list of the different features that the pupils have identified. Discuss why it might be important for map readers to know about each of them.

Colour symbols: Look in an atlas to see how colour is used in physical maps of regions or continents. Make a table to show these different colours and their meanings, using the following three columns: name of colour; drawing of colour; meaning of colour.

Plenary
Ask pupils to draw their own mystery maps, showing a journey across an imagined landscape. They should add symbols to show features along the way but deliberately 'forget' to add a key. See whether a partner can puzzle out what each symbol means and reconstruct the story.

Lesson 3 Compass directions

What can we learn from compass directions?

You will need
- a globe and an atlas
- card, scissors, coloured needles and split pins
- square sheets of paper
- a magnetic compass
- an Ordnance Survey map of the local area.

Key vocabulary

- cardinal points
- compass
- east
- north
- North Star
- south
- west

Getting started

Introduce the pupils to the notion of compass directions. The simplest way in which to do this is by identifying the North and South Poles on a globe. At any point on the Earth's surface, the direction to the North Pole indicates the north point. The other cardinal points are arranged clockwise at 90 degree intervals.

Class activities

Cardinal points: Tell pupils that there are four cardinal compass directions: north, east, south and west. You can help them to remember this sequence with a mnemonic, such as 'Naughty Elephants Squirt Water'. It is helpful to make a drawing for the children to copy. You can then add the intermediate or ordinal directions: north-east, south-east, south-west and north-west.

North and south walls: Establish with the pupils which wall or corner of your classroom faces north. Ask them to make drawings of creatures and places that lie in this direction for a class display. On the opposite side of the classroom, set up a display of creatures and places that lie to the south. You might divide the class into two groups for this activity.

Compass model: Ask pupils to make their own compass models using a circle of light card for the base, a coloured needle and a split pin. Go out into the playground or find a wide empty space where the pupils can 'navigate' and go in different directions. If you establish the north point before you start, they will be able to play games that involves going a set number of paces in different compass directions.

Compass panorama: Give each pupil a square sheet of paper. Ask them to fold the corners into the centre. They should write the letters N, E, S and W clearly on each point to represent the cardinal directions. Go outside to a place where there is a clear view in each direction. Establish the direction of north using a magnetic compass or the compass on a mobile phone. The pupils should now orientate themselves and make drawings of what they can see in each direction to create a compass panorama.

The North Star: Discuss how, in the past, sailors who were far away from land used to rely on the stars to establish compass directions. Polaris, or the North Star, is directly in line with the two stars that mark the far end of a very bright constellation, which is variously called the Plough, the Big Dipper or the Great Bear. Wherever they might be, sailors who were able to see Polaris knew the direction of north, and hence which way they were heading. You might select one of the short YouTube films about the North Star to show the pupils, and get them to make diagrams showing its location.

Around your school: Look at an Ordnance Survey map to find some of the different places that are located to the north of your school and its immediate environment. See whether the pupils can work out a mixture of physical and human features. Next, repeat this exercise looking in the other cardinal compass directions. Compare the features that different groups have selected.

Plenary

Look at a map in an atlas to find some of the places that are located to the north of the UK. A world countries map will be a good map to start with, but continental and regional maps will also be helpful. Then find places that lie to the east, south and west of the UK. Ask pupils to list three places in each direction.

Fieldwork and further investigations

- Get the children to draw a map of their journey from home to school, showing key places that they pass along the way. Alternatively, ask them to draw a map (you could call it a picture) of the places that matter to them in and around their home and school.

Cross-curricular links

English: Ask pupils to write a short story, entitled 'The Lost Map'. As well as writing about the map and its significance, the children might make a drawing of it. Perhaps the map is the clue to a crime. Perhaps it shows events from many years ago, now long forgotten.

Mathematics: Download a vertical overhead photograph of your area, using Digimap for Schools. Ask pupils to trace different routes and journeys in the local area, such as their route from home to school. Can they calculate its distance using the measuring tool?

PE: Play a compass direction game with the pupils when you are next in the hall for PE. Ask pupils to run and touch the north wall, hop to the south wall, jump five times to the west and so on.

Themes

Sustainability: One of the principles that underpins sustainability thinking is that we will only care for the things that we love. Maps and map work in the local surroundings engage children in a positive way. Even apparently unremarkable environments have meaning and significance.

Values and wellbeing: Developing their map-reading skills is one way of helping pupils to build their self-confidence. It builds their knowledge of their surroundings and the wider world, enhancing their sense of belonging and place attachment.

Progression and assessment

By the end of this area of study, children will have begun to understand some of the key principles that will enable them to interpret formal maps. They will know that maps use plan views to show places from overhead, they will be able to explain why compass directions are important and they will be able to recognise some commonly used map symbols. They will also have gained a greater knowledge of the features of their local area.

Useful books and websites

Catling, S. (2017), 'Learning about places around the world', in Scoffham, S. (ed) *Teaching Geography Creatively* (2nd edn). London: Routledge.

Hodgkinson, L. (2022), *Martha Maps it Out*. Oxford: Oxford University Press.

Richardson, P. and Richardson, T. (2016), *Everyday Guide to Primary Geography: Maps*. Sheffield: Geographical Association.

Ordnance Survey children's website: www.ordnancesurvey.co.uk/mapzone

North Star: search for 'How to find the North Star'.

2 Continents and oceans

What does the curriculum say?

Pupils should be taught to:

- *name and locate the world's seven continents and five oceans*
- *use world maps, atlases and globes to identify the continents and oceans studied at this key stage.*

What do I need to know?

The most basic division of the Earth's surface is into land and water. Water covers over 70 per cent of the total surface area, which is why Earth is sometimes called a 'blue planet', as the water shows up from space. Land occupies the remaining 30 per cent, although a significant proportion of this lies permanently beneath a covering of ice and snow.

Oceans

An ocean is defined as a vast expanse of salt water. Oceans are also very deep, unlike seas, which are comparatively shallow. In order of size, from largest to smallest, the major oceans on Earth are: Pacific, Atlantic, Indian, Southern and Arctic.

Continents

A continent is defined as a very large block of land. Asia is by far the largest continent. Defining the boundaries between continents is not always easy. For example, Asia is joined to Europe for historical rather than geographical reasons. Islands present a special problem, especially if they are far from the coast. One continent (Oceania) is made up almost entirely of islands scattered across the Pacific, which stretches the concept almost to breaking point.

Over geological time, the continents have been carried from one place to another by forces beneath the Earth's surface. At one time in the past (between 500 and 600 million years ago), all the land was joined in a supercontinent called Gondwana (or Gondwanaland). It is believed that the continents will join up again at some point in the very distant future. As people have explored the world, their knowledge of its geography has expanded. The Greeks thought that there were just three continents. Christopher Columbus is known for his journeys to the Americas in the fifteenth century, and Captain Cook for his journeys to Australia and the Pacific Islands in the eighteenth century. However, It wasn't until the nineteenth century that Europeans first sighted and began to explore Antarctica.

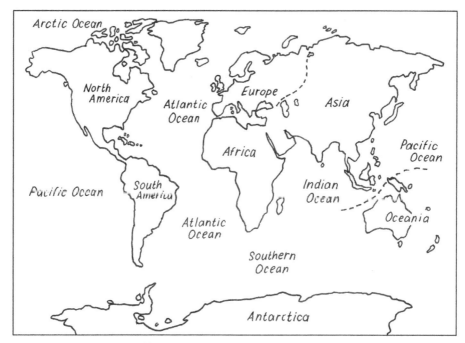

Figure 4: There are seven continents and five oceans.

Maps, diagrams and models

Geographers try to represent the Earth's surface using maps, diagrams and models. When it comes to accuracy, globes have a particular advantage, as they show the world in three dimensions. Flat maps are much more versatile but, whatever projection they use, they will inevitably distort either shape or direction. Modern maps seek to achieve a compromise. A quick test is to compare the size of Greenland and South America. Greenland is actually only about a ninth of the size of South America, but it is often portrayed as being almost equal.

Misconceptions and research

Young children have considerable difficulty accepting that the Earth is a sphere, and often subscribe to a 'flat Earth' theory. Evidence from satellite images can help to challenge their misconceptions, but may only partially dislodge their earlier common-sense notions. For example, it is hard for them to comprehend that people in Australia are standing upside down in relation to Europeans, which is something that even some adults find hard to accept.

Interesting facts

- The Pacific Ocean is bigger than all the world's continents put together.
- Africa is home to four out of five of the world's fastest land animals.

Key questions

1. Does the Earth have a top and a bottom?
2. What do the children think is most remarkable about the Earth?

Lesson 1 The globe

What can we learn about the world from a globe?

You will need
- an inflatable globe – a wide selection is available, some highlighting countries, some focusing on rivers and mountains and others including drawings of animals and habitats, but any of these will work for these kinds of activities.

Key vocabulary
- continent
- equator
- globe
- North Pole
- ocean
- South Pole
- names of the continents and oceans

Getting started
Introduce the globe as a model of the world. Talk about how a large part of the globe is coloured blue: what does this represent? Ask children to point out oceans and large land masses. Tell the pupils that the Earth spins as it travels through space (you can demonstrate this). See that you point out key reference points, such as the North and South Poles and the equator.

Class activities
Continent names: Explain that continents are very large areas of land. Tell the pupils the names of the seven continents and show them on the globe. Point to the UK and explain that we live in the continent of Europe.

Continent shapes: Have a discussion about which is the biggest continent and invite pupils to talk about their different shapes.

Continents rhyme: Teach the children the continents rhyme (below) to help them to remember the names of the continents.

Continents rhyme

Get out the map, and what do you see,

Seven continents, where can they be?

Europe and Asia lie northwards on the sphere,

Africa is shaped liked an elephant's ear!

Around the South Pole lies Antarctica,

Australia and some islands make up Oceania,

North and South America are joined in the middle.

Can you solve the continent riddle?

Globe tossing: Toss the globe to one of your pupils and ask another pupil to call out a continent name. The child with the globe has to point to it, maybe with the help of a partner. Continue this game. You might also extend the game by focusing on oceans instead of continents.

Ocean names: Explain that oceans are very large bodies of water. Tell pupils the names of the five oceans of the world and show them on the globe. Have a discussion about their sizes and where they are on the globe.

Plenary

Ask the pupils some questions about continents and oceans, e.g. 'Which continent would you find at the South Pole?'. Can they name a continent that lies on the equator? In which continent do we live?

Lesson 2 World maps

What can we learn about the world from an atlas?

You will need

- world maps and atlases designed for young children
- continent outline shapes duplicated on paper
- dice.

Key vocabulary

- atlas
- country
- desert
- features
- mountain range
- river
- world
- names of the continents and oceans

Getting started

Tell the children that a book of maps, known as an atlas, can show much more information than a globe. The drawback is that any two-dimensional map will involve distortions. Look at a world map to locate the continents and oceans studied in the previous lesson. Ask children to also find the equator and the North and South Poles. Where is Europe? Can they spot any other features that they know?

Class activities

Continent facts: Divide pupils into small groups and ask them to use their research skills to find out three or more facts about a given continent. For example, they might name different cities and countries or identify some rivers and mountain ranges. Alternatively, they might talk about the shape of their continent and whether it is joined to another one or not. Give the children continent outline shapes to record their findings.

Animals worldwide: Give pupils a list of iconic animals and ask them to find the most appropriate continent for them to live. Pupils draw and/or write the animal names on a map of the world, e.g. penguin (Antarctica), kangaroo (Oceania), grizzly bear (North America), elephant (Africa and Asia), giant panda (Asia), condor (South America) and badger/Scottish wildcats (Europe). As an alternative, pupils could take one continent and make a list of animals found there.

Continent features: Ask pupils to find and map some significant global features on a world map, e.g. mountain ranges (Himalayas, Rockies, Andes), rivers (Nile, Amazon, Mississippi) or deserts (Sahara, Gobi).

UK in the world: Ask the pupils to find the UK on the world map. Talk about its position, e.g. between the North Pole and the equator, on the edge of mainland Europe, next to the Atlantic Ocean.

Holiday chance: Working in pairs, pupils write a list of the continents, excluding Antarctica. Ask them to put a number next to each one. Give one child in each pair a single die. The number that they throw will tell them the continent that their partner is going to visit. Their partner finds this continent on a map and describes what they would like to see there. Swap roles and repeat.

Plenary

Review the children's learning and ask them to use their new knowledge to say how the continents are different. Which one would they most like to visit and why?

Lesson 3 Images of the world

How do we find out about the Earth?

You will need
- access to the internet and appropriate software and apps, e.g. Google Earth.

Key vocabulary
- astronaut
- digital
- feature
- image
- space
- webcam

Getting started

How do we know about planet Earth? Explain that in the past, people depended almost entirely on what they could see as they travelled around. Today, space travel and satellite images have revealed vast quantities of information about the planet on which we live. What do the pupils think that Earth might look like from space? Display an image of 'Earthrise', which shows a view of the Earth as seen from the Moon, and discuss what it shows. How does it make the children feel?

Class activities

Google Earth: Using Google Earth, zoom out to a whole-Earth view and gently spin the Earth from west to east. Pupils take turns to shout 'stop' and try to guess what can be seen. Can they name any visible continents, oceans or other features?

Webcams: Webcams offer an instant view into other parts of the world, as varied as a beach, city centre or the research station at the South Pole. See what different places you can visit with your pupils and discuss some of the evident similarities and differences, e.g. weather, landscape, people, clothes and time of day.

Digital games: Use interactive digital games for pupils to test their growing knowledge of the names and locations of the continents. A brief online search will quickly locate a range of suitable online games.

Zoom: Read *Zoom* by Istvan Banyai (see Useful books and websites, p. 33) and/or watch a video version on YouTube. Discuss how each image shows details of a larger scene, ending up with a view of the Earth from space. What does this now make the pupils think about the Earthrise image?

How did the Earth begin?: There are numerous creation myths from different cultures and religions, which you can share with the children. You could also take a scientific approach and explain how the Earth was formed out of rock and dust as part of the solar system over four thousand million years ago. Learning about the planets follows naturally from this.

Plenary

Make a class wall display using a world map as a base. Pupils can add all their researched material, including personal information, to compile an ongoing record of their learning. Use labels to name the continents and oceans. Hint: use a data projector to project a world map image onto the board and draw around the outline, rather than use a bought map.

Fieldwork and further investigations

- Many images of the Earth from space are remarkably beautiful. The NASA website has a vast range of easily accessible and helpful examples, e.g. see 'Image of the Day' (www.nasa.gov/multimedia/imagegallery/iotd.html) and 'Earth As Art' (www.nasa.gov/connect/ebooks/earth_art_detail.html). Either allow pupils to browse these images online or print and laminate some examples and keep them in your book box; some could be labelled. Use them to promote discussion and understanding about the Earth's surface.

Cross-curricular links

English: Talking about the continents and oceans provides ample opportunities to develop specialised vocabulary. Pupils could use these terms either in speech or in creative writing to describe an imaginary journey. Challenge them to add details about landscape, animals and weather as they 'visit' different continents.

Mathematics: Comparing the sizes of the continents introduces young children to the concept of area. Lesson 3 also involves the idea of scale. Both these ideas can be developed at a basic level in mathematics.

Science: Finding about the creatures that live in different continents links directly to work in science on living things and their habitats. The development of specialised vocabulary in geography also supports the science curriculum.

Computing: Lesson 3 will help pupils to develop their computing research skills to access digital information and use technology purposefully to create, organise, store, manipulate and retrieve digital content.

Themes

Colonialism and social justice: The knowledge of the world that Europeans developed from the late fifteenth century onwards led to an era of colonialism, which is reflected in the world map today. Names that include compass directions, such as the old colonial term 'West Indies' and Middle East, only make sense when viewed from European locations. Meanwhile, city names such as New York, Kingston and Sydney are obvious clues to the colonial past.

Sustainability: Images of the Earth from space have alerted people to the fragile nature of the planet and inspired them to think more carefully about their actions. Explore the impact of these images on children's knowledge and feelings about the world in which we live. Note: emotive and cognitive learning work together to deepen paths of learning.

Values and wellbeing: Recognising that we all live on the same planet, whatever our faith or beliefs, and that Earth is our only home, emphasises our unity as a species and the importance of values such as inclusion and equality.

Progression and assessment

By the end of this area of study, all pupils should be able to name the five oceans and seven continents; being able to describe some of their features demonstrates a growing understanding.

The ability to locate the continents and oceans on a globe or world map indicates a higher level of achievement, for which all children should be aiming by the end of Key Stage 1.

Useful books and websites

Banyai, I. (1995), *Zoom*. London: Penguin (also available on YouTube).

Burleigh, R. (2016), *Solving the Puzzle Under the Sea*. London: Simon and Schuster.

Dyer, S. (2002), *Five Little Fiends*. London: Bloomsbury.

Otter, I. (2020), *Dear Earth*. London: Caterpillar Books.

Owens, P. (2011), *Little Blue Planet: Investigating Spaceship Earth*. Sheffield: Geographical Association.

How the Earth was formed: search for 'Big Bang and birth of Earth' on YouTube.

Photographs of the Earth from space: search for 'Earth from space NASA photos'.

3 The school and its surroundings

What do I need to know?

The term 'local area' has a loose definition but in educational circles generally refers to the environment around the children's home and school. How this is interpreted is likely to be affected by variables such as access, safety, population density, services and everyday activities. At Key Stage 1, the local area is usually defined as the area that can be easily reached on foot around the school. At Key Stage 2, this usually extends to mean the area in which the majority of a school's pupils live, including places that they can see in the distance.

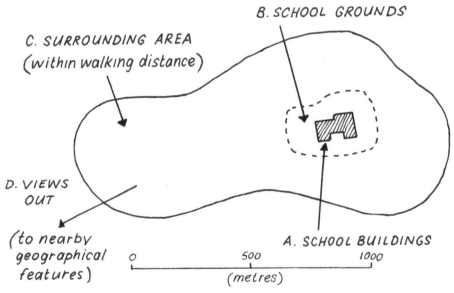

Figure 5: **The locality can be thought of as having a number of different components**

Schools

The physical features of a school consist chiefly of built structures such as walls, fences and paths. Plants and wildlife add another dimension. Different areas in a school site include the classrooms, playground, car park and lunch hall. The human features refer especially to the pupil profiles, with gender, ethnicity, age and socio-economic groupings being some of the aspects that are often studied by geographers.

The location of a school can be described by its position on a map, address and postcode. Schools also have other specific characteristics, such as size, setting and catchment area. These features provide extra information about what a school is like and form part of a valid geographical enquiry, as does finding out how children feel about their school and how they might like it to change in the future. Fieldwork is the best way in which to develop enquiries into the geography of a school and its grounds, and offers a good deal of scope to investigate these different aspects.

The local area

It is valuable to explore the area around your school on foot. This will help you to find out about different places that you can safely access with pupils, and how long it takes to get there. You will also need to do your own risk assessments and to follow any established procedures that your school has devised for outdoor work. For example, it is considered good practice to carry out a shared risk assessment in class with children before taking them out on any field trip.

It is important to remember that even the most seemingly ordinary street can be a valuable teaching resource with a good deal of geographical potential. House types, signage, patterns of bricks, windows, doors and drain covers all provide interesting points of discussion for geography and help with associated vocabulary development. Practical work in the local environment harnesses children's personal knowledge and natural curiosity. Many children also find it memorable and enjoyable. Local streets and buildings are a free resource and are literally on the doorstep and available for use on a regular basis. Direct experiences and the first-hand observations that result are a central part of good practice acknowledged by Ofsted.

Misconceptions and research

Children today are more likely to be brought to school by car or public transport and less likely to walk than in the past. As a result, they may have limited knowledge of the environment between their homes and their school. One of the key factors seems to be the extent to which adults talk to them about the journey. Without first-hand investigation, young children may also have misconceptions about the school grounds and believe that dangerous creatures such as lions and bears live there.

Interesting facts

- Some children who live on islands such as the Scilly Isles (South West England) and the Hebrides (western Scotland) have to travel to school by boat.
- Schools can be very different sizes. In Cumbria, Milburn Primary School has just five pupils, while Barclay Primary School in London has more than 1,300.

Key questions

1. Where is our school and what is it like?
2. What do we like about our school and how could we make it better?
3. What are the key features in our local area?

Lesson 1 The school and its grounds

Where is our school?

You will need
- a letter addressed to the class and school
- an aerial image of your school
- access to the internet
- chalk (different colours)
- paper and digital maps
- junk-modelling materials.

Key vocabulary
- address
- buildings
- grounds
- postcode
- school

Getting started
Show a large envelope with the school address on it and discuss the postcode. What do the letters mean? Make postcards addressed to the school and visit a local post office to

post them, to show how an address ensures that post is delivered to the right place. Do the children all have the same postcode?

Class activities

Overhead view: Using Google Earth or Google Maps, enter the school address or postcode and find your school. Talk about what can be seen from this perspective and help pupils to identify some of the nearby features by zooming in and out. Switch to oblique view and Street View to help children to make connections between what they see from above and from the ground.

Activity places: Ask pupils to identify the best place within the school to do a specific activity. Provide some examples and ask children to come up with some of their own. These might include ideas such as: eat a packed lunch, get a drink, read quietly and play football. Make an activity map of the school.

Favourite place outside: Take the class outside and walk around the school grounds. Stop at different points around the school and identify features that you can see and what you might do there. Ask pupils to say which parts they like best and why. Add these to a map and compare choices.

School improvement: Walk around the school and look for areas that could be improved or that need repairing. Ask pupils to mark each spot with coloured chalk or a sticky label and take a photograph of the feature in question. They could also record a video message, giving the location and the name of the feature, and saying what needs improving. Add this information to a map of the school. Include the routes taken on foot around the school.

Looking north: Go outside and ask pupils to use a compass to find which way is north. Use coloured chalk to draw an arrow on the playground. Discuss what makes north a significant direction. Add arrows for the other cardinal compass directions.

3D map: Create a 3D map or model of the school and its grounds using junk-modelling equipment and ask pupils to include new features that they'd like to see. What would the features be and where would they put them?

Plenary

Create a fact-file for the school with the class and decide on the best headings. Add essential information together, such as the address, a map, directions to the front entrance and any relevant images. You might do this by using the annotation tools in Digimap for Schools on a class whiteboard, on shared laptops or tablets, or using paper maps and pens.

Lesson 2 Getting to school

How do we get to school?

You will need
- maps of the local area.

Key vocabulary
- environment
- journey
- pollution
- road safety
- route
- transport
- travel

Getting started
Ask pupils how they get to school. Discuss how far pupils live from school and how this affects how they travel in. If there are children who live very near to school, do they travel on foot or by scooter? Do those who live further away always have to travel by car? Discuss road safety and the ways in which people stay safe.

Class activities
Graph it: Create graphs showing the different ways in which pupils get to school.

Memory maps: Ask pupils to think about their routes to school and map them from memory. Tell them about this activity a day in advance so that they can pay special attention to their journeys to school the next morning. Share some observations and vocabulary ahead of the task.

TripGeo maps: TripGeo.com is a program that allows you to input a start and finish destination and will then play an animated street-view image of your journey on a split screen. While one part of the screen shows the animated view, the other shows the progress being made on a map. Select one child's journey and show it to the class, comparing it with their map from memory. Stop the 'journey' at various points along the route and ask pupils to say what they can see. Invite the child whose journey it is to give a spoken commentary of part of the route.

Walking to school: Discuss ways in which walking to school could be made safer for those who live close to school. Find and map the safest routes. Discuss how you can encourage more pupils to walk to school.

Road safety: Walk around the school site and investigate how busy the roads are at different times of the day, and how safe the parking is. Map the danger spots on Digimap for Schools using the annotation tools, and make a report for parents, governors and even the local council or press.

Other journeys: Investigate how other children get to school in this and other countries. Ask pupils to select a favourite story and create a poster showing the location, route and type of transport used. Provide links to some YouTube examples, using appropriate search terms to show children who travel by boat or who make very long journeys.

Plenary
Working in small groups, ask the pupils to select one journey and create a presentation using TripGeo, taking it in turns to give a spoken commentary.

Lesson 3 Local features

What are the key features in our local area?

You will need
- aerial images and maps of the school and its surrounding area
- access to Digimap for Schools
- audio and visual digital recording devices
- paper and crayons
- magnetic compasses.

Key vocabulary
- building
- hospital
- path
- road
- shop
- street
- train station

Getting started
Tell the pupils that you will all be going out for a walk around the school to explore the local area. Ask them what they think that they will see on their walk and make a list with

the class. Encourage them to think about a range of features but don't give them any clues as to whether they are right or wrong. Ask what they would like to find out about and select the best questions to try to answer during the walk. Having brainstormed the initial list of expected features, explain the importance of staying safe and working carefully together while outdoors.

Risk assessment: On the class interactive whiteboard, use images taken from your own risk assessment or captured views from a street-view map, or go directly into the map using the internet. Show the route that you will be walking and stop at points that you consider to be dangerous, such as crossing a road or where a pavement is too narrow. Working from an image, ask pupils to identify any risks with a partner and suggest what they could do to stay safe. Establish some useful answers and develop vocabulary as appropriate. Repeat with some other images and then ask children to draw or write a brief risk assessment for each image shown and suggest a safety action.

Class activities

Locality walk: Have an informal walk around the local area, stopping at some selected points to note what can be seen and to help pupils to identify features. Collect feature names by using a scribe or a voice recorder and compare these with what was imagined before the children went outside. Take photographs of interesting signs and features too, and add these to a digital map on return.

Tweetmaps: Using a class X (formerly Twitter) account, ask the class to describe a feature along the route using less than 280 characters, thinking carefully about accurate vocabulary and choice of descriptor. Add an image too and enable location tagging to create a virtual record and map of the journey.

Sound maps: Stop at a given point and listen carefully to the sounds that you can hear. Map these on a piece of paper, using one colour for 'built' and another for 'natural' sounds, and draw the direction from a central point to show from whence they came. Add these to a class map.

Touch maps: Take chunky wax crayons and small squares of paper for rubbing patterns found on buildings, other objects or trees. Add these to your locality map.

Teddy draping: Use a small toy or teddy and select sites along the route to place them and photograph them. Then describe their position carefully using the feature name and phrases such as 'next to', 'beside', 'on top of' and 'beneath'. You could also take magnetic compasses so that children can establish the direction in which they are looking.

Feature words: Use a word-cloud generator program such as Word Art, Mentimeter or Tagxedo to produce a class word cloud of feature names gathered before and after the walk, and compare the difference. Programs like Tagxedo will let you import the words into different shapes, such as trees or hearts. You can also import your own templates. These can be used to illustrate booklets or maps or even be used as badges.

Plenary

Ask the pupils to review their learning against their initial ideas and compare the new to the previous vocabulary. Use aerial images and large-scale maps to help to identify these features. Ask the children to say what most surprised them and why. Did they answer their initial enquiry questions and what new questions do they have?

Fieldwork and further investigations

- Make models of your own and other streets using building blocks and bricks. Make a large-scale model out of boxes that pupils can 'jump into'.
- Devise a street trail for pupils to follow, looking out for clues and answering questions along the way, or support pupils to make their own.
- Draw a poster highlighting the best points of your local area and persuading people to come and live in the area.
- Create a playset in the classroom to represent a local feature, such as the village shop or a local supermarket or bank.
- Invite someone who works in the local community, such as a local police officer, to your class to talk about their work.

Cross-curricular links

English: Investigating the school and what goes on within it, as well as what it is like, involves a good deal of specialised vocabulary to name and describe features. Using purposeful contexts, such as reports to parents and governors, also provides motivation for writing.

Mathematics: Measure the playground or school field in different ways. Pupils might walk the perimeter and count the footsteps needed to do this, and also measure the time that it takes using a stopwatch. Use a trundle wheel to measure the same distance in metres. Create a large map for display, adding photographs and sketches of key features.

Science: Looking closely at the school grounds requires knowledge of different creatures and other living things and their habitats. Investigating and mapping the school also requires naming and describing materials and their properties.

Design and technology: As part of their work on improving the school grounds, pupils could design and make simple nesting and bat boxes or bird feeders.

Themes

Biodiversity: Even in built-up areas, the school and its surroundings can be surprisingly rich in plant and animal life. There will be trees and bushes in nearly every city street and, depending on how they are maintained, gardens can contain huge numbers of different species. Birds often catch children's attention, especially in spring, when they are more active. Some people put up bird feeders and bird boxes. This raises questions about how to improve biodiversity and could easily lead to a discussion about wildlife in and around the school building.

Sustainability: Investigating what they like about the school grounds and how they might be improved will help children to develop notions of environmental stewardship and care. It is also empowering, as it helps children to realise that they can change and improve their surroundings.

Values and wellbeing: Using local streets and buildings as a teaching resource can be highly affirmative. Pupils appreciate the way in which it validates their local environment and attributes meaning to the world around them. The enhanced sense of identity and belonging that can result boosts their self-esteem and self-confidence – these qualities are an important part of spiritual, moral, social and cultural development (SMSC). Thinking about road safety raises questions about self-care and respect for life. Learning about how others get to school in very different environments helps children to appreciate diversity, while comparing what they each like and don't like about their school supports tolerance and understanding of other viewpoints.

Progression and assessment

By the end of this area of study, all children should be able to locate their school on an appropriately scaled map, give the school address and talk about key features of the local environment. They will be able to describe the layout of the school and the different activities that go on within it. Children should also be able to explain how they get to school, what they see along the way and explain why some roads around the school might be more dangerous than others.

By the end of this area of study, children will have developed enough vocabulary to describe and talk about the different features in their local environment. They will be able to identify some of these features on a map and explain why some are where they are. Children will be able to name the different types of housing in the local area and recognise these types on a large-scale map. They will be able to describe some of the activities that people do in the locality and say which ones are leisure and which ones are jobs.

Useful books and websites

Baker, J. (2008), *Belonging.* London: Walker.

Pickering, S. (ed) (2017), *Creative Learning Out of Doors.* London: Routledge.

Sweeney, J. (2018), *Me on the Map.* New York: Ballantine Books.

Digimap for schools: http://digimapforschools.edina.ac.uk

Google Earth: https://earth.google.com

Google Maps: https://maps.google.co.uk

Journey to School: www.journeytoschool.com

Street View: www.instantstreetview.com

Local information: search for 'Neighbourhood statistics'.

Word clouds: www.wordart.com, www.mentimeter.com or www.tagxedo.com

'25 of the most dangerous and unusual journeys to school in the world': www.boredpanda.com/dangerous-journey-to-school

4 The United Kingdom

What do I need to know?

The United Kingdom is made up of four countries that have been joined together for hundreds of years. England and Wales became united in 1284. Scotland joined the Union in 1707 and Northern Ireland was added in 1921. Each country has its own flag, which is represented in the Union Jack, and its own capital city, culture and traditions.

England

Capital city: London

Patron saint: St George

England is the largest country in the UK and is about the same size as all the other countries put together. London, with a population of around nine million people, dominates the south. It is a global centre for banking and commerce, and Heathrow is one of the busiest airports in Europe. In northern England, there are many old industrial areas that flourished in the nineteenth century.

Scotland

Capital city: Edinburgh

Patron saint: St Andrew

Scotland is the most northerly country in the UK. It has high mountains and a large numbers of islands, especially along the west coast. Most people live in the Central Lowlands, where Edinburgh and Glasgow are the chief cities. The Southern Uplands and Highlands are the emptiest and most remote areas, with extensive moors and mountains.

Wales

Capital city: Cardiff

Patron saint: St David

Wales lies to the west of England and is noted for its valleys and mountains, including Snowdonia. It has a population of just over three million people, one-sixth of whom can speak or understand Welsh. In the past, most jobs in Wales used to be in farming, mining and heavy industry. Today, many of the factories have closed, and tourism and service industries are increasingly important.

Northern Ireland

Capital city: Belfast

Patron saint: St Patrick

Northern Ireland covers about a quarter of Ireland. It is sometimes referred to as Ulster. Apart from the capital city, Belfast, most parts of Northern Ireland are deeply rural. Northern Ireland has a long history of conflict between the Protestant and Catholic communities.

Figure 6: (a) The UK (b) The British Isles (c) Great Britain

Misconceptions and research

A country is a largely abstract concept, with many facets and dimensions. It is not surprising, therefore, that throughout the primary years children find it hard to say what a country really is. Concentrating on distinguishing features such as the flag and national emblems is one way of establishing national identity. Learning about the UK on a regular basis will help to build and deepen children's understanding.

Interesting facts

- Great Britain is the world's eighth-largest Island.
- Edinburgh, the capital city of Scotland, is built on the remains of an extinct volcano.

Key questions

1. What is the United Kingdom like?
2. What are the key differences between the countries of the United Kingdom?
3. Where is the United Kingdom in relation to other countries?

Lesson 1 UK countries and capitals

What are the countries and capitals of the United Kingdom?

You will need
- a simple map of the countries of the UK
- art and craft materials, including modelling clay and gardening sticks
- blank playing cards.

Key vocabulary
- England
- Northern Ireland
- Scotland
- Wales
- United Kingdom

Getting started
Look at a map of the four countries of the UK. Discuss it with the pupils and help them to understand that each country is shown in a different colour and that the sea is shown

in blue. Read the names of the capital cities and explain that these are very important places, with lots of buildings. Can children work out approximately where they live on this map? Have any of them visited the different countries or capitals? What do they notice about the shapes of the different countries?

Class activities

UK map: Make a large outline map of the United Kingdom for a wall display. Pupils could then add labels with names of the different countries, capitals and seas. If possible, add postcards, flags made by the children and photographs to show different places and features.

Flags: Ask the pupils to make little flags for the different UK countries. They should colour them carefully and fix them to gardening sticks. Display the flags, along with other items from the country concerned, on tables around the classroom. Use small lumps of modelling clay to make solid bases to stop the flags from falling over.

Digital maps: Pupils use a digital mapping program that they can use to search for the capitals of the different countries of the UK and mark them on the map.

Countries snap: Make up some playing cards based on the names and outline shapes of the countries of the United Kingdom. You will need eight cards in each set – four for the names of the countries and four for the shapes of the territories. Put several sets together for the pupils to use for games of snap.

Countries game: Make large flags for each country of the United Kingdom and put them in the corners of the school hall before beginning a movement lesson. When the pupils are ready, play some music and ask them to dance. Every so often, you should stop the music and call out the name of the country. The children then have to run to the correct corner. You can make the game more atmospheric by using folk music from the different countries.

Plenary

Ask the pupils to say one thing that they now know about each country of the United Kingdom. Their answers might focus on names of the countries and their capital cities, but could also include their size, shape and location. Thinking about how the four countries are both similar and different is one way of developing a deeper discussion.

Lesson 2 UK coasts, seas and oceans

What are the seas and oceans around the UK?

You will need
- picture books with seaside settings
- access to the internet
- a map of the UK, naming surrounding seas
- labels to add to the UK map
- short strips of Velcro™.

Key vocabulary
- beach
- cliff
- coast
- island
- ocean
- sea
- names of seas and oceans around the UK

Getting started
Talk with the pupils about the places that they have visited in the UK. Have any of them been to the seaside? What was it like? Explain that the UK is surrounded by sea. This means that if you travel by land, you will end up at the coast in whichever direction you travel.

Class activities
Seaside story: Read the pupils a story about the seaside. There are some excellent picture books to choose from, and the combination of text and images is often very effective in conjuring an image of the seashore.

Coasts: The UK has one of the most varied and dramatic coastlines in the world, with long, sandy beaches, great banks of shingle and rocky cliffs and caves. Children love finding out about beaches and the seaside. You might start by making a collection of 'seaside words'. Get children to make a simple drawing to go with each one as a way of developing their vocabulary, using words such as 'beach', 'cliff' and 'sea'.

Seaside 'I spy': Ask the pupils to imagine that they are at the seaside and you are playing a game of 'I spy'. What do they imagine that they can see? For example, the answer to 'I spy with my little eye something beginning with F' might be 'fish'.

Seas and oceans: Talk with the pupils about the difference between seas and oceans. Oceans are very large and deep. Seas are smaller and relatively shallow. Look at a map of the UK. Can they point to an ocean and say what is it called? Can they point to the seas around the UK and say what they are called? Are there any areas of water that have a special name, such as 'bay' or 'channel'? Next, ask the pupils to pick up one of the seas and oceans labels that you prepared earlier. Get them to add each one using Velcro™ in an appropriate place on the UK wall map that you devised in the previous lesson.

Plenary

Play a game in which pupils pool their knowledge about the UK. Working collaboratively, can each child in the class think of a different fact or piece of information?

Lesson 3 UK and the wider world

Where is the United Kingdom in relation to other countries and places?

You will need
- an inflatable globe
- a computer or tablet and internet connection
- blank maps of the world and Europe at different scales.

Key vocabulary
- capital city
- Europe
- journey
- migration
- overseas

Getting started

Engage the class in the globe-tossing game. Throw the globe to one pupil and ask them to find the UK with the help of a partner, and add a sticker to mark its location. Repeat this with other children, asking them to label the continents and oceans. This might be presented as a 'beat the clock' activity. Alternatively, if you are using a blank outline globe, pupils could label the UK, continents and oceans using a marker pen.

Class activities

Where are we?: Using a globe or world map, talk with the pupils about the location of the UK. It is approximately halfway between the equator and North Pole, and it is on the edge of the Atlantic Ocean, alongside the mainland of Europe. Which continents are closest to the UK? Which continents are furthest away?

Overseas links: Find out whether the pupils already have personal links with mainland Europe and other continents. For example, some children may have been born or lived in other countries. Others may have travelled abroad for holidays or have links with friends and families overseas. Showcase this information using bar graphs, maps, diagrams, infographics and storybooks.

Bird visitors: A significant number of the birds that we see in the UK migrate here from different countries on a seasonal basis. For example, cuckoos, swifts and swallows come from Africa in the spring, while swans, geese and blackbirds come from the Arctic in the autumn. Find out about some of these seasonal migrations. Why do birds need to make such long journeys?

City journeys: Using a digital mapping program such as Google Maps, give pupils different journeys to investigate between London and other capital cities in mainland Europe. Ask the children to consider different ways of travelling, e.g. road, rail and water as well as air. They might also note any special features along the journey. Are there any rivers, mountains or seas that they need to cross?

Plenary

Discuss and decide as a class the best three facts to describe the location of the UK. Encourage pupils to use the names of countries, continents, seas and oceans in their answers.

Fieldwork and further investigations

- What countries are the nearest neighbours to the UK? Look at an atlas to make a list. Extend the activity by drawing a distance ring, centred on your locality. You will need to select a suitable distance (e.g. 500 km) and use a pair of compasses to draw the ring on the map. If possible, add photographs or postcards to illustrate some of the places that are found within the distance that you have chosen.

Cross-curricular links

English: Activities relating to the sea and coastline are a natural opportunity to develop pupils' vocabulary and to help to link new meanings to known vocabulary. Setting up a word book is one way of helping to consolidate pupils' knowledge and will prove useful throughout the year as they embark on other topics and lessons in geography.

Mathematics: Working from a map of the UK, ask the pupils to find Belfast and the other capital cities of the UK. Get them to compare the distances from Belfast to the other capitals and to put them in order, with the closest first and the most distant last. Discuss what this might mean for the people of Northern Ireland.

Design and technology: Finding out about the development and building of lighthouses around the UK coast is fascinating. The Eddystone Lighthouse, 14 miles off the Devon coast, has a particularly dramatic story. Watch one of the videos available on YouTube about the construction of the lighthouse, before asking the pupils to construct their own lighthouse models.

Music: Listen to the different national anthems for England, Scotland and Wales, and learn to sing them. Discuss which ones the children enjoy most and why.

Themes

Colonialism and social justice: The United Kingdom is itself the product of colonialism. Wales, Scotland and Ireland were all conquered and colonised by invaders from England at different times over the past thousand years. While the process of assimilation has forged a united country, with common values and beliefs, the different countries have retained distinct cultural traditions. Listening to traditional folk music is one way of exploring these with young children.

Biodiversity: Although the UK has lost around half its biodiversity in recent decades, the different habitats, such as mountains, woodlands, grasslands, marshes, coasts and oceans, still support a great diversity of wildlife. Exploring this diversity is a powerful way in which to engage children and helps them to learn about the geography of the UK and its regions.

Progression and assessment

By the end of this area of study, all children should be able to name the four countries of the UK and their capital cities. They will also have gained increasing familiarity with the outline shape of the UK and its surrounding seas and oceans. Those who are exceeding expectations will have also begun to appreciate some of the features that make the countries of the UK distinctive. They will also have a basic knowledge of the location of the UK in relation to other countries.

Useful books and websites

Rosen, M. (2009), *The Bear in the Cave*. London: Bloomsbury.

Rotchell, E. (2014), *Barnaby Bear Investigates the UK*. Sheffield: Geographical Association.

Explore the ocean using Google Earth: www.google.com/earth/explore/showcase/ocean.html

The story of Eddystone Lighthouse: search for 'The story of Eddystone Lighthouse (BBC Coast)' on YouTube.

Extracts from the BBC *Wild Isles* series: search for 'BBC Wild Isles' on YouTube.

5 Weather and seasons

What does the curriculum say?

Pupils should be taught to:

- *identify seasonal and daily weather patterns in the United Kingdom and the location of hot and cold areas of the world in relation to the Equator and the North and South Poles*

- *use world maps, atlases and globes to identify the United Kingdom and its countries, as well as the countries, continents and oceans studied at this key stage.*

What do I need to know?

The weather varies from day to day. It is made up of a combination of wind, rain, temperature and other factors. Climate is the pattern of weather that occurs over a period of many years. In the United Kingdom, and at similar latitudes north and south of the equator, there are four seasons: winter, spring, summer and autumn. Each of the seasons has its expected patterns of weather, which vary in different parts of the UK. A helpful way in which to describe the difference between climate and weather with young children is to say that climate is what you expect in a given place and weather is what you get.

There are official dates for the starts of the seasons, although in practice these are not precise. A simple approach is to link the seasons to specific months. In the Northern Hemisphere, March, April and May are the spring months, summer occurs in June, July and August and so on. The situation is reversed in the Southern Hemisphere, where the Sun appears highest in the sky in mid-December when it is over the Tropic of Capricorn.

Pupils need to be able to identify the different weather elements, name and measure them, and know at what time of the year they are most likely to find certain weather patterns. They should be able to use simple maps and symbols to describe weather on a given day and interpret simple charts and diagrams. Recording simple weather data that they have collected for themselves is an excellent way in which to engage with these activities.

Pupils also need to be able to make the connections between the weather and everyday lives. This means knowing how to dress for different kinds of weather, how extreme weather events can be disruptive and how weather affects people's jobs, especially those who rely on it, such as farmers, builders and others who work outside. Periods of very dry, wet or windy weather are often memorable, as are heatwaves and cold snaps. You can use such weather events as a natural introduction to this area of study.

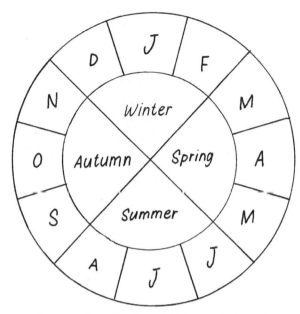

Figure 7: The UK has a temperate climate. Rain is distributed fairly evenly throughout the year and there are no great extremes of temperature. There are four seasons of roughly equal lengths

Misconceptions and research

Children often do not understand that weather is localised and variable. If they are experiencing a particular kind of weather in their locality, they can find it hard to realise that in another part of the UK – or even in the same county – there could be different weather events taking place. Due to their limited understanding of the water cycle at this age, they can also be confused about where the weather comes from or why it happens. Some known misconceptions include children believing that rainbows are a sign from God and that the movement of leaves in the trees or the blades on wind turbines cause the wind to blow.

Interesting facts

- Eastern England is the driest part of the UK, with less rain on average than many parts of Greece.
- During the Great Frost of 1683–4, the worst frost recorded in England, the River Thames in London was covered with ice up to 25 cm thick.
- The hottest ever temperature in the UK (over 40 degrees centigrade) was recorded at Heathrow airport in July 2022.

Key questions

1. What is the weather like today?
2. How do we measure and record the weather?
3. What do we expect the weather to be like in different seasons?

Lesson 1 Recording and forecasting the weather

How does the weather change?

You will need
- a map of the UK weather symbols and whiteboard
- access to the internet
- art materials.

Key vocabulary
- cloud
- cold
- fog
- gale
- hot
- rain
- showers
- snow
- Sun
- warm

Getting started

Ask the pupils what the weather is like today and begin a discussion, noting down some of the best descriptions and explaining any relevant vocabulary. Find out what the pupils know, and explain additional terms as needed.

Class activities

Weather symbols: Ask the pupils to make weather symbols showing different conditions, such as sunshine, sunshine and showers, clouds, rain, snow, fog and gales. You could use these to create a visual record of weather conditions over a week, recording the weather first thing in the morning, at midday and last thing in the afternoon. Add in wind direction using simple hand-held weather vanes or hand-held streamers.

Electronic weather diary: Keep an electronic diary using an online form or weather app, and record temperatures at the same time each day in the same place outside the classroom. Make simple graphs and link this to your location on a UK map. To extend the activity, use either Met Office data or links with another school to compare the daily temperature graph in another locality in the UK.

Weather forecaster: Choose a pair of pupils to be the daily weather forecasters and to give short presentations to the class, using a map of the UK and weather symbols. As an extension, you could ask them to give forecasts for a location in one of the other countries of the UK, researched by using the Met Office website (see Useful books and websites, p. 61).

Play corner: Turn the play corner into a weather centre, with maps and a hand-held video camera for pupils to record each other talking about the weather and giving forecasts.

Weather recording: Use simple equipment to measure different weather criteria outside once a week, and use the data to support work in mathematics. Investigate where the windiest/warmest/shadiest parts of the school grounds are and map them on a plan of the school. Create information panels outdoors identifying these areas, giving average termly measurements and using symbols.

Cloud watchers: Download a cloud chart from the Met Office website that identifies different cloud types. Go outside and get the children to take pictures of clouds that they can see using tablets or digital cameras. A day with part cloud and some sunshine is often best. **Remind the children never to look directly at the Sun**. Talk with the children about the different shapes, colours and cloud forms that they see.

Plenary
Ask pupils to summarise the day's weather in your locality, referring to the temperature, wind and cloud conditions, and discuss what the weather is likely to be the following day.

Lesson 2 Seasonal change

How do the seasons change?

You will need
- large sheets of light card
- a plan of the school and surrounding area

- a digital camera/video-recorder
- an app like FreezePaint that will collect a palette of colours from the landscape.

Key vocabulary

- autumn
- change
- spring
- summer
- winter

Getting started

Discuss the four seasons and the differences between them. Find out whether pupils can name and sequence them. Which season do they like most and why? Display the season names in order, in a cyclical diagram. Explain that the four seasons describe the changes in temperature and day length that happen in the same order every year. Establish the name of the current season and show the sequence. In practice, this is something that pupils learn best by constant reinforcement through everyday talk about the weather and seasonal change in real time, and hence this learning is ongoing.

Class activities

Seasonal activities: Ask pupils to brainstorm and sort seasonal-specific activities, e.g. building a snowman in winter, swimming in the sea in summer, picking daffodils in spring and kicking leaves in autumn.

Seasonal clothes: As a class, sort out a collection of clothes and accessories into season-appropriate wear. Ask pupils to draw pictures of themselves wearing appropriate clothing for each of the four seasons. Provide a dressing-up box and play area with different clothes, seasonal labels and a camera for children to photograph each other dressed for an identified season.

Seasonal clocks: Cut out large circles from a sheet of card and divide each into four quadrants, one for each consecutive season. Ask pupils to decorate each quadrant with appropriate weather vocabulary and other seasonal words and images. Add one clock hand at the centre to show the time of year, and ask them to turn it throughout the year to indicate the changing seasons.

Seasonal clues: Ask pupils to go outside and look for seasonal clues by using all their senses and looking carefully all around. Pay particular attention to trees and other plants, birds and other animals, and the weather. Take photographs and gather words and phrases to describe what children can see, smell, touch and hear. Point out things that are particularly indicative of the current season and weather-related.

Seasonal word clouds: Paste the words and phrases that the pupils have gathered into a word-cloud program such as Tagxedo. Select an appropriate outline shape for the word cloud to characterise the season being investigated.

Seasonal palette: Using an app such as FreezePaint, which samples colours from the landscape, walk around the school grounds and do just that. Allocate a different area to each of several small groups of pupils, using a map plan of the school grounds, such as that from Digimap for Schools, to pinpoint the location. Upload the resultant colour swatches to the map at the correct locations. This could also be done using standard photographs of features showing seasonal change.

Hint: The most important activity is to experience a season at first hand by going outside and doing some fieldwork. It is helpful to stay within the school grounds and use the same observation points to observe change throughout the year, but this can be augmented by walks outside of school too.

Plenary
Create a class seasonal display using words, images, drawings, maps and other artefacts linked to appropriate weather data and vocabulary.

Lesson 3 Extreme weather

How are we affected by extreme weather?

You will need
- atlases and digital mapping tools such as Digimap for Schools
- YouTube clips of extreme weather events
- a sand tray
- plastic guttering
- different-sized stones
- sand and gravel
- little figures
- building bricks and watering cans.

Key vocabulary
- blizzard
- flood
- gale
- heatwave

- hurricane
- tornado

Getting started

Ask the pupils whether they can remember a serious weather event, when the weather was so bad that it caused flooding or people were snowed in. You could show some news footage or a YouTube clip from recent severe weather events in the UK. Alternatively, have some images available to discuss that show people in extreme weather conditions. Have a discussion and explain some of the extreme terminology, like 'storm' or 'hurricane'. Reassure pupils that unusual weather events like these are very rare and that, even if they happen, there are plans in place to keep people safe. Ask pupils to think of ways in which the weather might disrupt their daily lives and make a list. Are some more dangerous than others?

Class activities

Extreme weather: Give pupils photographs of severe weather events and ask them to write captions. Provide weather vocabulary, such as 'flood', 'storm', 'gale' and 'blizzard', and a list of geographical feature names to match with some of the images, e.g. 'road', 'river', 'coast' and 'railway line'.

Dress for the weather: Make a list of clothes and items that you would take away for a week's holiday if it was forecast to be very hot / cold. Ask the pupils to find real weather data for a pretend holiday in the UK in the next few days, and use this information when they decide what to pack.

Comic strip: Ask the pupils to draw comic strips to show an extreme weather event and the problems that it causes. They might include a map as one of their drawings. Pupils could also draw themselves doing some of their favourite activities in ideal weather conditions.

Where was this?: Find out where some severe weather events took place and find them in an atlas or on a map of the UK. Use a digital mapping program to add labels to show the location and the name of the extreme weather involved, such as snow or fog.

Making landforms: Ask pupils to create landscapes in the sand tray using available materials, such as sand and gravel and guttering pipe for river channels. Add small-world play figures and houses, e.g. made from building bricks. Using a watering can or similar, simulate varying levels of rainfall and discuss what happens. Provide laminated feature-name labels to add, and then photograph the scenes. You could video some of the sequences and make news reports.

Plenary

Show some images of extreme weather events in the UK and ask pupils to describe the weather and the disruption that it might have caused.

Fieldwork and further investigations

- Invite someone whose job relies on the weather, such as a builder, farmer or fisherman, to talk to the class about how the weather affects them. Alternatively, you might invite a travel agent to talk about their work and the ways in which people choose holiday destinations where they can expect certain weather conditions, e.g. snow in Alpine ski resorts and sunshine for beach holidays.

- Take photographs of the same scene during a term or school year to record seasonal change. For example, you might take a picture each week of a tree in the school and edit it to create a short time-lapse movie. Doing this over the course of a year can involve all pupils and provide a record created by them of seasonal change. Note the location and the direction of view.

Cross-curricular links

English: Ask pupils to write short imaginary stories about a day when the weather spoilt their plans. They will need to say where they were, what the weather event was and how it ruined the day.

Mathematics: Measure, graph, chart or record weather data in different and interesting ways. Record the daily temperature at different points in the school grounds for a week and map it. Collect weather statistics from around the UK and add them to a map.

Science: Finding out the weather and season links directly with work on seasonal changes in science. The observations that pupils make and the measurements that they record will provide evidence that they are working scientifically.

History: Find out about extreme weather events that have affected the UK in the past. Examples include the North Sea floods of 1953, the seventeenth-century frost fairs on the River Thames and the year without a summer (1816).

Music: Listen to some music that relates to the weather and seasons, e.g. Vivaldi's *Four Seasons*, or let the children use instruments to recreate the sound of a weather event, e.g. a thunderstorm.

Themes

Climate change: Climate change appears to be making the UK wetter in winter and hotter in summer. It is also leading to more extreme weather events, including droughts, floods and storms. Some pupils may have personal experience of such events. You will easily be able to find out more about what is happening, both locally and globally, from reports and internet searches.

Sustainability: Monitor the classroom temperature in different weather conditions. How can you use less energy in cold weather? Are outside doors kept shut to prevent heat from escaping? Are the windows, walls and ceiling well insulated? Can you put an extra jumper on rather than turning up the heating?

Personal development: Taking responsibility for wearing the right clothing for the weather and knowing how to stay safe in adverse weather conditions enable children to develop their self-knowledge, self-esteem and self-confidence.

Progression and assessment

By the end of this area of study, children should be able to recognise and name common and some extreme weather phenomena using correct vocabulary, and describe some effects that the weather can have on everyday lives. They should know which symbols to use and how to locate them on a UK map to give information about local weather events. They will be able to make simple weather measurements and relate them to expected conditions for the season and time of year. Children will be able to name, sequence and describe the key characteristics of each season.

Useful books and websites

Carter, J. (2018), *Once Upon a Raindrop*. London: Caterpillar Books.

Usher, S. (2018), *Storm*. London: Templar Publishing.

Walters, C. (2007), *When Will it Be Spring?*. London: Myriad Books.

Wildsmith, B. (2007), *The North Wind and the Sun*. Oxford: Oxford University Press.

Digital mapping: http://digimapforschools.edina.ac.uk

Met Office website: www.metoffice.gov.uk

Word clouds: www.tagxedo.com

6 Hot and cold places

What do I need to know?

The Sun plays an essential part in supporting life on our planet. It provides the energy that allows plants and creatures to flourish and it heats the atmosphere, which in turn drives the world's climate. Generally, the hottest places are at or near the equator, where the Sun is high in the sky at midday. The coldest places are around the North and South Poles, where the Sun never rises very high above the horizon. In practice, this pattern becomes more complicated as cloud, wind and ocean currents distribute the Sun's energy unequally, creating different regions and climate zones. This area of learning considers three very distinctive regions and the plants and creatures that are associated with them. The ideas that are presented here are then developed in subsequent lessons. There is a direct progression to lower Key Stage 2, where pupils are introduced to climate zones, and to upper Key Stage 2, where they learn about global climate change.

Polar regions

These are found around the North and South Poles. Here, summer temperatures barely rise above freezing and winters are intensely cold. There is ice and snow throughout the year and frequent fierce storms and winds. The Arctic Ocean covers the northern polar regions, so there is water beneath the ice. By contrast, the continent of Antarctica covers the southern polar regions, and some parts of the surface rise to several thousand metres above sea level. This makes Antarctica the coldest place on Earth.

Hot deserts

These are extremely dry and they also receive large quantities of sunshine, which can raise the temperature to great heights. Few plants and creatures can survive in these regions known as hot deserts, which cover nearly a third of the surface of the continents. The Sahara Desert (North Africa) is the largest in the world. The Great Victoria Desert (Australia) and Kalahari Desert (Southern Africa) also cover vast areas.

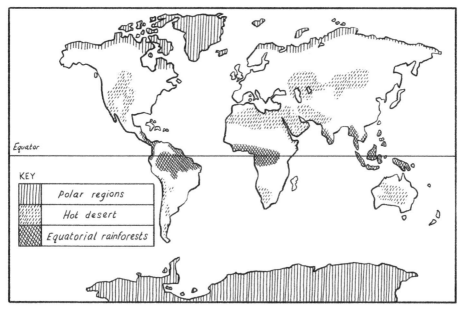

Figure 8: More than half the world's dry land consists of equatorial rainforests, hot deserts and polar regions

Equatorial rainforests

These are found around the equator. Here, rising air currents create heavy rainfall throughout the year, allowing dense rainforests to grow. Great numbers of plants and creatures thrive in the damp, warm conditions – many of them are still undocumented by scientists. The Amazon and Congo river basins, together with the islands of Indonesia, are the main rainforest regions of the world. However, the forests are being rapidly cleared for agriculture and development, which contributes to climate change and endangers wildlife.

Misconceptions and research

Children often think that the reason why equatorial regions are hot is because they are closer to the Sun. This simply isn't true. The key factor affecting global temperature is the amount of solar radiation that they receive. Due to the tilt of the Earth on its orbit around the Sun, equatorial regions receive more overhead sunlight than any other part of the world, which causes them to be hot; the polar regions receive the least, causing them to be cold.

Interesting facts

- The Sahara Desert is only slightly smaller than the entire continent of Europe.
- Around 25 per cent of the medicines in use today come from rainforest plants.
- Scientists in Antarctica have drilled into ice that is 2.7 million years old.

Key questions

1. Why don't all places have the same conditions?
2. How have people adapted to living in hot and cold places?

Lesson 1 Polar regions

What are polar regions like?

You will need

- an atlas or globe
- A5 sheets of paper and scissors
- access to the internet.

Key vocabulary

- Antarctica
- Arctic
- hibernate
- midnight
- Northern Lights
- North Pole
- penguin
- polar bear
- South Pole

Getting started

As a class, look at a globe or atlas map to locate the polar regions. Talk about the cold, snow and ice. Explain that the winter nights are very long and that in many places the Sun never rises for months on end. It is also exceptionally cold. In summer, the situation is reversed: there is a lot of daylight and sunshine, even at midnight. Using an atlas, identify similarities and differences between the Arctic and Antarctic.

Class activities

Polar bears: Watch the David Attenborough video clip of a mother bear and her cubs taking their first steps after the Arctic winter (search for 'Attenborough polar bears' on YouTube). Discuss with the pupils how some animals hibernate to help them get through the winter. Ask the pupils to work in pairs to decide on three things that interest them about this video to share with the rest of the class.

Midnight Sun: Give the pupils each a sheet of A5-size drawing paper. They fold the paper to create five vertical strips. Ask pupils to draw the same polar scene in each frame to show the position of the Sun at 12 noon, 6.00 pm, 12 midnight, 6.00 am and again at 12 noon. Add the time to each small drawing and the title 'Midnight Sun' at the top.

Antarctic explorers: Although it had long been suspected that there was an unknown southern continent, Antarctica wasn't actually sighted by Europeans until the nineteenth century. Using the internet, ask the pupils to find out about some of the explorers who went on expeditions to Antarctica in the past, such as Captain Scott, Roald Amundsen and Sir Ernest Henry Shackleton. Find out too about how explorers are still making journeys to the North and South Poles, sometimes walking solo for months at a time. In January 2022, British Army medical officer Preet Chandi became the first woman of colour to ski solo to the South Pole.

Emperor penguins: Emperor penguins are some of the very few creatures that can survive in the intense cold of Antarctica. Here are some penguin facts:

- Emperor penguins live to be about 20 years old.
- They weigh between 20 and 40 kilograms.
- They grow to be slightly over a metre tall.
- They eat lots of fish.
- They live in colonies of between 500 and 20,000 pairs.
- They have a black head, back and upper wings, and a white front.

Ask pupils to draw the outline shape of a penguin on a sheet of paper and then use the space inside to make up their own collection of penguin facts. Extend the activity by looking at some of the excellent videos that are available online. Why are animals like penguins only found on the edges of this continent and not inland?

Plenary
Talk with the pupils about whether they think that they would like to visit the polar regions. What would they need to take with them for a short expedition? What do they think that they would find particularly challenging?

Lesson 2 Hot deserts

What are hot deserts like?

You will need

- an atlas or globe
- a small cactus pot plant
- access to the internet
- materials to make collage paintings.

Key vocabulary

- cactus
- camel
- drought
- dune
- indigenous
- legend
- meerkat
- oasis
- palm tree
- saguaro

Getting started

As a class, look at a globe or atlas map to locate desert regions. There are hot deserts in every continent, apart from Europe and Antarctica. Where are they? Talk about the distinctive features of this climate. Explain that while many hot deserts are extremely dry, there may also be periods of rain, and some of the nights are cold.

Class activities

Desert images: Many people have strong images of deserts, which they associate with camels, sand dunes, palm trees and oases. Ask the pupils about their images to see what they already know. Use this as an opportunity to point out that there are many different types of desert. They can be hot or cold, not all are sandy and in many places cars have replaced camels. Point out that deserts also conceal great riches. Much of the world's oil comes from desert areas, and that links us to them in a very significant way.

Hot desert landscape: Ask pupils to make a painting or collage of a hot desert landscape. They could incorporate different materials such as sand, gravel, wood, cloth and bark. The textures that they use are one way in which to communicate the harshness that characterises these desert regions.

Plants: Plants and animals have to adapt to cope with hot desert conditions. Bring a small cactus pot plant into the class and talk about how the spikes help to protect it and how the thick skin helps it to survive long periods of drought. Extend the work by looking at photographs of the spectacular cacti from Arizona (saguaros), which grow 20 m and live for several hundred years. Encourage pupils to make their own drawings.

Meerkats: Meerkats are a form of mongoose and live in the Kalahari Desert and Southern Africa. They are extremely lively and sociable, and collaborate in order to survive in hostile desert conditions. While some meerkats dig in the sand looking for insects and other small animals to eat, others take on guard duty, looking for predators. There are lots of films showing meerkats in the wild that appeal to young children (see Useful books and websites, p. 71). Watch one of these and talk with the pupils about the meerkats' qualities. Do they think that these little animals are to be admired? What makes them special?

Indigenous people: The indigenous people of Australia are thought to have the longest continuous culture on the planet. Before British colonists arrived, there were around 250 nations in Australia, each with its own unique mixture of culture, customs and language. Find out more about the stories, songs, art and dance that made up these cultures. You could begin by reading creation myths and legends to the pupils and sharing some picture books, such as *Rainbow Bird* (Eric Maddern) and *Tiddalick the Greedy Frog* (Nicholas Wu).

Plenary
Consolidate the work that you have done in this lesson by asking pupils to write down and illustrate six words that describe the desert and desert life.

Lesson 3 Equatorial rainforests

What are equatorial rainforests like?

You will need
• an atlas or globe

• art materials

• a net, crêpe paper, rainforest photographs and picture books for the jungle corner

• a wall map showing vegetation or climate zones.

Key vocabulary

- avocado
- canopy
- deforestation
- equator
- rainfall
- rainforest
- season
- spice

Getting started

As a class, look at a globe or atlas map to locate rainforest regions, such as the Indonesian islands, Congo and Amazon river basins. Point out that rainforests are only found close to the equator. Talk about the equatorial rainforest climate; it is always hot but, unlike the hot desert, temperatures stay remarkably steady. Close to the equator, rainfall is also distributed fairly evenly. There are no particular seasons and the days are very similar in length throughout the year.

Class activities

Equatorial rainforest display: Create an equatorial rainforest wall display. Begin by drawing some trees viewed from the side, and then ask pupils to add animals to one of the four main layers listed below:

- the top layer, where the tallest trees emerge into the daylight around 50 m high
- the main canopy of dense foliage, 30–40 m above the ground
- the understorey, consisting of small trees, creepers and vines
- the forest floor, with tangles of mosses, ferns and fungi.

There are many creatures to choose, ranging from parrots and monkeys to tigers, toucans, snakes and frogs. Every child should be able to contribute at least one animal. Remember that there are lots of ants in the rainforest too!

Jungle corner: Turn a corner of your classroom into an equatorial rainforest environment. Use a net strung across the ceiling to represent the canopy of trees. Suspend lengths of green crêpe paper to suggest creepers. The walls could be decorated with pictures of rainforest plants and animals. There are plenty of picture books about the rainforest that you could display for children to read. Don't forget to include a world map. Pupils can then consult this to find out where they might 'go' or to see where the places that they 'visited' are.

Equatorial rainforest products: Make a display of food and other items that come from these rainforests. You could include the following food items: coffee, chocolate, bananas, pineapples, nuts (e.g. cashew nuts and Brazil nuts), pepper, cinnamon and other spices, avocados, coconuts and oranges. Products such as rubber, palm oil and timber provide other examples of rainforest links. How do the children think that these products are brought to the UK? Why can't we produce them here?

Deforestation: Organise a short class discussion on deforestation. Divide the class into two groups: one group to think about why the rainforest needs to be cleared for farming and industry, and the other group to focus on the importance of retaining the forest as a home for wildlife and local people. See whether each group can put forward three arguments to support their case. They might also come up with a banner or slogan to promote their views. Can the groups work together to think of some solutions that help people to make a living and also preserve habitats?

Plenary
Ask pupils to say what is special about the equatorial rainforest environment. Why does it support so many different plants and creatures?

Fieldwork and further investigations

- Set up two simple bottle gardens in glass or plastic jars arranged on their sides. Fill one jar with earth and try to keep it warm and damp to replicate the rainforest climate. Fill the other jar with sand and keep it dry to simulate the desert. Add a number of suitable plants to each jar or make drawings to illustrate them. As an extension, find out about how the domes at the Eden Project in Cornwall recreate distinctive biomes. If possible, visit a local botanical garden, where pupils can visit different greenhouse environments.

- Make a survey of plants, either in and around your school or that the children have at home. Can pupils find any cacti or palm trees that originate in desert environments? Can they find any orchids, ferns or other equatorial rainforest plants? See whether you can set up a display table showing how we use plants from both the hot desert and the equatorial rainforest to decorate our environment.

Cross-curricular links

English: Ask pupils to make simple books, each with four or eight pages, about the creatures that live in one of the three climates featured in this area of study. Each page could contain information about a different creature: what it eats, where it lives and how it responds to the climate. Invite the pupils to decorate the covers and put their names and a title on the front.

Mathematics: Ask pupils to research climate records around the world. What is the highest/lowest temperature ever recorded? Which places are the driest/wettest on Earth? Can they find any surprising statistics?

Music: Invite pupils to compose a short piece of music to illustrate the features of the three climates featured in this area of study. The rainforest climate might contain the sound of raindrops; the desert could be harsh and angular; the polar regions might focus on winds or the gentle magic of the ice sheets.

Art: Look at images of the Northern Lights on the internet. Pupils may use these as inspiration to make their own Northern Lights paintings.

Themes

Colonialism and social justice: Voyages of exploration revealed the equatorial rainforests and large areas of previously unknown hot desert to European adventurers. From the sixteenth century onwards, the plants, minerals and human resources of these areas were systematically exploited, and thousands of indigenous people lost their lives as a result. Some groups, such as the First Nations of Canada and the indigenous tribes of Australia, have survived, however, and they give us a fascinating glimpse of a way of living and relating to nature that is completely different to mainstream Western practices that children can explore.

Biodiversity: With over three million species, the Amazon is one of the most biodiverse places on Earth. We also know that the Earth is losing vast numbers of plants and creatures and that we are witnessing a period of mass extinction, which is the direct result of human action. Talk with the children about why this matters so much.

Sustainability: In many parts of the world, there are concerns that hot deserts are expanding: sub-Saharan Africa, parts of South Asia and the Andes are among the areas affected. Over-cultivation, over-grazing and the clearance of trees for firewood are some of the causes. Shifting climate patterns are another factor. You might discuss with pupils the way in which hot deserts are spreading, partly due to deforestation and poor land management.

Progression and assessment

By the end of this area of study, all children should be able to talk about the differences between equatorial rainforest, hot desert and polar regions. The ability to name specific examples and/or locate them on a globe or world map will be evidence of higher levels of achievement. Pupils who are exceeding expectations will have a growing understanding of how plants, creatures and people respond to the environments that they have studied.

Useful books and websites

Bailey, E. (2015), *One Day on our Blue Planet… in the Savannah*. London: Flying Eye.

Cowcher, H. (2009), *Antarctica*. London: Macmillan.

Harvey, R. (2006), *In the Bush*. London: Allen and Unwin.

Maddern, E. and Kennaway, A. (1993), *Rainbow Bird: An Aboriginal Folk Tale from Northern Australia*. London: Frances Lincoln.

North, W. and Hamblen, A. (2012), *Australia Here We Come! Exploring a Distant Place*. Sheffield: Geographical Association.

Richardson, P. and Richardson, T. (2012), *Living in the Freezer: Investigating Polar Environments*. Sheffield: Geographical Association.

Wu, N. (2013), *Tiddalick the Greedy Frog: An Aboriginal Dreamtime Story*. Huntington Beach, CA, USA: Teacher Created Materials.

Desertification: search for 'Desertification – a visual disaster' on YouTube.

Meercat videos: search for 'Meerkat BBC' on YouTube.

Polar bear video: search for 'Mother polar bear and cubs emerge from den' on YouTube.

7 Mountains, rivers and coasts

What do I need to know?

The shape of the land is always changing – sometimes quickly but sometimes very slowly, over millennia. In addition to direct human influence, the landscape is worn away due to the combined effects of water, wind and temperature. It is also affected by the movement of tectonic plates deep beneath the surface, which cause the land to be pushed up to create mountains or pulled apart causing trenches to develop.

Mountains

Mountains are elevations on the Earth's surface, usually higher and steeper than hills and usually more than 600 m high. Mountains can be found on every continent and even under the sea. They can be generally described as having sloping and often steep sides and sharp or rounded peaks. Some mountains have snow on their summits, even though they are found at warm latitudes. A well-known example is Mount Kilimanjaro in Kenya, which is Africa's tallest mountain. Due to the effect of altitude, the temperature at the top of Kilimanjaro is much lower than that at the base. On some mountains there is what is called the 'tree line', above which the temperature and growing conditions make it impossible for trees to survive.

Rivers

Rivers usually begin in hills and mountains, often rising out of the ground in a spring. They grow larger as they flow downhill and are joined by tributaries. Further downstream there may be lakes, waterfalls and gorges. Although a few simply end in a lake, the vast majority eventually flow into an estuary and join the sea. There will be towns along the way, especially at bridging points. Ask pupils to name any streams and rivers that they know of, either locally or further afield. Are they aware of any famous rivers such as the Thames, Nile or Amazon?

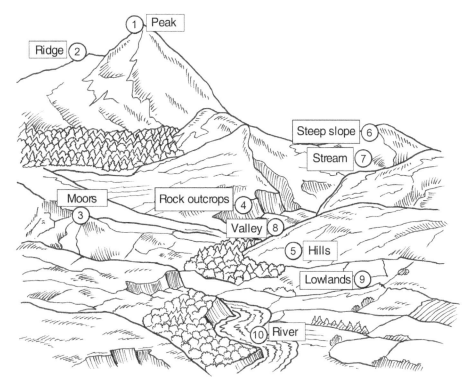

Figure 9: Mountain landscapes have many distinct features

Coasts

Coasts are where the land meets the sea; they form natural boundaries. They are continually being shaped by the sea or ocean that meets them and are affected over longer periods of time by sea-level change. Coasts can be very different in physical appearance and can take the form of marshland, cliffs, estuaries or sand dunes, depending on the local geology and the processes shaping them. The coast is traditionally a good place to settle: most major cities are located on the coast. It's where trade from other countries arrives and goods are exported abroad. Places on coasts that offer safe and easy access for ships can become harbours and ports. Many jobs, from tourism to fishing, are located at coastal resorts and villages.

Misconceptions and research

Primary school children, especially those in Key Stage 1, make little sense of general terms such as 'human geography' and 'physical geography'. However, identifying the names of physical features and learning about their properties is entirely appropriate for the age range. There is a good deal of vocabulary to develop if children are to feel confident talking about and describing landscapes. Placing children's learning in context is crucial when developing their knowledge and understanding, and fieldwork should be used wherever possible so that they can study features at first hand.

Interesting facts

- Mount Everest is the highest mountain, but the world's tallest mountain is Mauna Kea, as it is more than 10,000 m from the ocean floor to its peak.
- Canada has the world's longest coastline – five times as long as the equator.
- Although millions of people live on its banks, there are no bridges over the Amazon River.

Key questions

1. What are the most important landscape features?
2. What is the difference between a hill and a mountain?
3. At what point does a river end and the sea begin?

Lesson 1: Mountains

What are the world's highest mountains?

You will need

- an electronic world map
- an atlas
- sticky notes and felt pens
- modelling clay and paint
- Unifix® cubes
- photographs of hills and mountains from different regions of the UK.

Key vocabulary

- cliff
- hill
- peak
- ridge
- river

- rocky outcrop
- stream
- valley

Getting started

Ask whether pupils know the name of the world's highest mountain. Where is it? Can they find it on a globe or mark it electronically on a digital map? Explain that you are going to research and find out the names of the highest mountain in each continent. You are also going to find out about mountain landscapes.

Class activities

Mountain words: Project a large view of a mountain onto the interactive whiteboard and discuss with the pupils the features that they can see. Annotate the picture with mountain words, such as 'peak', 'ridge', 'steep slope', 'cliff', 'stream' and 'rocky outcrop'. Complete the activity by giving each pair of children an image to annotate themselves, using sticky notes and felt pens. You might decide to give pupils a suitable word list to help them with this task.

Mountain building: Make models of mountains out of modelling clay and other materials. Paint the models to show rivers, vegetation, rocky outcrops and so forth, to make them look realistic. Add labels of the key features and give the mountain a specific name as appropriate.

UK mountains: Explain that mountains are normally more than 600 m high. Provide the children with some pictures of mountains in the UK, together with details of their heights and locations (e.g. Ben Nevis in Scotland, 1,344 m; Snowdon in Wales, 1,085 m; Scafell Pike in England, 977 m; and Slieve Donard in Northern Ireland, 852 m). Get the children to locate the mountains on an atlas and mark them on their own blank outline maps, and ask them to add some more examples of their own. Which of the four countries in the UK has the largest number of high mountains?

Scale models: Provide the names of some of the tallest mountains from each continent and give their heights in metres. Ask pupils to help you round their heights up or down to the nearest 1,000 m. Build scale models of the mountains using a Unifix® cube to represent each 1,000 m. Pupils should first compare the mountains, ordering them from highest to lowest, before placing their labelled models on the correct continents as accurately as possible.

Dressing for mountains: Make a kit list for a day out on Ben Nevis/Snowdon for a summer's day walk to the summit. Explain why you would need to pack waterproof and warm clothes even if it was a very hot day. Why is a map a vital piece of kit?

Plenary

Toss an inflatable globe to pupils in turn and ask them to identify one of the major rivers or mountain ranges on it, say what feature it is and point to its location. Each time one is mentioned, find and label it on a digital map on the interactive whiteboard or a large paper map of the world. Search for some webcams online or video clips showing climbers on British mountains or some of the world's major peaks.

Lesson 2 Rivers

What are rivers like?

You will need

- an atlas
- a water tray, sand and a watering can
- a video clip of the credits from *EastEnders*
- inflatable globes
- access to the internet and digital mapping software.

Key vocabulary

- bank
- flow
- mouth
- river
- source
- stream
- tributary

Getting started

Is there a stream or river near you? Where is it and what is it called? Explain that streams and rivers flow downhill and find their way to the lowest point on land, before returning the water to the sea or ocean. If you have a water tray, you could build a sand model of a hill and use a watering can to water the top, and watch how the water runs down the slopes to find the lowest point.

Class activities

River Thames: Show the pupils the famous scene of the loop of the Thames in London used for the credits of *EastEnders*, and ask whether any of the children recognise what it is. Explain that the Thames is the longest and most famous river solely in England (and the second longest in the UK, after the Severn). The Thames starts from small springs near the town of Cirencester in the Cotswold hills; it flows through London and then out into the Thames Estuary and the North Sea. Remind pupils that the Thames is the river on which the capital city is built. Can they find it on a UK map? Can they map it on a blank outline map?

River habitats: Explain that the plants and creatures that live near a river form a distinct habitat and that they all depend on the water that it brings and the soil that accumulates on its banks. Read the pupils an extract from *The Wind in the Willows* by Kenneth Grahame. Explain that this famous story is based on the Thames and introduces a range of different characters. Ask pupils to make drawings of a riverside scene featuring some of these creatures.

River acrostic: Discuss words that describe a river and its surroundings. As a class, work collectively to devise an acrostic using either single words or phrases structured around the word 'river'. Next, challenge pupils to make their own acrostics structured around the names of specific rivers, such as the Thames, Severn, Trent or the name of a river in your locality.

UK rivers: Help pupils to build up their knowledge of rivers around the UK by looking at Ordnance Survey or atlas maps, as well as digital aerial imagery. Ask pupils to complete tables listing the names of the rivers, the hills/mountains where they begin and the sea into which they flow. Are there any major towns along their banks?

Plenary
Read a story book about a river and ask pupils to comment every time that they hear a special river word. Ask them what they think it means.

Lesson 3 Coastal sights

What is the coastline like?

You will need
- an atlas
- access to the internet
- photographs of different coastlines in the UK and other parts of the world
- a water tray with materials and figures for small-world play.

Key vocabulary

- beach
- cliff
- coast
- dune
- headland
- marsh
- mudflat
- ocean
- rock stack
- sea

Getting started

Show the pupils a Google Earth image of the UK and them to identify the land and the sea. Explain that the coastline is where the land meets the sea or ocean. Ask them to look carefully to see whether they can find areas where there are lots of islands, places where the land juts out into the sea to form headlands and stretches of coastline that appear to be straight. Next, show the pupils some pictures of different coastlines, e.g. cliffs, rock stacks, beaches, mudflats, sand dunes and so on. Talk about these different features and the differences between them. What do they all have in common?

Class activities

Tactile display: Make a tactile display using objects found on a beach that pupils can touch and smell, such as sand, pebbles, shells and seaweed. Label the items and add information books and magnifying glasses. See whether you can find any picture books to add to the display.

My coast: Do you have a beach near you? If not, ask where the pupils have been on holiday. Ask pupils to bring in photographs of themselves at the beach and add them to a map of the UK or the wider world. Ask pupils to describe what the beach was like and what they did there.

Coast or not?: Ask pupils to use an atlas to find countries that have a coastline all around them, those that have some coastline and those that are landlocked. Record the results in a table with three columns. Conversely, give pupils the names of some countries and ask them to investigate into which category they fall.

Coastal play: Use the water tray to recreate coastlines and features using materials such as modelling clay, sand and pebbles. Add small-world play features and ask pupils to make annotated maps of their coastal places once complete. Provide some images of different coastal features, such as sandy beaches, marshland or cliffs, for the children to copy.

Plenary

Ask pupils to find a photograph of a beach, either in the UK or abroad, that they would like to visit. Ask them to use this in a holiday poster that explains what the coastline is like, using some of the terms about which they have learned in the lesson.

Fieldwork and further investigations

- If there is a stream or river that can be easily reached nearby, visit it for formal and informal fieldwork. Take photographs and/or sketch features that can be found there. Determine the directions of the river flow, and the sea and the source using a compass. Note the different plants that you can see. Can the pupils spot any fish, birds or insects? How do people use the river? Make a list of activities and facilities and whether there are any nearby access points, such as car parks or bridges. Back in class, create a large map of the river and add feature names and images to make a display. Add images electronically to an Ordnance Survey map using Digimap for Schools. **Devising a risk assessment is particularly important for all river fieldwork, as the water level can change from day to day and there is always a danger that a child will slip or fall into the water.**

Cross-curricular links

English: Make a vocabulary wall featuring names of images as you undertake this area of study. Paste the words you have learned about into a word-cloud program, such as Tagxedo. You could arrange mountain words in a mountain shape and arrange river words in a sequence to represent a river.

Mathematics: Comparing the lengths of different rivers and the heights of mountains involves the pupils in practical mathematical problems relating to measurement, sequencing and scale.

Science: Finding out about mountains, coasts and rivers provides ample opportunities for investigating plants and their habitats and comparing the range of creatures that are found in different environments.

Art: Rivers and riverbank scenes have been popular with artists through the ages. You might either look at some famous examples, such as Constable and Monet, or ask pupils to do their own paintings, perhaps after a fieldwork visit.

Themes

Climate change: Scientists believe that sea levels are currently rising by around 3 mm a year, due to climate change. This will have significant impacts on coastlines over a period of time. Around one-sixth of the land in Bangladesh could be lost by 2050, and the Pacific Ocean island nation of Tuvalu may disappear entirely. Discuss this with the class but try to avoid disaster scenarios. Sea levels are always changing, but we have to do what we can to mitigate climate change and care for those who are affected by it.

Sustainability: People enjoy going to the beach, especially in summer, but they sometimes leave litter behind them. Discuss the importance of keeping rivers and beaches clean and recycling rubbish. Think about the impact on creatures as well as people. Will some types of pollution last longer than others?

Values and wellbeing: Developing a better understanding of the physical features of the UK and other parts of the world introduces children to inspiring and iconic landscapes. The wonders and beauties of the world are a powerful reason to care for and nurture the environment. Nature has inspired poets, artists and musicians throughout history, and is often a key factor in spiritual development.

Progression and assessment

By the end of this unit, children should be able to recognise and name a good range of geographical features. They should be able to name some of the highest mountains and longest rivers in the world and the UK, and explain in simple terms the properties of mountains, rivers and coasts. A few children will be able to make the connection between physical landscapes and what people do there.

Useful books and websites

Clulow, H. (2016), *The River: An Epic Journey to the Sea*. London: Caterpillar Books.

Grahame, K. (1993), *The Wind in the Willows*. London: Wordsworth Editions.

Marting, M. (2017), *A River*. San Francisco: Chronicle Books (also see online video versions).

Oswald, P. (2021), *Hike*. London: Walker Books.

Peet, M. (2017), *The Treasure of Pirate Frank*. London: Nosy Crow.

Turney, A. (2014), *Investigating Rivers*. Sheffield: Geographical Association.

Digimap for Schools: www.digimapforschools.edina.ac.uk

Photos of mountains, rivers and coasts: search on Google Images.

Tagxedo: www.tagxedo.com

8 Villages, towns and cities

What does the curriculum say?

Pupils should be taught to:

- *use basic geographical vocabulary to refer to key human features, including: city, town, village, factory, farm, house, office, port, harbour and shop*

- *use aerial photographs and plan perspectives to recognise landmarks and basic human and physical features; devise a simple map; and use and construct basic symbols in a key.*

What do I need to know?

Villages

Villages are one of the most basic and ancient forms of human settlement. By living in small groups, people were able to pool their labour and share their skills as they farmed the land or harvested fish from the sea. Until relatively recently, most villages were more or less self-sufficient. In the UK, the church, post office, inn, school and shop formed the heart of the community. Nowadays, new houses are being added to many villages to cater for people who work in towns or for those who come to the countryside to retire.

Towns

Towns are significantly larger than villages, with many more facilities. They have offices, banks, restaurants, pubs and places of entertainment. They may also have factories and trading estates. Many towns started off as villages and developed as centres of trade and commerce, perhaps due to their favourable position. They then developed and grew rich on the produce from the nearby countryside. Today, the high street or marketplace still forms the historic core of many towns, and it is there where the oldest buildings are to be found. Housing estates, schools and sports grounds tend to be located in surrounding areas, where there is more space and land is cheaper.

Cities

Cities are the largest of all settlements and have regional, national or international significance. They serve as centres of government and have specialist facilities, such as hospitals, universities and research centres. They are also major transport hubs, with extensive road, rail and air connections. People have always been attracted to cities by the opportunities that they offer. In Britain, many cities developed in the nineteenth century, as the Industrial Revolution brought new forms of prosperity based on manufacturing.

However, problems such as pollution, derelict spaces and deprivation now affect these older industrial centres. In other parts of the world, shanty towns and very rapid development are presenting considerable challenges.

Urban growth

Until the beginning of the present century, most people in the world lived in villages and rural communities. Now, for the first time in recorded history, urban life has become the dominant mode of living. Towns and cities are growing ever larger, as people migrate from the countryside to seek security or a better life. By 2050, it is predicted that three-quarters of the population will be living in urban areas. Newly developed countries in particular have seen spectacular urban growth. China, for example, has over 100 metropolitan areas, each with over a million people, and in some places, such as the Pearl River Delta, cities have merged together to form conurbations. Greater Tokyo, the area around New York and the Ruhr in Germany are other examples of extensive urban areas.

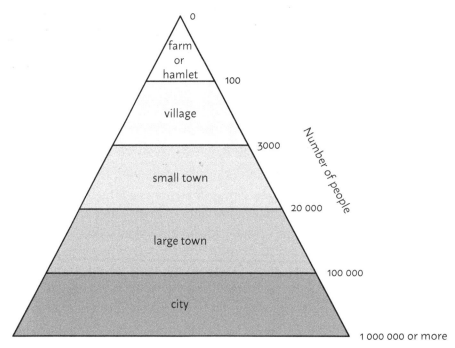

Figure 10: People live in settlements of different sizes. Places are called hamlets, villages, towns or cities, depending on the number of people who live there. The figures in this diagram are not definitive but give a general idea of settlement size

City life is now the dominant form of living, both in the UK and around the world. Approximate population sizes for the different settlements are as follows:

- small village: 50–500
- large village: 5,000–3,000

- small town: 3,000– 20,000
- large town: 20,000–100,000
- city: 100,000–one million
- conurbation: several million plus.

Misconceptions and research

Although children may be able to talk convincingly about villages, towns and cities, they may still be confused about the status of their own settlement and believe that they live in a village when they actually live in a town (or vice versa). This may be because the terms are generalisations that are difficult to visualise.

Interesting facts

- St David's in Pembrokeshire has a population of less than 2,000 people but is classed as a city because it has a cathedral.
- Lancing in West Sussex, with a population of around 19,000, claims to be the largest village in England.
- After the Second World War, 'new towns' were built across the UK to replace poor or damaged homes.

Key questions

1. What are the differences between villages, towns and cities?
2. Are there villages in other countries apart from the UK?

Lesson 1 Villages

What are villages like?

You will need
- strips of light card that can be folded into eight panels to make zigzag books
- access to aerial photographs showing different villages
- a map of your area or a rural location elsewhere in the UK.

Key vocabulary
- city
- detached house

- shop
- terraced house
- town
- village

Getting started

As a class, discuss the differences between villages, towns and cities. What do pupils think are the main features of each? Can they name any villages, towns and cities that they have visited or know about? How many people do they think might live there?

Class activities

Village names: Talk about villages either in your area or in other parts of the country. Working from a map, make a list of village names. You might sort the names using different criteria, e.g. in alphabetical order, by size or by distance. Look at a local map as an extension activity to discover other villages to add to your list.

Village portrait: Give pupils some long sheets of card, which they should fold into a zigzag to make a simple book with eight panels. Ask them to make a labelled drawing of a key building or place on each of the panels. They could choose from the following: place of worship, school, inn, garage, farm, shop, village hall, playground, detached house and terraced house. They could also add ideas of their own and pictures of people or animals, as appropriate.

The view from above: Look at photographs of villages taken from the air. Using Google Earth or Digimap for Schools, you can zoom in and out to see increasing levels of detail. Discuss what you can see in each image. Can pupils find the roads, houses, surrounding fields and woodlands? What other significant features can they spot, e.g. streams, ponds, parks or coasts?

Village plans: When you look at aerial photographs and maps, the pupils may notice that villages have different plans or shapes. In some villages, the buildings are clustered together, almost in a circle. In others, they are stretched out along a single street. Discuss the different plans that you discover.

Village visit: Arrange a visit to a nearby village. It will be best if you plan a route beforehand, linking the places and features that you want the pupils to see. If possible, try to arrange access to a place of worship or an interview with a shopkeeper. Talk about what you discover with the class and take photographs to record the key features as you investigate.

Plenary

Ask pupils to make a large collage picture as a class display. Suggest that they work in groups to make drawings and label the key buildings. Around the edge, add pictures of the people who live there and the jobs that they do.

Lesson 2 Towns

What are towns like?

You will need
- information about local services
- paper and art materials.

Key vocabulary
- council
- inputs
- outputs
- services
- shield
- traps and gratings

Getting started

Ask the pupils to name some of the towns that they know, either locally or further afield. Make a list on the interactive whiteboard. Confirm that all the places that they have named have a range of shops and lots of houses. Explain that many towns grew up as trading centres and some still have street markets.

Class activities

Inputs and outputs: Discuss with the class the inputs and outputs of towns. Explain that people who live in towns depend on others to provide the things that they need for their survival on a daily level. Food, water and resources such as building materials are key inputs that are essential in supporting modern life. So too are electricity and other forms of energy, such as oil and gas. At the same time, town and city dwellers generate outputs that need to be disposed of in one way or another. Foremost among these are rubbish, sewage and atmospheric pollution. Ask pupils to make a diagram to show inputs and outputs in action. They should place themselves at the centre of the page, with arrows showing inputs and outputs to the left and right.

Town services: A short walk along a local street will provide plenty of clues to the infrastructure that supports town life. Discuss with the pupils the different traps and gratings that they discover in the pavement (probably mostly water and gas), the overhead wires and cables that they see, and the bins that store rubbish awaiting collection. What would happen if any of these services broke down? Are some services more important than others?

Two sides: Towns can have many contrasting areas, with different characters and functions. Even two sides of the same street may be very different. Investigate and compare similarities and differences within a small area through fieldwork.

Town council: Who keeps a town running? Talk about some of the services provided by the local council. Children will be aware of refuse and rubbish collection. Prompt them to think about repairs to roads and pavements, the maintenance of parks and gardens, and public services such as museums, libraries and sports centres. Extend this activity using leaflets and newsletters provided by your local town council or district authority.

Town shield: Ask pupils to imagine that they have been asked to design badges or shields for a competition. Divide sheets of paper into four and ask them to make drawings of four features that they think are significant about their local town. Next, see whether they can simplify these drawings and combine them in shields that are divided into four quadrants like the paper with which they started.

Plenary
Consolidate pupils' understanding of towns and their facilities. Using the headings below as prompts, see whether pupils can name any local examples.

- **Commerce:** shops, cafes/restaurants, banks
- **Services:** schools, doctors' surgeries, fire stations
- **Employment:** offices, factories
- **Transport:** bus stations, garages, car parks
- **Leisure:** parks, sport centres, theatres

Lesson 3 Cities

What are cities like?

You will need
- images of cities
- an atlas
- corrugated card, paper and paint
- sticky notes.

Key vocabulary

- landmark
- silhouette
- skyscraper

Getting started

Explain to pupils that a city is much larger than a town. Download some photographs of cities from the internet and discuss what they show. How many skyscrapers can children see? Are there any particularly interesting-looking buildings? Do the pictures make them feel excited or frightened?

Class activities

Landmarks: Many cities are famous for their landmarks. Examples include the Eiffel Tower (Paris), Statue of Liberty (New York), Kremlin (Moscow) and Sydney Opera House (Sydney). Young children sometimes find the Leaning Tower of Pisa particularly fascinating, but they will also discover many other examples that will appeal to their imaginations. Using the internet, challenge pupils to download photographs of different examples for a group display. See that each landmark is linked to the city where it is found on a simple world map.

Tallest buildings: The world's tallest buildings are all to be found in great cities. At 830 m (2,717 feet), the Burj Khalifa in Dubai (United Arab Emirates) takes the record at the time of writing – it is about the same height as the mountains of Wales and northern England. Ask pupils to investigate other examples – the outlines are sufficiently distinctive to make interesting silhouettes for a display.

Comparisons: Explore cultural similarities and differences using the picture book *Mirror* by Jeannie Baker. This tells the story of parallel lives in Sydney, Australia and a rural village in southern Morocco, and how they are connected. There are also video versions of the book available on YouTube (see Useful books and websites, pp. 89–90).

World cities: Give pupils an atlas and ask them to find six or more cities in different parts of the world. They should write down the names so that they can share what they have discovered with the rest of the class. To make this activity more competitive, you could get pupils to name the country or continent where their cities can be found.

Cities of the future: Discuss with the class how they think that cities might change in the future in response to new technology and inventions. Ask them to focus on one specific change that captures their imagination, and ask them to make drawings to show their ideas.

Plenary

As a class, discuss the advantages and the disadvantages of living in a city. Ask pupils to write down what they think on sticky notes to pin to a class display. Discuss what the pupils have written and their views on city life.

Fieldwork and further investigations

- Make some flashcards with the names of different villages, towns and cities about which the pupils have learned in this area of study. Ask pupils questions about each place. Is it a town, village or city? Is it in this country? Is it famous in any way?
- Make a class list of all the things that pupils know or associate with London. As well as buildings and well-known sights, think about famous people who are either alive today or who lived in London in the past. Divide the class into small groups to create a collage of their images.

Cross-curricular links

English: As a class, discuss the advantages and disadvantages of town life. Then read them Aesop's tale of the town mouse and country mouse. Do they agree that town life is hurried and stressful? What would they say if the story was told the other way around, i.e. from the point of view of the town mouse visiting the country?

Mathematics: Find out about the number of people (round number of millions) living in different world cities. Show these figures in a simple bar chart and add data for London to help the children to make comparisons.

Art: Towns and cities often have striking skylines, which have been celebrated by artists to good effect. The London skyline, centred on St Paul's, is one that will be particularly familiar for people in the UK. Ask the pupils to create their own skylines, real or imaginary, using black paper for the buildings, which can be set against a colourful sunset for added impact.

History: The oldest towns in the UK can trace their origins back to Roman times. Look at a map of Roman Britain in a book or atlas. What are the main towns shown? How many of these towns are still in use today? Have any been abandoned? Which is the nearest Roman town to the place where you live?

Music: Songs often mention places, especially cities, so there are good opportunities for singing one or two of these with pupils to broaden out this area of study. You may have your own personal favourites, but you can also refer to websites to support this work (see Useful books and websites on the following page).

Themes

Biodiversity: In 2019, London became the world's first National Park City. It has over eight million trees and around 15,000 different species. What would pupils do to increase biodiversity in their own area? Where would be a good place to plant new trees? Are there any areas that could be set aside for wildlife?

Climate change: Fumes from petrol and diesel cars contribute to climate change and cause people to have breathing problems. How could traffic in your area be reduced? Are there are roads that could be closed to traffic? Find out about the Ultra Low Emission Zones that are being introduced in some towns and cities.

Sustainability: Cities make a huge demand on resources. They need to be supplied with water and they create waste that needs to be processed. They are supplied with food, which often comes from distant places. They need electricity and power to keep them running. Gather some ideas from the children about how this 'footprint' could be reduced. You might begin by listing the resources that they all use each day and the demands that we all make on the environment.

Progression and assessment

By the end of this area of study, all children should be able to talk about the differences between villages, towns and cities. They should also be able to name a few key cities worldwide and in the UK. Those who are performing at higher levels will have begun to develop opinions about the relative merits of rural and urban life. Recognising that there are multiple factors to consider is a further indicator of achievement, as is the ability to relate classroom learning to personal life circumstances.

Useful books and websites

Baker, J. (2010), *Mirror*. London: Walker Books (also available on YouTube).

Browne, A. (1990), *Voices in the Park*. London: Random House.

Ringgold, F. (1996), *Tar Beach*. London: Dragonfly Books.

Aesop's fable: search for 'The town mouse and the country mouse' on YouTube.

Cities from above: search for 'Cities at night from space'.

Songs about cities: search for 'Wikipedia, list of songs about cities'.

9 Routes and journeys

What does the curriculum say?

Pupils should develop knowledge about the world, the United Kingdom and their locality. They should understand basic subject-specific vocabulary relating to human and physical geography and begin to use geographical skills, including first-hand observation, to enhance their locational awareness.

What do I need to know?

There is a subtle difference between 'route' and 'journey'. A journey is about travelling from one place to another and a route is a precise description of how you get there – it is something that can be mapped and measured. A journey is a concept that encompasses both purpose and mode and can apply to people, animals or things. A route is much more direct in meaning. This area of study is an opportunity for pupils to bring together and consolidate various aspects of the geography programme of study from across Key Stage 1.

Local routes

There are various familiar and repetitive routes that we make in our normal day-to-day lives and that are closely linked to our culture, community and geographical setting. Children will have similar experiences in that they travel to school, accompany family to the shops, visit other members of the family nearby and make trips for leisure and play. Investigating the spatial component of these everyday trips allows them to deepen their knowledge of their local area, which will then enable them to make a better comparison to a contrasting area elsewhere.

Roads and railways

When people travel between places, they usually want to take the route that is quickest and easiest. Roads and railways mark out permanent ways that are suitable for different types of transport. In mountainous areas, they follow valleys and avoid steep slopes. Elsewhere, they skirt marshes, lakes and forests. Sometimes, roads and railways deviate to avoid areas of high landscape quality or cultural significance. Bridges and crossing points are particularly important in determining the best route from one place to another and tend to bring routes together, creating traffic bottlenecks.

Migration routes

When people and creatures move from one place to another with the intention of settling, either permanently or temporarily, they are said to migrate. Animals often make very long migrations each year in their search for food and in response to global weather and climate patterns. They usually follow established routes, and children enjoy finding out about the journeys that they take. For example, some birds, such as swallows and cuckoos, migrate north from Africa to the UK for the spring and summer months. Others, such as redwings, fieldfares, blackbirds and robins, migrate south to the UK from Scandinavia in the winter months, when their food becomes covered by snow.

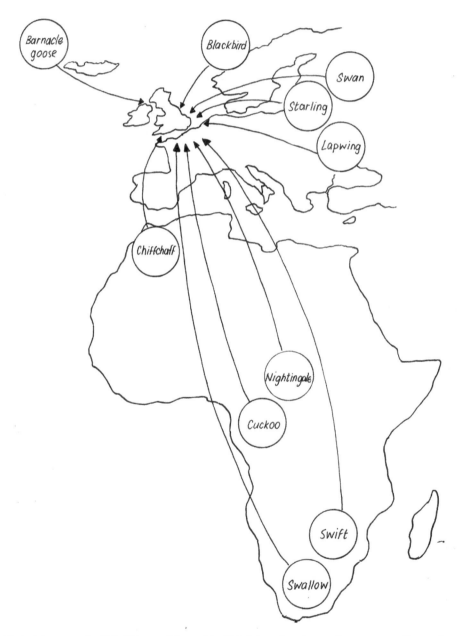

Figure 11: Bird visitors to the UK. Winter visitors: blackbird, lapwing, barnacle goose, starling and swan. Summer visitors: swift, swallow, cuckoo, nightingale and chiffchaff

Misconceptions and research

The ability to navigate and find the way from one place to another is a basic survival skill that develops at an early age. Research has shown that even children as young as three or four have remarkably good wayfinding ability, and that they can retrace a route and point out landmarks that they have been shown by an adult several days earlier. Similarly, young children perform well in experiments in which they are asked to find a hidden toy using just a map or plan of a room. There is a long-standing debate about whether boys and girls perform equally well at tasks of this kind. There is also discussion about whether any differences are innate or culturally mediated.

Interesting facts

- The Suez Canal almost halves the distance by sea from Mumbai in India to London in the UK.
- The shortest route from the UK to Japan involves going over the Arctic, rather than crossing the USA.
- Arctic terns migrate from the Arctic to the Antarctic and back again over the course of a year. This is the longest migration of any bird – a distance of 70,000 km and nearly twice the circumference of the Earth.

Key questions

1. What is the difference between a route and a journey?
2. What is the best way in which to convey a route that we know to another person?
3. Why do routes sometimes twist and bend rather than taking straight lines?

Lesson 1: Everyday journeys

What journeys do we make in our locality?

You will need
- Ordnance Survey digital and/or paper maps of the local area
- access to Digimap for Schools
- string, coloured pens and paper.

Key vocabulary
- code
- direction

- journey
- route
- symbol
- travel

Getting started

Ask pupils to think about the trips that they make during a day or a week. Where do they go to? Why do they go there? How do they get there? Establish that they come to school every day and hence will each have the same destination but different starting points. Where else do they go? Are they allowed to go and call on friends in their streets? What family trips do they make, e.g. to the shops, the doctor's, the cinema, the park or Grandma's house?

Class activities

Everyday journeys: Ask pupils to make lists of the journeys that they take in a normal week. They will need three columns: where they start, where they go and how they travel. They might also add whether they think that it is a short or long journey.

Different destinations: Explain how you can use symbols and codes to show the different forms of travel. For example, you can use one colour for a route that you walk and another colour for a route that you follow in a car. Ask pupils to draw a symbol for their house in the centre of the page. They should then use a colour code of their choice to draw lines in different directions to the places that they visit. Can they think of symbols to represent these different destinations? Remind pupils that they are constructing a diagram and not a map.

Local routes: Ask pupils to focus on local journeys that they know well. Now, using a program like Digimap for Schools, ask the pupils to mark the exact routes that they take using the 'draw line' tool. Note particularly any changes of direction, road crossings and landmarks along the way. Children could also measure the distances that they travel.

Routes in school: Using plans of the school, map journeys for display in the corridors, such as how to find the library or the lunch hall.

Within a kilometre: Ask pupils to look carefully at an Ordnance Survey map showing their school and surrounding area within a radius of a kilometre. Tell them that they are going to write a guide about a place that is less than one kilometre from their school and worth visiting. They have to identify the feature on a map and say why they would visit it, and then advise people of the best route to take to get there. This will involve close examination of a map of their local area, and they will need to use the key to identify the features there first.

Plenary

Summarise the everyday journeys that people make and why. Which ones are essential and which ones are for fun? Discuss reasons why it's good to walk whenever it's safe and reasonable, and consider how you could encourage others to walk for short journeys rather than take the car.

Lesson 2 Holiday journeys

What journeys do we make when we go on holiday?

You will need
- an atlas
- digital and paper maps
- blank postcards
- blank maps of the UK.

Key vocabulary
- destination
- holiday
- journey
- motorway
- route
- terminal

Getting started

Ask pupils to say where they have been on holiday in the UK and mark places on a map as you talk. Then ask about holidays overseas and mark these too. Ask pupils to say how they got there and whether they have an idea of how long the journey took. Did they use different forms of transport and if so why? If they flew, why did they need to take a plane, rather than drive or take a train? Establish that some places are so far away that it would take a very long time to get there over land. Also establish that some places are across large expanses of sea or ocean (using the map to show this), and hence alternative transport is necessary.

Class activities

Motorways: Most children will have travelled down a motorway during journeys in the UK. Ask pupils whether they know the number of any motorways on which they have been. Look at a map and establish that many motorways go to London, which is itself ringed by a motorway – the M25. Once children have noticed this pattern of routes, ask them to draw their own maps, either on a blank outline of the UK or digitally, in which they label two or more motorways.

Travel terminals: Investigate different travel terminals in the UK using maps, images and YouTube clips – for example, Heathrow Airport, St Pancras International Station and Folkestone Channel Tunnel. Mark the major terminals on a map of the UK using an appropriate key.

Holiday destinations: Using paper and/or digital mapping, ask pupils to identify where they went on holiday and how they got there. Provide some holiday destinations for pupils who have not been abroad and also let children work in pairs so that they can share one destination. Pupils should identify the start and finish of their journey and say how they travelled. Can they name the countries that they passed through or flew over?

Dream holiday: Ask pupils to imagine that they have won a free trip to anywhere in the world. Where would they go and why? Ask pupils to map their destinations and explain how they would get there. Next, ask them to think of the 'greenest' ways in which they could travel there. Would it be different to their original plans? Can you get there by train, for example?

Postcards: Ask pupils to write imaginary postcards back from their chosen destinations. Talk about what they think the places look like, the weather conditions and nearby sights. Ask them each to describe a journey that they have made on foot, bicycle or some other form of transport during their holiday, and to make a drawing of it on the front of the card.

Plenary
Discuss as a class the advantages and disadvantages of different forms of transport – road, rail, sea and air. Make a list of children's ideas on the interactive whiteboard.

Lesson 3 Animal journeys

What journeys do animals make?

You will need
- access to the internet
- a globe and atlases
- picture books about journeys.

Key vocabulary

- journey
- migration
- osprey
- route
- swallow
- wildebeest

Getting started

Explain that migration means travelling from one place to live somewhere else. Ask pupils whether they know of any animals that migrate, and explain that they often want to find a better life and feed their young at different times of the year. Sometimes, animals migrate permanently because of changes in temperature and growing conditions. Others, like swallows, migrate from Africa to the UK each spring and return in the autumn. See whether you can find some images of these tiny birds and show the pupils a map of the huge journey that they undertake.

Class activities

Farmyard walk: *Rosie's Walk* (Pat Hutchins) tells the story of a chicken's journey around a farmyard. Read the story to the pupils or show them an animated version set to music (see Useful books and websites, pp. 99–100), and ask them to remember the things that Rosie passes as the fox chases her. Ask pupils to make drawings of the farmyard, showing all these places along a route.

The Owl and the Pussy-Cat: Read Edward Lear's poem 'The Owl and the Pussy-Cat' to the pupils or show the children a YouTube version that is set to a song (search for 'Lear owl and pussy-cat' on the internet or on YouTube). What risks do they think that the owl and the pussy-cat took in making their journey? Ask the pupils to make their own drawings of the land where the bong tree grows.

Migration routes: Find out about some famous migration routes taken by animals. For example, wildebeest migrate between the Serengeti and Masai Mara in Africa each year, as they seek the rains and fresh grass to eat. Meanwhile, the monarch butterfly travels over 4,000 km across the USA to Mexico each autumn. For further information, visit the animated map at the RSPB website (see Useful books and websites, pp. 99–100).

Osprey watch: Research some facts and figures about the osprey and why it migrates each year to warmer climes. Create a fact-file and map its journey. Find some webcams to watch ospreys online (in the UK from late spring to early autumn) and make a diary of developments.

Swallow watch: Note the date on which the first swallows are spotted in your area. Keep a log of when they disappear too, and use this as an addition to your mapped routes. Using the internet, research from which countries they have come and, on either digital or paper maps, map the routes that they take. Pupils could research other birds too and map these in a similar way.

Plenary

Read the pupils a picture book story about an animal journey. *The Snail and the Whale* (Julia Donaldson) is a classic that links together lots of different environments and places. Talk about the journey with the pupils and ask them to draw pictures showing where the animals went. Using these drawings as a prompt, ask the children to talk about the route. Perhaps they can invent names for the different places and the landmarks along the way.

Fieldwork and further investigations

- Go on a short walk in the school grounds. Provide pupils with lengths of string and ask them to gather items along the way that will remind them of the route that they took. The items that they collect can be fixed to the string by tape, tied on or pushed through the weave, if the string that you are using is thick. Back in class, ask pupils to make a diagram (simple linear map) showing the sequence in which they found the items that they collected. Use this 'journey string' to help them to recount the route.

- Identify a walk around the local area from the school and assess it in terms of safety and hazards. For example, you might identify busy roads, narrow pavements and badly lit areas that could be difficult at night-time. Use this information to create a hazard map, with advice about keeping safe in the local area. Mark key features on the map and name them.

Cross-curricular links

English: Write the instructions for a short route, such as a treasure trail, in the school grounds. Depending on their ability, pupils could use terms such as 'left' and 'right' to identify changes in direction. However, they might also refer to the four main points of the compass – north, east, south and west.

Mathematics: Find out more about how the Suez Canal has shortened sea journeys. Using pieces of string, ask pupils to trace and measure routes between cities in India/ East Africa and Europe via the Suez Canal and via the Cape of Good Hope. Compare the distances. Next, find out how the Panama Canal shortens the sea journey between the ports on the east and west coasts of the USA. The impact is even more dramatic!

PE: Devise some orienteering routes for the pupils to undertake in the school grounds.

RE: Special routes and journeys feature prominently in religious life. Ask pupils to find out about some famous pilgrimages and religious gatherings, such as the hajj, the Kumbh Mela or the trail to Santiago de Compostela in Spain.

Themes

Colonialism and social justice: From the seventeenth century onwards, Europeans established plantations around the world to grow the plants that they had discovered on their travels. Coffee, tea, cotton, sugar and tobacco are among the most-famous examples, and it is fascinating to discover where they first originated and the journeys involved.

Biodiversity: Many garden flowers and tree species have been deliberately introduced to the UK, but others have arrived by chance. Invasive species such as Japanese knotweed are an increasing problem, as they spread easily and pose a threat to native biodiversity. The seeds are often carried along transport routes by boats, aircraft, trains and cars.

Sustainability: Discuss how some forms of transport cause much more harm to the environment than others. Cars, planes and boats that burn fossil fuels are particularly damaging and make a significant contribution to carbon emissions. Find out how people are trying to reduce these problems. Electric vehicles are currently replacing those that run on petrol and diesel. Can the children think of any other solutions? What might they consider when they themselves go on a journey?

Progression and assessment

This area of study will consolidate work carried out in the previous lessons: it encourages pupils to apply and deepen their knowledge of places in the UK and wider world, it reinforces geographical vocabulary and it develops mapping skills and the use of directional vocabulary. By the end of this unit, children will also have an appreciation of everyday journeys, know how to represent them on simple maps and be able to talk about routes at both a local and a global scale.

Useful books and websites

Archer, M. (2021), *Wonder Walkers*. London: Penguin.

de Brunhoff, L. (2005), *Babar's World Tour*. New York: Abrams.

Donaldson, J. and Scheffler, A. (2004), *The Whale and the Snail*. London: Macmillan.

Hutchins, P. (2018), *Rosie's Walk*. London: Bodley Head (also see video versions).

Milne, K. (2017), *My Name is Not Refugee*. Edinburgh: Barrington Stoke.

Bird migration: search for 'Garden Wildlife Direct' and scroll to 'Where do UK birds migrate to?'.

Osprey migration: search for 'Osprey migration map UK'.

RSPB bird migration: search for 'RSPB migration of birds'.

10 Learning about Sri Lanka

What does the curriculum say?

Pupils should be taught to:

- *understand geographical similarities and differences through studying the human and physical geography of a small area in a contrasting non-European country*

- *use aerial photographs and plan perspectives to recognise landmarks and basic human and physical features; devise a simple map; and use and construct basic symbols in a key.*

What do I need to know?

Sri Lanka lies off the coast of India, a few degrees north of the equator. It is slightly smaller than Scotland but, with a population of 22 million, it is more densely settled. Colombo, the capital, is the biggest city. There are other towns around the coast. In the north, there are extensive archaeological sites, which date from the great civilisations that developed in Sri Lanka several thousand years ago. From the sixteenth to the eighteenth centuries, Portuguese and Dutch traders began to arrive from Europe, after which Sri Lanka was ruled as a British colony (Ceylon) for around 150 years. It has been independent since 1948, but English is still quite widely used, especially in government.

Sri Lanka is known for its natural beauty and charm. The coast is fringed with long sandy beaches and coconut groves. Inland, the mountains of the central highlands rise to several thousand metres in dramatic wooded peaks. The climate, which is dominated by the monsoon, shows considerable variations. The northern areas are dry and hot, there are patches of rainforest in the south and the mountains are relatively cool. A wide variety of plants and creatures live in these different environments. Sri Lanka is also well known for gems such as sapphires, rubies and moonstones.

Population

The population of Sri Lanka is diverse. About three quarters of the population is Sinhalese, speaks Sinhala and follows Buddhist customs and practices. Tamils form an important minority. They have a different language (Tamil), write in a different script and have their own religion (Hinduism). There is a smaller number of Muslims, some of whom are descended from Arab traders, and a Christian community that is largely Catholic. Conflict between the Sinhalese and Tamils, which had been suppressed under British rule, gradually developed into a civil war in the 1980s and 1990s. By the time it finished in 2009, tens of thousands of people had lost their lives, leaving a bitter legacy.

Economy

Agricultural products are an important part of the Sri Lankan economy. The plantations that were established by the British in the past made Sri Lanka famous for tea, rubber, cinnamon and other spices. Today it remains the world's most-important tea exporter. The country has also developed an important textile industry, and tourism is also recovering strongly after the devastation caused by the civil war and the 2004 tsunami.

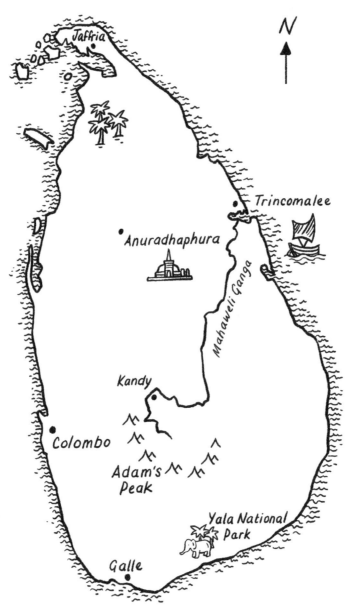

Figure 12: Sri Lanka has many contrasting environments

Misconceptions and research

Children sometimes think that places that are far away in terms of distance are also far back in time. Such perceptions can be unwittingly reinforced by colourful and exotic images of traditional practices and lifestyles. When teaching children about the geography of a contrasting country or region, it is important to be aware of the need to challenge rather than reinforce stereotypes. Presenting children with multiple images will help to guard against the dangers of a single-story approach.

Interesting facts

- The world's oldest documented tree was planted in Sri Lanka in the third century BC.
- Sri Lanka was the first country in the world to elect a female prime minister.
- Sri Lanka has had a number of other names in the past and was originally called just 'Lanka' (island).

Key questions

1. What is Sri Lanka like?
2. In what ways is Sri Lanka similar to and different from the UK?

Lesson 1 Introducing Sri Lanka

What is Sri Lanka like?

You will need
- a globe or atlas
- a range of items that are either from or linked to Sri Lanka
- sheets of A4 paper containing the outline shape of Sri Lanka.

Key vocabulary
- Buddhist
- cinnamon
- coconut
- island
- Sinhalese
- Sri Lanka

Getting started

Set up a display table with a selection of items, all of which provide clues to life in Sri Lanka. Depending on what you can obtain, the display could include: a packet of tea, a coconut, some natural jute, gardening twine, a small ornamental elephant or turtle, a packet of rice, some packets of spice, a stick of cinnamon, a pineapple, bananas, a map of Sri Lanka, some photographs of Sri Lanka, some Sinhalese writing and a picture of a Buddhist monk. Most of the food items are readily available from shops and supermarkets, while the maps and images can be downloaded from the internet. If possible, cover the table with a traditional batik cloth. Talk with the pupils about what they think that this lesson and area of study is going to be about. Consider each item in turn and how it provides a clue to life in Sri Lanka.

Class activities

Introducing Sri Lanka: Help the pupils to find Sri Lanka on a globe or atlas. It is easy to locate, as it is just off the tip of India. Where else in the world can they find islands? Are islands all the same shape? How does Sri Lanka compare in shape and size with Britain and the UK? Explain that Sri Lanka is linked to Britain historically, as it was once a British colony, but it has been independent for many years. Both Sri Lanka and the UK are island nations.

How can you get to Sri Lanka?: Trace some of the different routes to Sri Lanka on a map or globe. What countries would you cross if you travelled by air? Could you get there over land? Is there a sea route? Ask the pupils to imagine what they might see on their journey.

Sri Lanka map: Make a large map of Sri Lanka for a class wall display. This will need to show tropical beaches, the mountains of the central highlands and a few key towns and cities, such as Colombo, Kandy and Jaffna. As the pupils learn more about Sri Lanka, they will then be able to add their own drawings or pictures.

Sri Lanka fact-file: Working in pairs, ask pupils to make a Sri Lanka fact-file. Encourage them to select a range of information, such as the name of the capital city, longest river, highest mountain, main language, religion and festivals. The pupils could also make a drawing of the flag and add notes about current issues (conservation and ethnic conflict).

More about Sri Lanka: Use the map and other items from the display table to think about what Sri Lanka is like. It is close to the equator, so it is hot, and some places get a lot of rain. This means that tropical fruit and vegetables grow well. In the centre of Sri Lanka there is a highland area, where the mountains rise to several thousand metres. The weather is cooler there and there are large tea estates. Ask pupils to make careful labelled drawings of four items that come from Sri Lanka.

Plenary

Give each child a blank outline shape of Sri Lanka on A4 paper. Ask them to add the title 'All about Sri Lanka' at the top. They should then write or draw some of the things that they know or have learned about Sri Lanka in the space inside the outline.

Lesson 2 Sri Lanka products and wildlife

What is Sri Lanka famous for?

You will need

- art and modelling materials, such as modelling clay or play dough
- matchboxes, silver foil and shiny coloured metallic paper
- paper and glue for papier mâché
- paints
- strips of paper or card.

Key vocabulary

- container ship
- jewels
- port
- rupee
- shop
- spices
- tea

Getting started

Discuss with the class how the goods that they buy in shops and supermarkets come from different parts of the world. Some of them come from Sri Lanka. Consider also the different plants and animals that they would expect to find in Sri Lanka. Children's preconceptions will provide a guide for your teaching and indicate the extent of their existing knowledge and understanding.

Class activities

Market stall: Set up a market stall selling fruit and other products from Sri Lanka, such as rice, bananas, pineapples, coconuts, spices, tea, sugar and dried beans. These items can be made from modelling clay or play dough, or created out of card or papier mâché in an art lesson. See that each item is clearly labelled with its name and price in rupees (give pupils details of the exchange rate – at the time of writing, there are about 400 rupees to the British pound).

Jewels: Sri Lanka is famous for jewels, particularly emeralds (green), sapphires (blue and yellow), moonstones (cloudy grey) and rubies (red). Pupils can make their own 'jewels' using silver foil and shiny coloured metallic paper. They could also turn small boxes (e.g. matchboxes) into decorated treasure chests. This might lead to a discussion about gems and minerals from other parts of the world. Are there any gems and semi-precious stones that come from the UK?

The story of tea: Ask the pupils to create picture sequences to show how tea is produced. Working in groups, they should illustrate the following:

- a harvester with a basket on their back, picking the top few buds from a tea bush
- the leaves being spread out to dry on trays
- sacks or chests of tea outside a tea factory
- a container ship carrying tea to the UK and other ports
- packets of tea for sale in shops
- a mug or cup and saucer with steaming hot tea waiting.

Complete the activity by fixing the pictures in a strip on a long piece of paper, with arrows between them and a title at the top.

Elephants: Ask each pupil to fold a sheet of A4 paper into three horizontal strips. In each strip they should draw an elephant to match these descriptions: 1. I live wild in the forests; 2. I carry heavy logs to help to build a house; 3. I am decorated with bells and cloth for processions. Now discuss whether it is better for elephants to be wild or tame. What arguments can the pupils think of, both for and against?

Plenary
Give the pupils blank sheets of paper with just the outline shape of Sri Lanka showing. Ask them to list or draw some of the things that they have learned about Sri Lanka in the empty space. This activity might be undertaken as a formative assessment or as a group activity, in which pupils simply consolidate what they have been doing in this area of study.

Lesson 3 Kandy: a town in Sri Lanka

What is Kandy like?

You will need
- a selection of photographs of Kandy, downloaded from the internet
- a map of central Kandy, showing the town centre, lake and Temple of the Tooth.

Key vocabulary

· festival

· lake

· market

· palace

· park

· pilgrim

· railway station

Getting started

Tell the pupils that they are going to find out about Kandy. Kandy was the last independent capital of the Sri Lankan kings and is in the hills, several hours by road from the coast. There is a lake built by one of the kings in the centre of the town and many fine buildings along the shore. Download some photographs of Kandy to share with the children and discuss what they show. You will find a good selection of images by typing 'Sri Lanka Kandy' into a Google search.

Class activities

Comparisons: Look again at the photographs of Kandy that you showed at the start of the lesson. Talk about each one in turn and consider what makes it different from the UK and how it is similar.

Key places: The key buildings in central Kandy include the royal palace, Queen's Hotel, railway station, market, shopping streets, lake and parks. The most famous place is the Temple of the Sacred Tooth, which houses one of the Buddha's teeth – a holy relic that attracts thousands of pilgrims. Discuss who might use each of these places. See whether you can locate them on a map of Kandy. Can pupils think of examples of similar features and facilities in your own area of the UK?

Current issues: Kandy suffers from heavy traffic and the roads are often congested. Air pollution is an increasing problem. Recently there have also been long periods of drought, which could well be associated with climate change brought about by increasing global CO_2 emissions. Tell the pupils about these problems and organise a short discussion in which one group of children talks about changes and problems in Kandy and another group talks about environmental problems in your own area.

News report: Ask pupils to imagine that they are presenting a news report about the festival that is held in Kandy each summer. The festival, which is called the Perahera, lasts many days and involves a nightly procession of highly decorated elephants. One of the elephants carries a golden casket containing a replica of the Buddha's tooth. Thousands of people gather by torchlight to witness this event, which is accompanied by drumming, acrobatics and sacred music. You can obtain further details from an internet search. The children might imagine that they are part of the crowd, one of the performers or even in charge of an elephant!

Plenary
Discuss whether pupils think that they would like to visit or live in Kandy. What do they think might be the advantages and disadvantages?

Fieldwork and further investigations

- Does your area have any links with Sri Lanka? See whether you can get in contact with someone locally who either comes from Sri Lanka or who knows it well. Invite them to come to visit your class so that the pupils can ask questions about daily life in Sri Lanka. They might touch upon a range of themes, such as weather, food, festivals, wildlife, environment, games and transport.

Cross-curricular links

English: There are many national parks in Sri Lanka. One of the most remarkable is at Mihintale, where the world's first wildlife sanctuary was established in the third century BC. Working in pairs or small groups, ask pupils to list the people who they think might be in favour of or against creating a national park.

Mathematics: Ask pupils to assemble some data about elephants. How tall is a typical elephant? How long do they live? How much do they weigh? How many of your friends make up the same weight? Use these data to make up a little quiz called 'Elephant fun'.

History: The inland area of northern Sri Lanka is home to some remarkable archaeological sites. The most famous remains are the Dagobas (huge semi-circular domes), old monastic buildings and the extensive network of water tanks. There is a spectacular royal palace perched on a platform at the top of a high rock. The children will be able to find images of these fascinating relics for a scrapbook or display.

RE: On the full moon in May, many Buddhist Sri Lankans make Vesak lanterns to celebrate the death of the Buddha. Pupils could make their own lanterns from paper, using light wooden sticks for the framework.

Themes

Colonialism and social justice: The impact of colonialism still shapes Sri Lanka today. The ethnic conflicts that have bedevilled Sri Lanka in recent decades date back to the colonial era, when around a million Tamils were brought over from India to work on plantations. Tea, rubber and other cash crops, which were originally set up by the British to supply the UK market, remain important economically. Meanwhile, English remains an influential language and is commonly used in government.

Biodiversity: Turtles are one of the species of endangered animals that can still be found in parts of Sri Lanka. Find out what the pupils know about these remarkable creatures by gathering their ideas as a class list. Next, fill in the gaps in their knowledge with the following information:

- Turtles live in tropical seas for 40 to 80 years.
- Female turtles lay eggs in deep holes in sandy beaches.
- Baby turtles hatch at night and go back to the sea.
- People collect turtle eggs to eat.
- People make jewellery from turtle shells.
- Tourists disturb nesting sites.
- Turtles sometimes get caught in fishing nets.
- Some of the coral reefs where turtles feed are dying.

Using this information, ask the pupils to write some conservation messages for locals and tourists. They might read these out or make them into a turtle conservation banner.

Values and wellbeing: Learning about Sri Lanka will help children to develop their image of a country that is many thousands of kilometres away from the UK and where there are different religious communities. This is a valuable way in which to build international understanding and respect for those with different traditions, faiths and beliefs.

Progression and assessment

By the end of this area of study, all children should be able to identify Sri Lanka on a globe or atlas map and be aware of its key human and geographical features. Those who are performing at higher levels will be able to identify some of the links between Sri Lanka and the UK. They will also have begun to engage at a basic level with some of the contemporary conservation issues.

Useful books and websites

Pathirana, A. (2022), *I am Sri Lankan.* Alexandria Pathirana Publishing.

O'Hara, M. (2018), *Elly Rose in Sri Lanka.* Elly Rose Publishing.

Padmanabha, S. (2020), *The ABCs of Sri Lanka.* St Paul's MN, USA: Beaver's Pond Press.

Perahera videos: search for 'Esala Perahera festival' on YouTube.

Part 2
Lower Key Stage 2

11 Mapping the world

What do I need to know?

As they progress through the primary years, children should become increasingly familiar with basic map conventions. This area of study introduces grids, longitude and latitude, with a particular focus on the latter and its relationship with climate zones. Familiarity and practice help children to make progress in using and making maps, especially when they have the opportunity to apply skills in different contexts and with different kinds of maps. Paper maps and GIS mapping software should both be employed in the making and using of maps.

Global reference points

There are a number of key reference points that provide a framework or structure. The North Pole and the South Pole mark the ends of the axis around which the Earth rotates. The equator marks the Earth's circumference. Places to the north of the equator are said to lie in the Northern Hemisphere. Places to the south of the equator are said to lie in the Southern Hemisphere. Lines of latitude measure distance in degrees north or south of the equator. They run in parallel, which means that they never meet.

An imaginary grid centred on the equator and poles enables people to define their location. Lines of longitude are measured in degrees east or west of the line that runs through Greenwich in London, UK (the prime meridian). They run from the North to the South Pole and are furthest apart at the equator. This means that they create wedges, rather like the segments of an orange or slices of a cake.

The idea of using a grid system to locate places on the Earth's surface dates back to Ancient Greek and Roman times, but it wasn't until the European voyages of exploration that the system that we use today began to fully develop. The key discoveries came from astronomy, which established beyond doubt that the Earth is a sphere that orbits the Sun and that it spins as it travels through space. It was this realisation that completely changed the way in which people thought about the world.

Latitude and seasons

Across the Earth, the lengths of day and night change with latitude and vary according to the seasons. This is the result of two factors: firstly, the Earth moves around the Sun as it spins, taking exactly a year to complete its orbit; secondly, rather than being vertical, the Earth's axis is tilted by around 23.5 degrees. This means that at some times of the year places are tilted towards the Sun and at other times they are tilted away from it. This gives rise to seasonal variations.

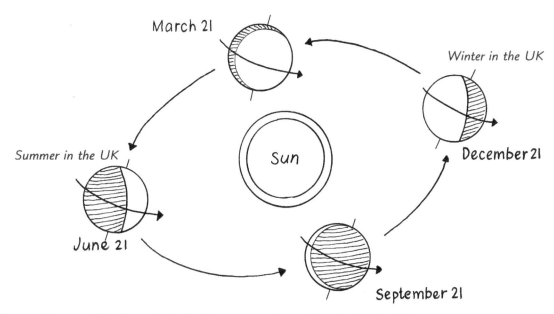

Figure 13: Places are tilted towards the Sun in summer and away from the Sun in winter

The places that experience the most-dramatic seasonal variations of day and night lie within the Arctic and Antarctic Circles. Here there is a period of perpetual daylight in summer and perpetual night in winter. At the other extreme, the regions within the Tropics of Cancer and Capricorn experience direct overhead sunshine at some point in the year. There are only minor seasonal variations between the lengths of day and night. These key lines of latitude that delineate the tropical and polar regions are usually marked with dotted lines on globes and atlas maps.

One of the other factors that is important to note is that the Northern and Southern Hemispheres experience exactly opposite conditions. When places in the north are enjoying the summer, it is winter in the south. Conversely, the northern winter is balanced by the southern summer. This explains why people in Australia and New Zealand are able to celebrate Christmas on the beach.

Misconceptions and research

Research indicates that while children may be able to manipulate a single variable (e.g. variations in height), they find it very much more challenging if a second variable is included at the same time (e.g. variations in height and width). When it comes to understanding the Earth in space, there are at least three variables to consider: the Earth spins on its axis, the Earth orbits the Sun and the axis is tilted. This suggests that it is important to break this topic into discrete stages and to consolidate learning over a period of time.

Interesting facts

- The Tropics of Cancer and Capricorn are named after the signs of the zodiac. In the time of the Ancient Greeks, the Sun appeared directly overhead at its most northerly point as it entered the astrological sign of Cancer. Similarly, the Sun entered the astrological sign of Capricorn when it reached its most southerly extent.
- Satellites and global positioning systems still depend on coordinates based on latitude and longitude.

Key questions

1. What is the significance of the Tropics of Cancer and Capricorn?
2. Why are grids useful?
3. How does the tilt in the Earth's axis cause the seasons?

Lesson 1 Grid squares

How are grid squares useful?

You will need
- sheets of cardboard and rulers
- Ordnance Survey maps of your area (1:25,000 or 1:50,000 scale is best)
- access to Digimap for Schools.

Key vocabulary
- column
- grid reference
- row

Getting started
Recap children's previous knowledge of grid squares, perhaps from Key Stage 1 teaching and also from computer games, board games (e.g. chess) and puzzles (e.g. crosswords). Some children may recall using grid references to find a street in an 'A-Z' or road atlas. A few may have experience of using grids in orienteering.

Class activities
Grid board game: This activity draws on the method used in the classic game 'Battleships'. Give each pupil a sheet of card and ask them to create a grid with eight rows numbered 1–8 and eight columns labelled A–H. Ask pupils to select six small objects, such as a paper clip, rubber or pencil sharpener, to place in the squares. Pupils now play the game in pairs. One child arranges the objects and hides their board from their partner. The other has 12 guesses to score as many direct 'hits' as they can. Reverse roles and play several rounds if time permits.

Treasure island map: Tell the pupils that they are going to devise a treasure island map, showing mountains, forests, rivers, marshes, cliffs, gorges, waterfalls, headlands, beaches and so forth. There may also be roads, buildings, castles, ruins, old churches and towers that people have built in the past. Ask pupils to draw an alpha-numeric grid over the map and to decide where the treasure chest is buried. Can they make up a set of clues using grid-square references that will guide others to their secret site?

Four-figure grid references: Look at an Ordnance Survey map of your area. It will be divided into grid squares numbered along the edge. To reference a grid square, first find the number of the column (the lines along the bottom), and then find the number of the row (lines along the side). Ask pupils to give grid-square references for different places in your area.

Local land use: Identify a section of the local Ordnance Survey map that is ten grid squares wide and ten grid squares deep (i.e. 100 squares in total). Ask the pupils to count up the number of squares that are mainly occupied by buildings, mainly occupied by woodland, mainly occupied by water and so forth. Record the results in a table or chart. The number of squares in each category will of course represent a percentage.

Comparisons: Using Digimap for Schools, select a grid square on the Ordnance Survey map of your area and discuss the features that it shows with the pupils. Next, look at a vertical overhead photograph of exactly the same area. What are the differences between the map and the photographic image?

Plenary

Ask pupils to look at the different grid squares on an Ordnance Survey map of your area. Can they find a square that looks busy, a square that looks empty or a square that looks dull? Ask them to locate a square that they would like to visit. Share ideas around the class. What squares have other children chosen and where are they on the map?

Lesson 2 In the tropics and around the poles

What are the tropics and polar regions like?

You will need
- a globe and atlas
- access to the internet
- sheets of card and paper.

Key vocabulary
- Antarctic Circle
- Arctic Circle
- Tropic of Cancer
- Tropic of Capricorn

Getting started

Using a globe, remind the pupils how the polar regions are tilted towards the Sun in summer and away from the Sun in winter. In the tropical regions, by contrast, the Sun is high in the sky throughout the year. Talk about how children think that this will affect the climate.

Class activities

Countries in the tropics: Working from an atlas map of world countries, ask pupils to make a list of five countries that lie along the Tropic of Cancer and five countries that lie along the Tropic of Capricorn. How many of these have they heard about before? Which continents and oceans lie wholly outside the tropics?

Inside the Arctic Circle: Ask pupils to make a zigzag book about the environment inside the Arctic Circle. They will need to include a map; many atlases include a map of the Arctic centred on the North Pole. On the other pages, they could make drawings and notes about an animal, bird, plant, natural feature (e.g. icebergs) and indigenous peoples.

They might also find out about explorers and current issues, such as the impact of climate change. They could finish with a page about the North Pole itself – they will find webcams that show what it looks like.

A to Z of the tropics: Pupils could compare what they have discovered about the Arctic by investigating the tropical environment. As well as producing zigzag books, pupils might see whether they can construct an A to Z of the tropics. There are plenty of plants and animals from which to choose, but they could also include countries and cities. Zambia and Zimbabwe are convenient solutions to the problem of finding an entry that starts with 'Z'!

Arctic and tropical links: Many birds migrate to the UK from tropical or polar regions. Cuckoos and swallows travel great distances across tropical Africa and the Mediterranean Sea on their journeys to Europe each spring. Starlings start to arrive in the UK from Scandinavia from the summer onwards. Barnacle geese traverse the North Atlantic from Greenland to reach the UK in the autumn. Bewick swans live over winter in the UK and fly back to Siberia to breed. Find out more about these incredible journeys using internet searches. The RSPB site is a good starting point (see Useful books and websites, pp. 120–121). You may also be able track the progress of individual birds that have been tagged or featured in research.

Plenary

Ask pupils to draw circles to represent the globe. Ask them to draw and name the five key lines of latitude: the equator, the Tropic of Cancer, the Tropic of Capricorn, and the Arctic and Antarctic Circles. Next, ask them to colour and label the polar and tropical regions and to write notes under their drawings about some of their characteristics.

Lesson 3 Lines of latitude and longitude

What are lines of latitude and longitude?

You will need
- a globe and atlas
- sheets of card and scissors.

Key vocabulary
- Antarctic Circle
- Arctic Circle
- latitude
- longitude

- prime meridian
- Tropic of Cancer
- Tropic of Capricorn

Getting started

Point out to the class the lines of latitude and longitude on a globe, atlas or electronic map. The lines of latitude go horizontally around the globe. They never meet and stay parallel to each other in hoops. The lines of longitude are the long lines that go from the North to the South Pole. They are furthest apart at the equator and make wedges. By combining latitude and longitude, we can specify the location of any place on the Earth's surface.

Class activities

At the same latitude: Find the UK on a world countries atlas map of the world. It is slightly closer to the North Pole than the equator – between 50 and 60 degrees north. What are the other countries of similar latitude that lie to the west and to the east of the UK? Ask pupils to make a list. What countries lie between 50 and 60 degrees south?

On the line: Ask the pupils to imagine that they are flying south from the UK along zero degrees of longitude (the prime meridian). Make a list of the countries that they would pass over and the seas and oceans that they would cross before reaching the South Pole.

Special latitudes: The regions between the Tropics of Cancer and Capricorn all experience direct overhead sunshine at some point in the year. The regions within the Arctic and Antarctic Circles all experience continual darkness in winter and continual sunshine in summer. Ask pupils to draw an outline of the globe, labelling the polar and tropical regions. Discuss the differences between their climates. Which is physically largest and which has the most countries and cities?

The United States: Many of the states that comprise the United States of America (USA) have boundaries that follow lines of latitude and longitude. The most obvious and dramatic is the northern border with Canada, which follows the 49th parallel. Working from an atlas, ask pupils to identify five or more states that have entirely straight borders that clearly follow grid lines. Can they think why there are no examples in the east of the USA?

Imaginary journey: Ask pupils to go on their own imaginary journey along a line of latitude of their choice. Ask them to tell the rest of the class what they saw and experienced.

Latitude and longitude game: Give the pupils a sheet of card and scissors so that they can make a set of playing cards as shown in **Figure 14**. Pupils should shuffle the cards and turn them over in pairs. For each combination, can they find the location in their atlas? Where have they ended up?

Equator: latitude 0 degrees	Prime meridian: 0 degrees
Tropic of Cancer: latitude 23.5 degrees north	Longitude: 40 degrees east
Arctic Circle: latitude 66.5 degrees north	Longitude: 80 degrees east
Tropic of Capricorn: latitude 23.5 degrees south	Longitude: 40 degrees west
Antarctic Circle: latitude 66.5 degrees south	Longitude: 80 degrees west
North Pole: 90 degrees north	International Date Line

Figure 14: **Cards for the latitude and longitude game**

Plenary

London and Cardiff are at a similar latitude, and Cardiff and Edinburgh have a similar longitude. Get the children to draw a map to show these cities and ask them to draw straight lines linking them together. What geometrical shape have they created?

Fieldwork and further investigations

- Identify significant features in the local area through fieldwork and show them on a digital map using four-figure grid references.
- Plan a treasure map for real, using local features and giving grid-reference clues for groups to locate using OS maps.

Cross-curricular links

English: Ask pupils to write a haiku about the tropics or the polar regions. A haiku is a poem with three lines: five syllables in the first line, seven syllables in the second line and three syllables in the last line. They often end with a question or a philosophical thought. For further information, visit the Poemhunter website (see Useful books and websites, p. 120).

Mathematics: The tilt in the Earth's axis may not sound a lot, but it means that the Sun appears to rise and fall by twice this amount between midsummer and midwinter – a variation of 47 degrees. Ask pupils to do a measured drawing to show what this actually means. They should start by drawing a square on a sheet on a paper, leaving some spare space on the right-hand side. Join the bottom-left and top-right corners to create a 45 degree angle. Now halve this to make an angle of 22.5 degrees, which is very close to the tilt of the Earth's axis.

Physical education: Representing the movement of the Earth in dance and drama offers rich possibilities for imaginative and creative responses.

Themes

Sustainability: Environmental problems are evident from the local to the global scale, and mapping them often reveals patterns and connections that might not otherwise be evident. A global perspective is especially important with respect to climate change and biodiversity loss, as they involve multiple connections over huge areas. These are complex issues, but when they are presented visually using satellite images, they can be understood by even quite young children.

Personal development: Knowing more about how the Earth works and their place within it enables children to develop their self-knowledge, self-esteem and self-confidence. This also awakens their spiritual awareness, as they come to see themselves in the wider scheme of things.

Values: It is important for pupils to develop their knowledge of the world (their locational framework) if they are to participate meaningfully in democratic processes and decision-making.

Progression and assessment

By the end of this area of study, all children should be able to locate the equator and other key features, such as the Tropics of Cancer and Capricorn, on a globe or atlas map and explain their significance. They will know about lines of latitude and longitude and how they can be used to locate places. Those who have a more-developed understanding will have begun to realise that the tilt in the Earth's axis accounts for the seasons.

Useful books and websites

Antarctic webcams: search for 'South Pole webcam'.

Earth's orbit: search for 'BBC Learning Earth's orbit of the Sun' on YouTube.

North Pole webcam: search for 'North Pole webcam' on YouTube.

Poemhunter: www.poemhunter.com/poems/haiku

RSPB: https://rspb.org.uk

World map: search for 'World map' using Google Images.

12 The shape of the land

What do I need to know?

The Earth's surface is subject to continual long-term change. Volcanoes and mountain-building processes build up the land, creating high mountain ranges. Meanwhile, the forces of erosion gradually wear them away. If no mountain building were to happen, theoretically the land would be worn flat over geological time. However, this process would be disrupted by changes of the sea level and other feedback mechanisms. The interaction of rocks and water happens in many ways over extended timescales. Ultimately, it accounts for the diversity of physical landscapes around the world.

Mountain building

Mountain building is driven by forces deep beneath the Earth's surface. Convection currents in the magma carry heat to the surface and draw cooler material back down again in massive long-term cycles. These currents carry the continents with them, pulling some areas apart and causing others to slide past each other or collide. The boundaries between different land areas are marked by fault lines, where earthquakes and volcanic eruptions are liable to occur. In some places, the land is raised up; in others, magma breaks out onto the surface, creating islands or mountain ranges.

Erosion

Erosion wears the land away in multiple ways. Rivers, for example, cut back into mountain and upland areas, carrying sediment downstream and depositing it in the sea or lakes along the way. Glaciers grind away at rocks to gouge deep mountain valleys. The wind blasts exposed surfaces. Meanwhile, repeated expansion and contraction brought about by changes in temperature cause rocks to crack, making them more exposed to the actions of ice, wind and water. Some rock strata are also vulnerable to chemical processes. Limestone, for example, dissolves slowly as it reacts with rainwater, resulting in dramatic landscapes with cliffs, gorges and caves.

Mountains and rivers

This area of study concentrates on two particularly important aspects of the physical landscape, namely mountains and rivers. Both have had huge impacts on the ways in which people live their lives. Mountains have their own climates and ecologies and create major barriers for road and rail routes. Rivers, by contrast, are almost always important lines of trade and communication. Many towns and cities are found on the banks of rivers. Agriculture and industry both benefit from ample supplies of river water but floods present a continual risk.

Continent	Longest river	Highest mountain
Africa	Nile – 6,695 km	Mount Kilimanjaro –5,892 m
Antarctica	No rivers (ice covers all the land)	Vinson Massif – 4,892 m
Asia	Chang Jiang – 6,350 km	Mount Everest – 8,848 m
Europe	Volga – 3,692 km	Mount Elbrus – 5,642 m
North America	Mississippi–Missouri – 5,969 km	Denali (Mount McKinley) – 6,194 m
Oceania	Murray–Darling – 1,472 km	Puncak Jaya – 5,030 m
South America	Amazon – 6,516 km	Aconcagua – 6,959 m

Figure 15: The Nile is the world's longest river. The Amazon is slightly shorter but carries much more water, since it flows through the rainforest. Many of the world's highest mountains are in the Himalayas

Misconceptions and research

Research indicates that children have many misconceptions about physical geography. These include:

- the idea that the physical landscape was created by people rather than natural forces
- confusion about the direction in which river water flows – some children, even upper juniors, believe that they flow from the sea into the mountains, rather than the other way around
- difficulty in understanding the words used to describe rivers that have alternative spellings and meanings, e.g. 'source' and 'sauce' and 'current' and 'currant'
- problems comprehending geological time (children, like adults, are prone to use human measures as a yardstick, even though the Earth is many millions of years old).

Interesting facts

- There are 14 peaks in the world at over 8,000 m high – they are all in the Himalayas.
- A fifth of all the river water in the world flows down the River Amazon.
- The Niagara Falls are moving backwards at a rate of about a metre a year.

Key questions

1. How are rivers and mountains made?
2. What do people use rivers for and why?

Lesson 1 Landscapes and physical geography

How are landscapes different?

You will need
- an atlas
- cardboard boxes, scissors, egg cartons, white paper, paper and glue for papier mâché and paints
- access to the internet and digital Ordnance Survey mapping.

Key vocabulary
- contour line
- gorge
- landscape
- moor
- slope
- tributary
- waterfall

Getting started
As a class, discuss different landscapes. Do you live in a flat or hilly area? Are there any mountains, rivers or marshes in your area? Think about dramatic landscape features, such as waterfalls, canyons, mountain peaks and rock faces. Explain that in this area of study, pupils are going to find out more about landscapes.

Class activities

Rivers and mountains worldwide: Investigate rivers and mountains worldwide using an atlas map. Ask pupils to find one river in each continent (excluding Antarctica). See whether they can complete a table listing the name of each river, the mountains where the river begins and the sea/ocean into which it flows. Extend the activity by adding information about the length of each river as a research exercise. Pupils might also compile a list of highest mountains.

Landscape photographs: Divide the class into pairs and ask them to find photographs showing different landscape features, such as mountains, moorlands, hills, valleys, waterfalls, gorges, marshes and estuaries. Ask them to select four examples to show to the rest of the class in a short electronic presentation.

Landscape model: Make a model of a mountain and river in a cardboard box. Start by cutting off the top of the box and one of the sides to make an open frame. Build up the model using layers of papier mâché over a loose base of egg cartons or screwed-up paper. As well as the main peak, try to incorporate river features, such as a lake, gorge, waterfall and estuary. Use clean white paper for the final layer and leave the model to dry. The children can then paint the landscape features and add the river. Ask them to add labels for place names that they have invented.

Mountain fingerprints: Explain that Ordnance Survey maps have contour lines, which show the shape of the landscape. Where the contours are close together, the slope is steep. Ask pupils to find and locate, using annotation tools and grid-reference numbers, the highest mountains in the UK. Children can then zoom in to look at the different patterns of each mountain made by the contour lines and choose one that they find interesting. They can then compare this with the 3D view on Google Earth.

Mountain safety: Make a poster about preparation for walking safely in mountain landscapes. Think about the clothes that you might need for different types of weather, the maps and equipment that you would need to navigate successfully, and ways in which you might attract attention in an emergency.

Plenary

Ask pupils which type of landscape they prefer and why. If they could travel to any part of the world to visit a special landscape, where would they choose to go?

Lesson 2 Mountain study

What are the features of a mountain environment?

You will need
- sticky notes
- blank outline maps of the UK
- a printed or electronic atlas
- access to the internet.

Key vocabulary
- barrier
- mountain pass
- mountain range
- national park
- peak

Getting started
Ask pupils to describe a mountain in their own words. Ask them to write down their ideas on sticky notes and to pin them up on a display board. Read out some of the definitions and talk about what they mean as a way of introducing this lesson on mountain landscapes.

Class activities
Mountains in the UK: Look at a map of the UK to find the main mountain areas in the UK: Dartmoor, Cambrian Mountains, Pennines, Lake District, Southern Uplands, Grampians, North West Highlands and Mourne Mountains. Give pupils a blank outline map and ask them to mark these mountain areas and to name a few individual peaks. They could also mark the locations of mountains and peaks using a digital mapping program.

World mountain ranges: Focus on one of the world's great mountain ranges. The Alps (Europe), Rockies (North America) or Andes (South America) would be particularly appropriate, depending on your regional place study. Ask pupils to write a descriptive paragraph about the mountain range that they have chosen, using an atlas, the internet and other sources of information. How long is the range? What countries is it in? What are the highest mountains? Are they famous in any way?

Crossing the mountains: Ask pupils to find a route across their mountain range. It might be from Bern to Milan (Alps), Vancouver to Calgary (Rockies) or Chile to

Argentina (Andes). What would they expect to see on the journey? What mountain passes would they cross? How high are they? Would there be any dangers? Ask them to draw a diagrammatic route map showing key features on the journey and places to stop. Share information around the class about how high mountains are formidable barriers to communication.

Mountain environments: High mountains have their own climates and distinctive plants and wildlife. There are many remote areas, some of which are designated as national parks. Ask pupils to locate a national park in the mountain range that they are studying. Ask them to report back to the rest of the class on what makes the park special, what they can see there, the range of wildlife, special trees and plants, and so forth. If they were to visit the park themselves, what would they plan to do?

Climbing Everest: Using research from the internet, find out about how Edmund Hillary and Tenzing Norgay became the first climbers confirmed to reach the summit of Mount Everest in 1953. Ask pupils to compile the front pages for their own imaginary newspapers reporting on this momentous event. They could include maps and photographs, as well as diary extracts, pretend interviews and comments from politicians and other world leaders. They might also 'look into the future' and anticipate the huge numbers of people who would want climb Everest in years to come and the impact that this would have on the environment.

Plenary
Invite a pupil to take the 'hot seat' and ask the rest of the class to think of good questions to ask them about mountains around the world. Discuss factual information and opinion, and the difference between the two.

Lesson 3 River study

What are the features of a river environment?

You will need
- an atlas
- access to the internet
- art and drawing materials.

Key vocabulary
- delta
- gorge

- lake
- marsh
- source
- tributary
- waterfall

Getting started

You can use the activities in this lesson alongside work that you are doing on a region in Europe, North America or South America. The pupils should focus on a river of their choice, such as:

- Europe: Rhine, Seine, Danube or Vistula
- North America: Mississippi, St Lawrence or Colorado
- South America: Amazon, Paraná or Orinoco.

Class activities

Sketch map: Ask pupils to draw a sketch map of the river that they are studying. They should identify the source and show any lakes, waterfalls and gorges, and name the sea/ocean into which it flows. What are the main cities along its banks? Are there are any tributaries or other notable features, such as a delta, that they want to add? Through what countries or regions does it flow?

Boat journey: Ask pupils to imagine that they are making a boat journey along their river. What different landscapes and places might they pass through? Are there any historic ruins, such as castles, or is there a link to the boats that used the river in the past? Ask pupils to use the information that they have collected for a brochure advertising a cruise. How many days do they think that it would take and where would it begin and end?

River wildlife: Ask pupils to find out about the plants and creatures that are found in and around the river. Are there any unusual fish? Does the river attract birds? The delta and marshes may be particularly rich in wildlife, especially butterflies and insects. Ask pupils to use the information that they have discovered to make careful drawings and notes about the river wildlife. Display their work in circles of a standard size, to look as though viewed through a telescope or microscope.

Famous city: Ask pupils to study of one of the famous cities through which the river flows. Is there a reason for its location and why did it grow and prosper? Ships and navigation will be an important part of this story. What goods passed through the docks? Where did they go to and come from? See whether the pupils can make a timeline telling the story of the city, using between four and six simple labelled drawings.

Dams: Many of the world's rivers have been dammed to generate energy and control the flows of water downstream. One of the most famous is the Aswan Dam on the River Nile, which generates a lot of Egypt's electricity but which flooded historic ruins and cost lots of money. In China, the Three Gorges Dam is the world's largest power station. This huge project has displaced lots of people. Organise a class discussion on the pros and cons of big river dams.

Plenary

Brainstorm a list of the uses of rivers around the world and encourage pupils to give examples based on the research and activities that they have undertaken.

Fieldwork and further investigations

- Find examples of different landscape features in your area. Hills and gentle slopes are common in most urban areas, and children are often aware of them because they use them in their games and outdoor activities. There may also be streams and shallow valleys. Sometimes these features are reflected in street names, e.g. Valley Road, Oak Rise or Church Hill. Some areas have ponds and small lakes. In other places, there are tunnels. If you live by the sea, there will be a range of coastal features, ranging from cliffs to beaches. Try to devise a walk in which the pupils can see different aspects of local physical geography. How have people made use of them and what challenges and opportunities do they present?

Cross-curricular links

English: Read to the class an extract from a novel that features a river, such as Mark Twain's *The Adventures of Huckleberry Finn*. Ask them to listen out for and write down the different words used to describe the water, riverbank and character of the environment. Challenge pupils to make up their own river poems using these words.

Mathematics: Ask pupils to compile a chart giving the names and heights of the highest mountains in each continent. Next, using lined paper, ask them to draw pictograms to represent this information visually. A scale of one centimetre for each thousand metres often works well. It is instructive to add a pictogram of a UK mountain, such as Ben Nevis, for comparison.

Art: Ask pupils to make a mountain landscape collage using pieces of fabric and cloth. You could use brown hessian or Binca™ for the background. Ask pupils to add clouds, rivers, trees and other items using a needle and knitting wool.

Themes

Climate change: Rivers have always caused problems, as they flow downhill from mountains towards towns, cities and fields. However, heavy and unpredictable rain caused by climate change (together with deforestation) is now making floods worse in many parts of the world. One terrible example occurred in 2022, when devastating flooding along the River Indus overwhelmed around ten per cent of Pakistan, killing thousands and making over two million people homeless.

Biodiversity: Mountain environments are often particularly fragile, as the plants and creatures that live there are at the edges of their biological ranges, and extreme weather conditions test them to the limit. As well as finding out about these unique habitats, pupils could consider how they are vulnerable to tourism, which can further erode their resilience.

Values and wellbeing: Finding out about famous mountaineers and their feats can capture children's imagination. The courage, determination and stamina of those who climb high mountains provide an inspiring example. More generally, learning how people forge a living in a range of challenging physical environments can enable children to deepen their respect for their own and other cultures.

Progression and assessment

By the end of this area of study, all children should be able to talk about how mountains and rivers contribute to the landscape. They should be able to name and locate some significant mountains and rivers, both in the UK and worldwide. Those who are working at higher levels of achievement will demonstrate an awareness of how mountains and rivers impact on human activity and their environmental importance.

Useful books and websites

Hooper, M. (2015), *A River Story*. London: Walker Books.

Twain, M. (2010), *The Adventures of Huckleberry Finn*. London: Collins Classics.

Whitburn, N. (2017), 'Landscapes and sweet geography', in S. Scoffham (ed), *Teaching Geography Creatively* (2nd edn). London: Routledge.

Mountains: search for 'BBC Planet Earth mountains' (20 short videos).

13 Water and the water cycle

What do I need to know?

Most of the water in the world is found in the seas and oceans, which cover more than 70 per cent of the Earth's surface. However, seawater cannot be used for drinking or irrigation, as it is contaminated with salt. Freshwater is much scarcer. Antarctica and Greenland have huge supplies, but these are locked up in snow and ice. This leaves rivers, lakes and water-bearing rocks as the main sources of supply.

With the growth in human numbers and increasing demand from agriculture and industry, water supplies are coming under more and more pressure. Global climate change is adding to this problem, disrupting established weather patterns and causing long-term droughts in areas as far apart as California, sub-Saharan Africa and Western Australia. As a result, millions of people around the world are at risk of water shortages. The burden falls most heavily on poor countries, where contaminated supplies spread disease. The World Health Organization (WHO) estimates that over four-fifths of all diseases are the result of unsafe water, poor hygiene and/or lack of sanitation.

In the UK, rainfall is distributed fairly evenly throughout the year. The south and east are the driest regions. In the north and west, where rainfall is heaviest, reservoirs store water for use in nearby cities. In other parts of world, particularly the Middle East, water security has become a highly contentious issue and the potential cause of conflict. If countries with control over the upper reaches of rivers construct dams and extract supplies, it affects those lower down, and in times of shortage the impact can be serious.

This area of study explores the importance of water as a natural resource. It also considers how water circulates in a continual process of evaporation, condensation and precipitation, known as the 'water cycle'. In global terms, the quantity of water in the world stays constant from one year to the next. What varies is the way in which it is distributed. Physical forces, especially weather systems, interact with human activity to make this an extremely complex process.

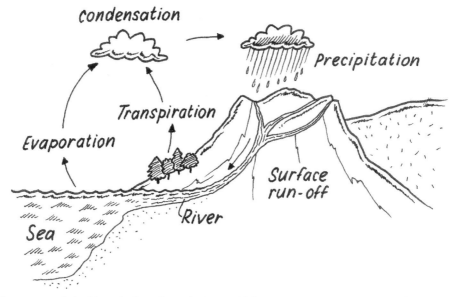

Figure 16: The water cycle is driven by heat from the Sun, which causes water to evaporate. The water vapour rises, cools and creates clouds. The clouds build up and shed water as rain. The rainwater flows downhill and back to the sea

Misconceptions and research

This area of study straddles geography and science. The processes involved in the water cycle are part of the science curriculum. How the water cycle influences climate and the impact that it has on people in different parts of the world introduces a geographical perspective. Children do not need to know how geography and science intertwine. However, they do need to appreciate two key ideas: the first is that a cycle is a process that is endlessly repeated; the other is that water, like other materials, can be a solid, a liquid or a gas, depending on its temperature.

Interesting facts

- Ninety-seven per cent of the world's water is stored in the oceans.
- The water that comes out of a tap is nearly as old as the Earth itself, even if it has fallen as rain in the last few weeks.
- Around the world, more people have a mobile phone than access to a flushing toilet.

Key questions

1. Is water the most important natural resource of all?
2. Why do we need to be careful about how much water we consume?

Lesson 1 Water in our lives

How does water affect our lives?

You will need
• access to the internet.

Key vocabulary
• borehole
• flood
• water butt
• waterworks

Getting started

Present pupils with a simple riddle: What runs but never gets tired? The answer, of course, is water. Explain to the children that this area of learning is about a key natural resource – without water, there can be no life. Astronauts are well aware of this. That's why space exploration will be boosted if people can find viable supplies of water or ice on Mars.

Class activities

Water survey: Ask pupils to make a survey of the number of times that they use water for drinking, washing, flushing the toilet and other activities during the day. They will need to devise a simple chart so that they can record the results. Next, get them to estimate the amount of water that they use based on the following figures:

| bath: 90 litres | washing hands: 3 litres | cooking: 12 litres | toilet (long flush): 8 litres |
| shower: 30 litres | brushing teeth: 1 litre | drinking: 2 litres | toilet (short flush): 4 litres |

Figure 17: The approximate volume of water used in day-to-day activities

Saving water: Discuss different ways of saving water at home and at school, e.g. using dual-flush toilets, turning off running taps, using taps that turn off automatically, taking a shower rather than a bath and catching rainwater in water butts. Find out more about saving water by visiting the Waterwise website (see Useful books and websites, p. 139). Ask the pupils to write a code for saving water.

Water supplies: Where does the water come from when we turn on the tap? The initial supply will probably be pumped from a river, lake or borehole and sent for purification and treatment in a waterworks. From there, the water will go into a reservoir or water tower, before reaching the houses, factories and farms where it is used. Ask pupils to make drawings of these four stages, showing how pipes link each part of the process. There are plenty of diagrams available on the internet showing various versions of water supply systems.

Floods: All areas suffer from heavy rain and floods at one time or another. Ask pupils to investigate incidents in their area over the years. Which areas were affected by floods and how high did the water come? What damage did the water cause and how did people respond? The pupils may well be able to track down some video footage showing what happened. Ask them to write short news reports about a flooding event, with clear headlines, brief summaries and pretend interviews with local residents, officials or experts.

Plenary
As a class, discuss what would happen if water supplies failed. What would pupils miss first? How would they respond? How long do they think that they would be able to survive?

Lesson 2 The water cycle

Where does water come from?

You will need
- access to the internet
- small mirrors.

Key vocabulary
- condensation
- deforestation
- drain
- evaporation
- water cycle

Getting started
In order to understand the water cycle, children need to understand that water can take different forms. It can appear as ice or in other solid forms such as snow, it can be

a transparent liquid or it can be an invisible gas. As a class, discuss the different forms that water can take. It is hard to understand that there is lots of water in the air in the classroom. Thinking about dehumidifiers and the condensation on windows may help to convince pupils.

Class activities

Water-cycle diagram: Explain to the class that water changes form as it warms and cools. The heat of the Sun turns liquid water on the land and sea into gas. As it rises into the atmosphere, the drop in temperature eventually causes this gas to condense as water particles, creating clouds. If the clouds become too heavy, the water particles fall back to Earth as rain. You can watch some excellent simple animations that show this process, such as those on BBC Bitesize (see Useful books and websites, p. 139). Ask pupils either to make their own individual diagrams in their books or to create a class wall display to illustrate the water cycle.

Down the drain: You can see parts of the water cycle in a very tangible form in the local environment. Take the pupils into the playground or a quiet side street. Ask them to trace what happens to water when it rains: it falls from the clouds onto the roof; it slides down the roof into a gutter; it flows to the ground in a gutter pipe; it makes its way into a drain, either in a pipe or by flowing along a channel. Ask pupils to make labelled and numbered drawings to show this sequence.

Clouds: Clouds are divided into three main types: cirrus clouds are thin wispy clouds made of ice crystals high in the sky; cumulus clouds tend to look a bit like cotton wool and build up into heaps and clumps; and stratus clouds form sheets at different levels and are often associated with rain. Ask pupils to find out different cloud types, and view different examples with them by projecting images onto the interactive whiteboard. See that you go outside into the playground to identify the clouds that you can see around you. Placing mirrors on the ground is one way in which to focus attention on a small area of sky. Cut-out cardboard viewers are another option. **Remind the children that they must never look at the Sun directly**.

Story of a raindrop: Ask pupils to think imaginatively about what happens to raindrops when they fall from the sky. What must it be like to hurtle down to the ground from a cloud, to land heavily on a roof and to slide down dark pipes to the ground? Would it be exhilarating, frightening or fun? Ask pupils to write their own imaginative accounts of the experience.

Broken water cycles: As a class, discuss how a lot of the water that evaporates into the air comes from plants, especially trees. When the trees are cut down, less water evaporates, so there is less cloud, and this means that there is less rain and the trees find it harder to grow. Deforestation is a particularly serious problem in the tropics, where the

Sun is very hot. Ask pupils to make a diagram or poster showing how cutting down large areas of trees can break the water cycle.

Plenary
Remind the class that the energy that drives the water cycle comes from the Sun. In polar regions, the Sun brings relatively little heat, which limits the amount of rain and snow. In equatorial regions, the Sun is much stronger and there is much more rainfall.

Lesson 3 Water worldwide

What are people doing to improve water supplies?

You will need
- access to the internet
- blank outline maps of the UK.

Key vocabulary
- borehole
- community
- reservoir
- water tank
- well

Getting started
Ask pupils how long it takes them to get to a tap when they need a drink of water when they are at home. They will probably be surprised by the question. Explain that in rural areas in Africa and other parts of the world, some people have to walk for several hours to get water. Many charities have videos showing water-improvement projects, which bring home what this really means. If you are happy with promotional material, the Oxfam video about a new borehole in the Tanzanian desert is well worth watching (see Useful books and websites, p. 139). *Hint:* Always ensure a balance of information and avoid building a 'charity mentality'. Outside help can sometimes be patronising and/or disempowering.

Class activities
Improving water supplies: There are many different ways of improving water supplies. These include: installing pipes linked to fresh water sources, harvesting rain in tanks and storage jars, building dams across streams and rivers, and digging new wells to access

supplies of ground water. Prepare your own presentation about a water-improvement project in a developing country to share with the pupils, using information from agencies such as Oxfam, Save the Children, WaterAid, Christian Aid and CAFOD. The pupils should then use this as a resource to compile their own summaries of the project.

UK reservoirs: Rutland Water, Kielder Water and the reservoirs in mid-Wales all store water for use in towns and cities. Ask pupils to mark and label them on a blank outline map of the UK. Extend the activity by getting pupils to draw detailed maps of one of the reservoirs, along with brief notes about why and when it was built.

New reservoirs: Building reservoirs can disrupt people's lives. Find out what happened to a community when it was flooded, by reading *Shaker Lane* by Alice and Martin Provensen to the pupils. Alternatively, you could show them the video version (see Useful books and websites, p. 139). Discuss who benefits and who loses when a reservoir is built. Are small reservoirs less damaging than big ones?

Water and health: Ensuring that everyone in the world has safe and affordable drinking water is one of the United Nation's (UN's) Sustainable Development Goals. Ask pupils to find out more about what these targets are and the ways in which they are going to be assessed.

Clean water drama: Divide the class into groups of six to eight and ask them to devise a short drama in which a group of villagers try to convince a government officer that they need piped water instead of relying on supplies from a river. Each child can take a different role, such as homemaker, child, farmer, older person, doctor, village leader and so on. Restrict the dramas to a maximum of five minutes each.

Plenary

Watch 'Our World, our water', a short video by CAFOD that summarises many of the themes in this area of study (see Useful books and websites, p. 139). Discuss why pupils think that water is important. Can they think of anything that they eat or use that doesn't depend on water in one way or another? Do they think that we are using it wisely enough?

Fieldwork and further investigations

- Find out more about the water company that supplies your school and homes in the local area. Ask whether you can arrange a visit from a member of their education service. Even better, you may be able to book a tour of your local water-treatment works. Explain that you are particularly interested in geographical issues and ask pupils to prepare questions in advance. They may want to ask about patterns of rainfall, the influence of rocks and the landscapes, changes in demand, environmental problems and so forth.

Cross-curricular links

English: Ask pupils to make up some riddles of their own about water and its importance in our lives.

Mathematics: Ask pupils to make bar charts showing how much water it takes to make different clothes, using these figures: jeans – 1,800 gallons, shirt – 400 gallons, socks – 100 gallons, cardigan – 500 gallons, shoes – 1,500 gallons. Extend the activity by asking pupils to research one or two more items to add to their charts.

Science: Conduct a simple experiment to illustrate evaporation. Select a part of the playground where puddles form when it rains. Choose a dry (reasonably warm) day and recreate the puddle by pouring some water from a watering can or jug. Draw around the outline of the puddle in chalk. Return to the puddle at set intervals to see how much water has evaporated, marking the edge of the puddle each time until it finally disappears. As well as discussing where the water has gone, look at the way in which the puddle got steadily smaller. Each outline will represent a contour line, providing a natural link to map work!

Themes

Climate change: In the Amazon and other rainforest regions, the vegetation helps to drive the water cycle. So much moisture evaporates from the trees that it creates thick storm clouds and causes heavy rain. If too many trees are cleared, it breaks the cycle, so that there are fewer clouds and less rain. Pupils can represent this diagrammatically, showing (a) the natural cycle and (b) the disrupted cycle.

Sustainability: Improving water supplies is a key issue in some of the poorest and most disadvantaged parts of the world and an essential element in sustainable development. Learning more about the UN's Sustainable Development Goals would be one way of building children's understanding of this theme.

Values and wellbeing: The UK is committed to working with other countries through the UN and other agencies to improve global living conditions. Learning about water and its importance as a resource is one way of developing children's awareness of how they can contribute positively to the lives of others, both locally and more widely.

Progression and assessment

By the end of this area of study, all children will have been introduced to the idea that water is a key natural resource and will understand its importance in our lives. They will also have begun to develop an understanding of the water cycle and be able to link it to their own experiences. Some children will be able to describe different global initiatives to improve living conditions. All children will know that they need to use water wisely.

Useful books and websites

Hooper, M. (2015), *The Drop in my Drink: The Story of Water on Our Planet*. London: Frances Lincoln.

Provensen, A. and Provensen, M. (1987), *Shaker Lane*. London: Viking/Kestrel (also available on YouTube).

Water in our lives: search for 'CAFOD: Our world, our water'.

Boreholes in Africa: search for 'Oxfam no water no life a new borehole in Turkana'.

Water cycle: search for 'Water cycle BBC Bitesize'.

WaterAid teaching resources: www.wateraid.org/uk/get-involved/schools

Waterwise website: www.waterwise.org.uk

14 Lake District

What do I need to know?

The Lake District is a region of mountains and lakes in the north-west of England, lying at a latitude of between 53 and 55 degrees north of the equator. The majority of it is designated as a national park. The park contains all the land in England above 910 m (3,000 feet), including Scafell Pike, the highest mountain in England. It also contains the deepest and longest lakes in England: Wast Water and Windermere, respectively. The towns of Workington, Whitehaven, Kendal and Barrow-in-Furness lie on the western coast of the Lake District but are outside the national park. Although the area of the Lake District National Park is clearly defined, the wider area known as 'the Lake District' is less precise.

The Lake District is one of the wettest places in the UK and certainly in England. The prevailing winds come from the west and cross the Atlantic, bringing with them a good deal of moisture. On reaching the shores of the Lake District, the clouds rise to cross the mountains, cooling as they do so and condensing to produce rain. This process is known as 'relief' rainfall.

The Lake District has much warmer winters than many other places at a similar latitude. This is because the North Atlantic Drift and Gulf Stream bring warm water from the Caribbean to the coasts of western Britain. The generally mild, wet climate has helped to create the bountiful lakes and rocky landscapes that we see today, as well as shape the main agricultural practice currently undertaken: sheep farming. Plentiful grass provides grazing for sheep that are hardy and agile enough to exist on mountain slopes, where tractors and farm machinery cannot easily reach.

The Lake District is a glaciated landscape. Glaciers carved U-shaped valleys during successive ice ages two million years ago. The action of the ice has left behind steep mountain peaks and narrow ridges. It also scooped out the valleys, creating depressions that

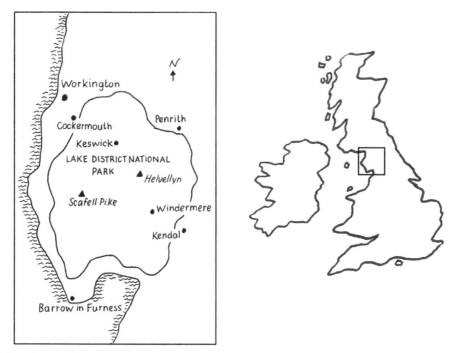

Figure 18: The Lake District is the largest and most visited of the 13 national parks in England and Wales

have now turned into lakes. These all radiate from the highest point, Scafell Pike. The beauty of these mountains and valleys is part of the reason why millions of visitors come to the region each year; the other aspect is the opportunity to enjoy outdoor pursuits, especially climbing and watersports.

While the geology and weather provide natural resources for industries such as mining, hydroelectric power and tourism, there are tensions between the tourism industry, jobs, the preservation of the natural environment and ways of life. The status of being a national park also makes homes less affordable, as they become more desirable. The Lake District was celebrated in British culture in part through the romantic poetry of William Wordsworth and his poet peers in the nineteenth century. The region's reputation for beauty and the notion of the idyllic landscape have endured to the present thanks in part to this legacy.

Misconceptions and research

Children sometimes find the term 'Lake District' rather confusing. They are surprised to learn that as well as having a lot of lakes, the region is also noted for its mountains.

Interesting facts

- Borrowdale is the wettest settlement in England, with over 3,000 mm of rain per year.
- Four hundred million years ago, the mountains of the Lake District resembled the Himalayas, with great mountain peaks towering into the sky.
- Around 16 million tourists come to the Lake District each year.

Key questions

1. Where is the Lake District?
2. What are the weather and landscape like and why?
3. What are the key issues affecting the Lake District?

Lesson 1 Introducing the Lake District

What is the Lake District like?

You will need
- an atlas of the UK
- paper and electronic maps of the UK and the Lake District
- internet access
- access to Tagxedo software.

Key vocabulary
- glacier
- lake
- mountain
- national park
- tarn

Getting started

Initiate a class discussion in which the pupils pool what they already know about the Lake District. Some children may have visited there, and many will have heard about it. Make a list of features and landscapes that you might see there and brainstorm words and ideas. Later, these can be revisited and checked against enquiry findings. You could put these beginning words and ideas into a Tagxedo word cloud to show the predominant ideas at the start of the enquiry, do a 'fly over' using Google Earth or create a TripGeo route animation. The animated route could play while pupils are carrying out their geographical enquiry during the main part of the lesson.

Class activities

What is the Lake District?: Ask pupils to work in pairs and produce paragraphs explaining where this region is and some key facts about what it is like in terms of landscape. Use a digital mapping program such as Digimap for Schools, as well as a key, to help to identify features. Give pupils access to the National Parks website too (see Useful books and websites, p. 148), for research purposes.

Map it: Ask pupils to add markers and annotate a digital map of the region, adding in key features such as highest mountains, largest lakes, significant towns and other human features, such as railway stations. Alternatively, they could use printed maps of the area to draw their own versions with keys. They might also mark and name the counties.

Weather: Use the Met Office website (see Useful books and websites, p. 148) to compare weather statistics between the Lake District and your own locality. Ask pupils to compile a table showing rainfall data and temperatures throughout the year. Then ask them to write a report advising the best time of year to visit the Lake District and explaining their views.

Measure it: Using a map of the area, ask pupils to mark the area encompassed by the Lake District National Park's boundary line. They could use the area-measuring tool in Digimap for Schools.

Place names: Using a map of the Lake District, ask pupils to collect interesting place names and identify where they are on the map. Can they find out their meanings and whether/how the names reflect what the landscape is like?

Plenary

Recap and consolidate the key physical and human features of the Lake District. Discuss with the class what they think makes the Lake District special and why it is so popular with tourists.

Lesson 2 The River Derwent

What can we find out about the River Derwent?

You will need

- images of Derwent Water
- maps of the Lake District, including digital maps for annotation

- atlases
- access to the internet
- sheets of A3 paper and colouring pens
- modelling clay and junk modelling materials.

Key vocabulary
- catchment
- Derwent Water
- mouth
- source
- tarn
- tributary
- weir

Getting started
Show some images of Derwent Water and ask pupils to describe what they can see. Recap what the pupils learned in Lesson 1, and how the plentiful rainfall helps to keep the lakes full. Where does the water come from and where does it go to? Explain that the streams and tributaries that flow into a river collect water from a wide area (its catchment area), and then identify the River Derwent on a map and on Google Earth. What tributaries join it on its journey to the sea? Which notable towns and villages can be found on its banks? Set up some enquiry questions with the pupils. The name 'Derwent' is derived from a Celtic word for oak trees – what does that tell us about the landscape at one time?

Class activities
Mapping the Derwent: Find the Derwent on a map and ask pupils to mark its catchment area and source, as well as its mouth. Mark major towns and villages along its route and note significant tributaries. Pupils could annotate a map electronically using a digital mapping program such as Digimap for Schools.

Picture the Derwent: Research and collect some images of the River Derwent at different stages of its journey, using a site such as Geograph. Add these digital images to the appropriate places on an annotated map and label any specific features shown, such as 'bridge' or 'weir'.

Measure the River Derwent: Using a measuring tool on a digital mapping program such as Digimap for Schools, measure the length of the Derwent from source to mouth.

Diagram of the River Derwent: Using a large A3 sheet of paper, ask pupils to work in pairs or as a small group to create a diagram showing the route of the Derwent and different kinds of physical and human features on its path. Annotate with notes in coloured pens. Modelling clay or junk modelling could be used to create a 3D map. Add compass directions to show the direction of travel, and label identified settlements.

Kilometre-square comparisons: The River Derwent rises near Styhead Tarn in the rugged mountains at the head of Borrowdale and reaches the sea at the port of Workington. Using an Ordnance Survey map or digital map of the region, compare a kilometre square of the river's mouth at Workington with a kilometre square at its source. Either capture the different sections electronically or use a paper map to create diagrams, identifying key similar and different features.

Plenary

Show some images of the River Derwent and identify which one would be best to illustrate 'A day out on the fells', 'A tourist brochure', 'A good place to live' and so on (you could determine your own categories), or ask pupils to suggest their own straplines for each image.

Lesson 3 Focus on Keswick

What is Keswick like and why?

You will need

- a map of the Lake District
- a large-scale map of Keswick and its surrounding area
- access to the internet
- A3 paper and pens.

Key vocabulary

- job description
- Keswick
- seasonal work
- tourism

Getting started

Recap work on the River Derwent from the previous lesson and note that the river passes through Derwent Water and close to the adjacent town of Keswick. This is a magnet for tourists. Discuss why this might be so. Brainstorm some jobs that you think people might do in Keswick to serve the tourist industry, and make a list. Pupils might be surprised to know that the pencil factory is the town's second-largest employer. Use Google Street View to take a virtual walk around the town and see what kinds of shops there are. Use an online booking site such as **LateRooms.com** or **Booking.com** to see how many hotels are listed for the town.

Class activities

Tourist brochure: Design a tourist brochure for Keswick, noting some of the activities and attractions nearby. Where could you advise people to visit if they were based in Keswick? Give information on weather and transport as well.

Infographic poster: Working in small groups, ask pupils to create A3 infographic posters about Keswick that include relevant maps and show numerical data as graphs. Use Keswick Information Centre website for information (see Useful books and websites, p. 148).

Estate agents: Look at some property sites and find out a range of house prices in Keswick, and then compare them with prices in your area. Write a short piece advocating moving to the Lake District and living in Keswick. What kinds of amenities are there? Are there schools nearby?

Pros and cons of tourism: Most people in Keswick are employed in the tourism industry, but what are the downsides of having so many visitors all year round? Ask pupils to identify some pros and cons. Ask what advice they might give if they were trying to keep money coming in from tourism but also preserve natural habitats and landscapes.

Job descriptions: Discuss some different jobs that you might find in the tourism industry in Keswick, such as hotelier, café worker, boat-cruise pilot, activity leader and tour guide. Ask pupils to write some job descriptions. Investigate the meaning of seasonal work and what kinds of tourist might come all year round. Why are artists and poets drawn to the region?

Plenary

Create a short quiz book about Keswick with the answers at the back. Draw comparisons with your own locality and any other regions that you have studied in Europe, North America or South America.

Fieldwork and further investigations

- The Lake District is one of only a few places in the UK where red squirrels can be found, and characters such as Squirrel Nutkin feature in books by the famous author Beatrix Potter, who lived and wrote in the Lake District. Pupils could investigate why red squirrels are only found in certain habitats and why they are under threat from grey squirrels. What conservation measures are being taken to help this animal to survive? This could then link to work investigating threatened species in your own school grounds or wider locale.

Cross-curricular links

English: Read the pupils the beginning of the poem by Proctor about the mountain peak 'Helvellyn' (see Useful books and websites, p. 148). Use this as a stimulus, as well as some images of the mountain and an Ordnance Survey map, to describe its landscape in a piece of extended writing. Extend the activity by reading some of the famous poetry by local poet William Wordsworth.

Mathematics: Use river facts and weather statistics to compile infographics and graphs. List and order the highest peaks and deepest/widest lakes. Compile facts on lakes using different measures, i.e. surface area, length, width and volume.

History: Look at historical maps of the region and explore how towns and villages have changed over time. Digimap for Schools has a historical 'slider' that will reveal the Ordnance Survey maps in the 1950s and the 1890s. How and why have places changed here?

Art: The Lake District has inspired artists through the ages. Show the pupils some paintings of the Lake District on the interactive whiteboard. Invite pupils to create pictures of their own using watercolour paints.

Themes

Biodiversity: Rewilding projects are being undertaken in many parts of the UK. In the Lake District, hazel dormice have been reintroduced to woodlands to create a 'northern powerhouse' that will rescue them from extinction. When a species is lost, it weakens the resilience of a habitat or ecosystem. Bringing them back makes it stronger.

Climate change: The relatively mild climate of the Lake District depends on warmth from the North Atlantic Drift. However, there are fears that this could be disrupted as climate change causes the Greenland ice cap to melt. Comparing average temperatures in the Lake District with those in places around the world of similar latitude (e.g. Ottawa and Vancouver) will open up discussion.

Sustainability: Investigate some of the strategies used to maintain and preserve the landscape in the Lake District against some of the threats from visitors. Discuss how your school is looked after, even though it is used by so many people each day. Identify actions that you can take to preserve habitats for animals and birds, for example.

Values and wellbeing: Developing a greater understanding of a shared heritage and passion to conserve beautiful landscapes and views is one way of helping children to gain an appreciation of their own and other cultures.

Progression and assessment

By the end of this area of study, children will have a greater understanding of a UK region (the Lake District) and be able to describe its key characteristics in terms of landscape, climate, weather and industry. Children will be able to talk in general terms about the region and describe a river that runs through it in more detail. They will know that tourism is a major industry and that towns like Keswick are tourist centres. Some children will be able to apply this growing understanding to make comparisons with other regions that they have studied.

Useful books and websites

Lake District facts and figures: www.lakedistrict.gov.uk/learning/factsandfigures

Lake District photo resources: https://www.lakedistrict.gov.uk/visiting/webcams-videos-and-photos

Keswick Information Centre: http://tinyurl.com/4vwr3c65

Met office website: www.metoffice.gov.uk

National Parks website: www.nationalparks.uk

Paintings: search for 'Lake District paintings'.

Poems: search for 'Lake District poems'.

15 Climate zones

What does the curriculum say?

Pupils should be taught to:

- *describe and understand key aspects of physical geography, including: climate zones, biomes and vegetation belts, rivers, mountains, volcanoes and earthquakes, and the water cycle*

- *identify the position and significance of latitude, longitude, Equator, Northern Hemisphere, Southern Hemisphere, the Tropics of Cancer and Capricorn, Arctic and Antarctic Circle.*

What do I need to know?

Weather and climate underpin much of the geography curriculum and are vital components in understanding why places are like they are. 'Weather is what you get, and climate is what you expect' is a helpful way to think about the crucial difference between the two. Weather is a snapshot in time of atmospheric processes and how they impact on a particular place. The weather can change from day to day and from hour to hour. Climate is the long-term pattern of weather, compiled using multiple data collections, usually over a period of at least 30 years.

Climate zones

Climate zones are areas with distinct climates. There is no agreed definitive of climate zones, in terms of either boundaries or terminologies. Similar zones may have different names, and while one classification set may have five or six categories, another set may have twice as many. In this book, we focus on the classical climate classification system developed by the climatologist Wladimir Köppen in 1884. Five key climate types are identified, based on temperature and rainfall:

- tropical climates
- dry climates
- temperate climates
- continental climates
- polar climates.

Tropical climates

Tropical climates are mainly found within the Tropics of Cancer and Capricorn. All are wet and warm, but there are distinct variations. Climates closest to the Equator are hot and wet all the year around, while others have distinct dry seasons. One particularly important variation is in the form of the tropical monsoon season, which is especially wet, influenced by seasonal winds that bring heavy rain.

Dry climates

Descending air masses at the northern and southern edges of the tropics create zones of continuous high pressure. Hot deserts are found here, with cloudless skies and very dry conditions. The Sahara Desert is located around the Tropic of Cancer and the Kalahari Desert around the Tropic of Capricorn. They are both in the same continent of Africa.

Temperate climates

Temperate climates have distinct seasons, with warm summers and cold, wet winters. They are found across Western Europe (including the UK), western and eastern regions of the USA and Eastern China. One variation is found in the Mediterranean, which has very warm, dry summers and mild, wet winters.

Continental climates

Continental climates are similar to temperate climates but with greater extremes of temperature. They are found mostly in the continental interiors of North America and Eurasia, which do not benefit from the temperature-regulating effects of the ocean.

Polar climates

Polar climates are found at and around the polar regions and are characterised by extreme cold and dry conditions, where no month averages above 10 °C. In the tundra, where the warmest month averages between 0 °C and 10 °C, some plants and low-lying shrubs are able to grow. Very high mountains, such as the Himalayas, experience a true polar climate. Alpine peaks, which are not so high, experience a tundra climate.

Misconceptions and research

Children are often surprised to find that the UK has a temperate climate. While it is sometime hot or cold in the UK, the climate is moderate in comparison with other places, which have much more extreme conditions. Understanding this can be challenging, but it deepens pupils' appreciation of averages and long-term trends.

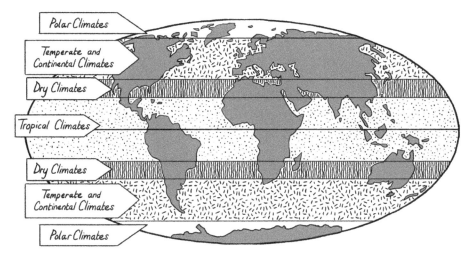

Figure 19: Simplified diagram of world climate zones as if the Earth was completely covered by continuous lowland or water

Interesting facts

- Ocean currents from the Caribbean have a big influence on the UK climate. Similar latitudes in East Asia and North America are much colder than the UK in winter.
- The Greek philosopher Aristotle divided the world into three climate zones: torrid, temperate and frigid. He thought that the torrid zone was too hot and the frigid zone was too cold for people to live in.

Key questions

1. What is the difference between weather and climate?
2. How does latitude influence temperature?
3. Why is it much colder at the poles?

Lesson 1 World climate zones

How are climate zones different?

You will need
- access to the internet
- a world climate-zone map
- blank world maps

- a globe
- a torch.

Key vocabulary
- climate zone
- equator
- latitude
- polar circles
- Tropic of Cancer
- Tropic of Capricorn

Getting started

Recap the names and locations of the equator and polar circles using a globe, and introduce other major lines of latitude: the Tropic of Cancer and the Tropic of Capricorn. Check that children can give a definition of 'climate' and revise Key Stage 1 knowledge about hot and cold places in the world, what they are like and where you can find them.

Class activities

Hottest places: Using a globe, or even a ball with lines drawn on it to simulate the major lines of latitude, demonstrate using a torch how energy is concentrated at the equator and spread over a wider area near the poles, because of the Earth's tilt on its axis. Note observations and ask children to draw diagrams with appropriate labels.

Global temperatures: Using a digital mapping program such as Digimap for Schools, select a world map and enable the lines of latitude to be visible. Choose a map layer that shows average global temperatures and ask children to work with partners to make lists of facts about global temperature:

- Where are the hottest average temperatures?
- Where are the coldest temperatures?
- Why do they think that the Antarctic Circle looks colder than the Arctic Circle? (The land mass of Antarctica is colder than the water mass of the Arctic Ocean.)

Global rainfall: Enabling a GIS map layer showing average rainfall, ask pupils to make a list of observations about the locations of the wettest and driest places in the world. You can toggle between layers to look at temperature and rainfall, and find out where the hot-wet and hot-dry areas of the world are. Explain that patterns like these help us to identify climate zones. Children can use blank world maps to draw and label some climate observations and/or add information digitally to a world map using mapping software.

Mapping climate information: Introduce some significant climate zones using a simple classification, discuss what each zone is like and give an example of a place found in that zone. Create a map showing these zones with a key. Locate Kilimanjaro and discuss why the summit is so cold even though it's near the equator.

Plenary

Using a climate classification map on the interactive whiteboard, give children a short true-or-false quiz about where a particular type of climate might be found, and ask them to respond with a thumbs-up or thumbs-down. Alternatively, they could write their answers and check whether they were right with a partner.

Lesson 2 UK climate

What climate do we have in the UK and how does it vary?

You will need

· an atlas with maps of the UK

· access to the internet.

Key vocabulary

· average

· pattern

· prevailing wind

· rainfall

· temperate climate

· temperature

Getting started

Recap the four seasons in the UK and the type of weather that you can expect in each one. Locate the UK on a globe and discuss why it hasn't got a hot-wet climate (not within the tropics) or a polar climate (not near the poles). Identify that the UK lies within the general classification of climate type called 'temperate'. Temperate climates have four seasons, with some variation, but they are not as extreme as continental climates. Revisit work on weather in Key Stage 1 and discuss how it can vary across the UK. Can children predict what they might expect in different parts of the UK as far as its climate is concerned? Where do they think that the coldest and wettest places, based on average readings, might be? Make a list of ideas to return to at the end of the lesson.

Class activities

Temperature variations: Use a Met Office map that shows the distribution of average temperatures in the UK, starting with the most recent full year (see Useful books and websites, p. 157). Ask children to work with partners to identify and note where the warm and cool places are in the UK and record this information using locational language and compass directions. They can then repeat this exercise using the drop-down menu to select other years at ten-year intervals – so, for example, looking at the average yearly temperatures of the year for 2024, 2014 and 2004. This way, they have scanned the data over a 30-year period, indicating climate patterns. What do they notice?

Mountains make a difference: Using an atlas showing the physical geography of the UK, can children explain some of the temperature differences that they notice? For example, it is on average colder in the north and warmer in the south and east of the UK. The mountains of Scotland, Wales and northern England are particularly cold. Revisit the idea of how temperature drops with altitude.

Rainfall variations: Repeat the 'Temperature variations' activity but using yearly rainfall maps for the same years. What do pupils notice now? Most rainfall is focused in the north and west of Great Britain, particularly over high ground near the coast. The south-east of the country has the driest conditions. Explain that the prevailing wind comes to the country from the south-west, across the Atlantic Ocean. This brings moist air, which falls as rain as it rises over hills and mountains. Discuss the impact that this has on people's lives. For example, how does the difference affect jobs and industries such as farming? The damper west coast is often used for rich grass pastures for dairy farming, while the wet uplands of Wales are more suited to sheep farming.

Plenary

Revisit the predictions made at the start of the lesson and discuss how accurate these were. Children can say or write three things that they have learned about the climate of the UK and offer an explanation for one of them. Discuss how even a globally small area such as the UK, which is in a single climate zone, can have distinct variations.

Lesson 3 Climate and forests

You will need

- access to the internet
- blank outline world maps
- digital mapping software
- photographs of biomes.

Key vocabulary
- biome
- boreal forest
- carbon sink
- equatorial rainforest
- taiga
- temperate rainforest
- vegetation belt

Getting started

Revisit work on climate zones, discussing the zone in the world with the warmest temperatures and the most rainfall. Name the major lines of latitude on a globe again, to ensure that all the pupils are familiar with the terminology. Use a software mapping package such as Digimap for Schools and look again on a world map at the layers showing average temperature and rainfall.

Class activities

Equatorial rainforests: Ask children where they think that they are most likely to find equatorial rainforests and why. Noting the warmest temperature on the map and the location of the wettest places (within the tropics), toggle off the climate data and select a layer showing vegetation and biomes. Identify the location of equatorial rainforests using the key. Can the children name some of the countries where these rainforests are found?

Manaus: Manaus is a major city located in the heart of Amazonia. Ask children to research climate data for Manaus and draw simple graphs of temperature and rainfall throughout the year. Two variables to use would be average rainfall and temperature per month. What do children think that it would be like to live there?

Temperate rainforests: Rainforests are found in all the world's continents except Antarctica. Although these forests are now very rare in the UK, they used to spread across many western coastal areas. Today they are mostly restricted to steep-sided valleys above rivers and lakes. Get the children to find out more about UK temperate (Atlantic) rainforests for a class display. See that they include maps and information about the plants and creatures that live there. What makes temperate rainforests so special?

Boreal forests: Boreal forests make up a large biome that stretches across much of the Northern Hemisphere, from the coast of Alaska in North America through northern Europe to East Asia. In these high latitudes just south of the Arctic Circle, freezing temperatures can occur for six to eight months of the year. These forests (which are also known as taiga or snow forests) provide environments where people live and work, with lumber resources and habitats for wildlife. Ask children to map and label these vast forests on a blank outline map of the world.

Did you know?: Boreal forests make up about 30 per cent of global forest cover and play an important role as a carbon sink. These forests also store 30 to 40 per cent of Earth's land-based carbon. Talk with the children about why they matter so much and what is happening to them today.

Matching images: Provide some photographs showing different biomes, such as the Amazon rainforest, the Atacama Desert in South America, Antarctica (with penguins) or the Arctic (with polar bears), and a temperate rainforest in the UK. Provide the locations unnamed on a map and ask children to match each image to a location, using their knowledge of climates, biomes and vegetation belts.

Plenary
Ask pupils to use partners to check whether they have correctly identified their images and locations, and give time for any corrections.

Fieldwork and further investigations

- Explore a local wood or park and map the kinds of trees that you find there. Depending on the location, the children could each adopt a tree of their choice. Ask them to keep a diary throughout the year, recording how it is affected by the weather. What creatures does it support? Does it look healthy?
- Compare climate zones on maps using atlases and digital maps, and talk about which ones are easier to understand and why.

Cross-curricular links

English: Compile a brief guide to climate zones. Write an account of a day in Manaus or devise a story set in a boreal forest. Use the recommended books (pp. 157–158) to help with this.

Maths: Investigate, create and compare climate graphs using data from different climate zones, e.g. compare Manaus with London.

Science: Investigate the requirements for renewable energy technologies, such as solar, wind and tidal power. Explain why certain climate zones are better suited than others. Explain the role of forests in acting as carbon sinks. Use the Ashden website (see Useful books and websites, pp. 157–158) to investigate alternative energy technologies and how people have innovated in ways to mitigate climate change.

Themes

Colonialism and social justice: A combination of fertile soils and good growing climates in the tropics contributed to colonisation around the world. In the Americas, for example, plantation agriculture focused on growing crops such as tobacco, sugar, cotton and coffee. Enslaved people provided the labour that made this possible.

Biodiversity: Climate, location and vegetation combine to create specific habitats and biomes. As a result, plants and creatures are closely adapted to their environment, and this explains why climate change is such a threat to them. Many forms of wildlife simply cannot adapt quickly enough to cope with rapidly changing conditions.

Values and wellbeing: We now know for certain that human activity is changing the balance of the atmosphere and disrupting climate zones around the world. The impact is already apparent in floods, storms, droughts and bush fires. The choices that we make can and do make a difference. This is a time to think carefully about values and what matters.

Progression and assessment

By the end of this unit, pupils will have learned about different climate zones and how they are related to latitude. They will have investigated variations in climate around the UK and appreciated what brings them about. The link between climate and vegetation, especially forests, forms another theme, as does the threat posed by climate change. There are multiple links to learning outcomes in both previous and subsequent units, which will support progression in map work and geographical knowledge and understanding.

Useful books and websites

Carmichael, L. E. (2020), *The Boreal Forest: A Year in the World's Largest Land Biome.* London: Kids Can Press.

Johnson, R. L. (2017), *A Walk in the Boreal Forest.* Princetown, NJ: Princetown Architectural Press.

Scoffham, S. (ed) (2023), *Collins Junior Atlas* (6th edn). London: Collins.

Ashden awards: www.ashden.org

Boreal forest: search for 'Boreal forest carbon sink'.

Canada's boreal forest: search for 'Boreal forests Canada NRDC'.

Climate maps: search for 'Met Office UK actual and anomaly maps'.

Global climate change: search for 'NASA Eyes on the Earth'.

Manaus climate data: search for 'Manaus climate data Met Office'.

UK temperate rainforests: search for 'Temperate rainforest UK Woodland Trust'.

16 Biomes and vegetation belts

What do I need to know?

A biome is a large geographical area or region with a distinctive community of plants and animals. Climate is a key factor in determining the nature and extent of a biome. Soil, relief and other elements also play a significant role. In very general terms, biomes stretch across the continents in belts that are loosely linked to latitude – the dense foliage of the equatorial regions contrasts with the sparse coverage nearer the poles. Biomes are not restricted to land; they also cover seas and oceans. Each biome contains a variety of ecosystems and habitats, which are adapted to local environmental conditions. There are five main biomes worldwide: forest, grassland, desert, tundra and aquatic.

Forest

Forests cover about a third of the land area of the world. In the tropics and equatorial regions, forests create a particularly rich habitat for plants and creatures. In mid-latitudes (including the UK), deciduous forests are widespread. Meanwhile, extensive regions of coniferous forest (taiga) are found in northern regions, particularly in Canada and Russia.

Grassland

Grasslands create open landscapes, which are used by animals for grazing and by people for farming. In the Northern Hemisphere, the prairies and steppes are planted with wheat. In Africa, the savannah is famous for its wildlife.

Desert

There are deserts in every continent of the world apart from Europe. The Sahara Desert, Arabian Desert and Great Victoria Desert are some of the largest hot deserts. The communities of animals and plants that live there are adapted to cope with harsh conditions. Antarctica and Greenland are also technically desert regions, but they support very few forms of life.

Tundra

The tundra is a very cold biome that is found particularly in northern Canada and Russia. There is a brief warm period in the summer months, which brings shrubs, lichens, mosses and flowers to life. Tundra is also found in high mountain areas around the world, such as the Andes and Himalayas.

Aquatic

Aquatic biomes include freshwater biomes, such as lakes, and the saltwater biomes found in the seas and oceans. Coral reefs form a distinct subdivision and are particularly important ecologically, as they support an abundance of plant and animal life.

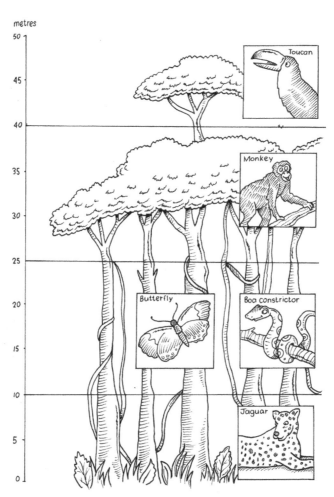

Figure 20: Half of the known species of plants and animals live in the tropical rainforest biome. 0–10 m: forest floor (dark and gloomy); 10–25 m: shadowy layer (trees struggle towards the light); 25–40 m: treetop canopy (thick leaves cut out most of the light); 40–50 m: tallest trees (tall trees grow through the canopy)

Changing biomes

Biomes are not fixed but are constantly evolving. The spread of deserts is particularly noteworthy and the cause of great concern in some areas. Similarly, rainforest regions are changing, as land is cleared for agriculture and industry. It seems likely that global climate change will bring about further modifications. Vegetation belts will need to shift their locations in response to new climate patterns. Rather curiously, this may mean that the areas currently designated as national parks will no longer be in the right areas.

Misconceptions and research

Vegetation belts are an abstract concept that children find rather hard to envisage. The fact that, in many countries (including the UK), large areas are no longer covered by their natural vegetation adds to the problem. A focus on animals and their habitats is one way in which to make this area of study more accessible.

Interesting facts

- The Atacama Desert (Chile) is the driest hot desert in the world, even though it is next to the waters of the Pacific Ocean.
- About one-third of the fish that live in the sea spend part of their life in and around coral reefs.
- In some parts of the tundra, the soil is permanently frozen beneath the surface, creating 'permafrost', which is used in the foundations for buildings.

Key questions

1. Why is climate the key factor in determining the nature and extent of a biome?
2. Which biomes are the most important ecologically?

Lesson 1 Rainforests

What are rainforests like?

You will need
- a world atlas
- light card, colouring pens/pencils, scissors.

Key vocabulary

- convection
- jungle
- logging
- rainforest
- ranching

Getting started

Find out what the pupils already know about the rainforest and gather their ideas on the interactive whiteboard. Use what they say to help to structure a set of enquiry questions about: where the rainforests can be found, the rainforest climate, the plants and creatures that might live there, what the rainforest looks like and how people use and benefit from it.

Class activities

Rainforest regions: Using a world atlas map of vegetation or climate zones, discuss with the class how the rainforests are found around the equator. The basins of the River Amazon and River Congo and the islands of Indonesia are core areas. See whether the pupils can name two or three countries in Asia, Africa and South America in the rainforest belt.

Rainforest weather: As a class, discuss the typical daily pattern of rainforest weather: the temperature rises in the morning, as the Sun rises steadily in the sky, heating the air; more and more moisture evaporates from the forest, leading to heavy clouds and thunderstorms in the afternoon; and in the evening, the skies clear. Ask pupils to create rainforest weather diagrams to illustrate this sequence. Show the time of day along the horizontal axes (x-axes) and illustrate them with relevant pictograms of the weather. Remind pupils how this pattern of convection links to what they have learned about the water cycle in other lessons.

Jungle book: Ask pupils to make their own booklets about rainforest creatures. Each page of each booklet should be about a different animal and its habitat. Encourage pupils to be inventive. How about using butterfly silhouettes as a border for written work, making a coiled-up snake or using a piece of cloth with a rainforest animal design? Pupils will also need to design attractive covers for the fronts of their books. Older children might structure their books according to the forest layers, with, for example, a double page on each of the following: forest floor, shadowy layer, canopy and emergents.

Rainforest research: Invite the pupils to conduct their own research into an aspect of the rainforest. Give them headings, such as 'A fascinating creature', 'An unusual plant', 'Surprising facts', 'Indigenous people' or 'An environmental issue' to provide a focus for their work. Give pupils an opportunity to share their findings with each other. You might also display what they have discovered around a world rainforest map as a class display.

Rainforest threats: Working in small groups, pupils write down each of the following problems on small rectangles of light card: forest fires, logging, mining, ranching and road building. Ask them to write a sentence about the damage that each one causes. Then ask them to arrange their cards in rank order, with the most serious problem at the top and the least serious at the bottom. Have all the groups come up with the same answer? Can they explain their choices?

Plenary

Ask pupils to review what they have learned in this lesson by completing an acrostic using the word 'rainforest'.

Lesson 2 Hot deserts

What are hot deserts like?

You will need
- access to the internet
- an atlas or electronic world maps
- a blank outline map of the world
- sand, glue and modelling equipment
- rectangles of card or hardboard.

Key vocabulary
- cactus
- date palm
- mirage
- oasis
- sand dune
- tropics

Getting started

Show pupils a short video about desert life, such as the YouTube film about the Arabian Desert (see Useful books and websites, p. 168). Talk about the plants and creatures that live in the desert and how they depend on each other.

Class activities

World deserts: Many of the world's hot deserts are found hundreds of kilometres away from the equator. In the Northern Hemisphere, the Sahara and Arabian Deserts lie on the Tropic of Cancer. The Thar Desert (India) and the Sonoran Desert (Mexico and USA) are also found at this latitude. In the Southern Hemisphere, the Atacama Desert (Chile), Kalahari Desert (Southern Africa) and Great Victoria Desert (Australia) lie on the Tropic of Capricorn. Give pupils blank outline maps of the world and ask them to show and label the Tropics of Cancer and Capricorn with dotted lines, and mark and label the hot deserts at these latitudes. They will need an image from the whiteboard or an atlas map to help them.

Desert adventure: Ask pupils to imagine that they are travelling through the desert. It is blisteringly hot by day, with fierce sunshine from dawn to dusk. The nights are cold, with bright stars. Sometimes there is a strong wind, which blows sand and dust in your face and makes you cough. You have plenty of nourishing dates with you from the palm trees and a large bottle of water from the well in the last oasis. Suddenly, your car breaks down and judders to a halt. What happens next?

Desert images: As a class, discuss some of the distinctive features of the desert environment. These include sand dunes, oases, sand storms, mirages, date palms, cactus plants, snakes, scorpions and camels. Ask pupils to divide or fold sheets of paper into four sections, where they can make drawings of four features of their choice. They should write a sentence under each drawing, saying what it tells us about the hot desert environment.

Desert diorama: Ask pupils to create a desert diorama. Start with a rectangle of card or hardboard for the base, which can then be covered with sand and glue to create a suitable surface. Ask pupils to decorate the scene with models of plants and creatures to make it as realistic as possible. You might use modelling dough as appropriate, and display the dioramas in an 'environment' corner, alongside photographs and information books.

Plenary

Working in small groups, ask pupils to consolidate their knowledge of the hot desert biome. Ask them to make a list of six or more features that give hot deserts their distinctive character.

Lesson 3 Savannahs

What are savannahs like?

You will need

- straws and paper clips (or some old coat hangers)

- access to the internet

- a pair of compasses for each pupil.

Key vocabulary

- Masai

- savannah

- season

- silhouette

Getting started

Explain that savannahs are found between the rainforests and hot deserts, where the climate is too dry for forests but there is enough rain for grass to grow. Show pupils an extract from one of the excellent wildlife films about the savannah. The David Attenborough programmes are particularly engaging (see Useful books and websites, p. 168).

Class activities

Savannah frieze: A great number of different animals live in the savannah, including elephants, zebras, lions, vultures and giraffes. Make a savannah animal frieze to display along a wall of your classroom. The pupils could each contribute a couple of drawings. Add silhouettes of scattered trees to create the background and show patches of green and brown grass in the foreground. You might also consider dividing the frieze into daytime and night-time sections.

Savannah mobile: Ask pupils to make savannah animal mobiles. They will need to colour and cut out some drawings of the animals that are found in the savannah. The simplest way in which to make each mobile is to attach three paper clips to a straw, suspend the mobile from a clip in the centre and ask the pupils to attach cut-out drawings of their savannah animals at each end. The pupils can add a second and third straw to create space for more creatures. They could also use coat hangers to create more-robust frames.

Masai herders: Most of the world's savannah is found in Africa and it is the home to many groups of people who herd animals for a living. One of the most famous of these groups is the Masai of Kenya and Tanzania. Find out about some of their traditional customs and ways of life from the internet. What do the children admire about the Masai? What do they think that they would find challenging about their lifestyle? Read them the picture book story *Bringing the Rain to Kapiti Plain* (Verna Ardeema) or watch a YouTube version (see Useful books and websites, p. 168).

Season dials: The savannah has just two seasons: there is a long, very dry season and a shorter, very wet season. Temperatures stay relatively high throughout the year. Make a season dial for Lusaka, the capital of Zambia. You will need to draw a circle with a ring on the outside divided into 12 equal sections – one for each month of the year. Starting at the top and going clockwise, write the first letter of each month's name in each space in the ring. Then draw lines to the centre, marking out the two seasons. The wet season in Lusaka lasts from November to March. The remaining seven months are the dry season. Colour and label the different sections. Next, make a second dial to show the comparison with the UK, where there are four seasons of equal length, starting with winter in December, January and February.

Plenary

Ask the pupils to say what is the most interesting thing that they have learned about the savannah from the activities that they have been doing. Gather their ideas together as a class list to display alongside the work that they have been doing.

Fieldwork and further investigations

- Ask pupils to look for examples of desert and rainforest plants around their school, home and local area. Many of the evergreens that are often grown as pot plants originated from the rainforest. The Swiss cheese plant (Central America) and African violet and zebra plant (Brazil) are good examples. Similarly, common desert plants include a wide range of cacti and palms that have been gathered from around the world. Ask pupils to research the different examples that they find. Discuss their locations in buildings and gardens, and the ways in which people try to recreate the climates that the plants need.

- As a class, discuss world climate zones using a globe as a visual aid. The basic pattern is relatively simple to explain: at the equator, convection currents carry moist air upwards, creating clouds and heavy rain; at the tropics, the air descends, bringing clear skies and very hot, dry conditions. The polar regions also have generally clear skies and dry air but, because the Sun never rises high in the sky, temperatures there are very low. The winds that blow between these three zones bring mixed weather and moderate rainfall to the places that they cross. Show the pupils annual world rainfall maps to confirm this pattern. Which places are very wet? Which are very dry? Which are in between?

Cross-curricular links

English: Ask pupils to fold pieces of paper into 16 squares. Working in pairs, pupils write down words that they associate with the desert, rainforest or savannah environment. Next, ask each pair to use these words in a poem. They don't have to use all of them and they can add others if they like. Share the poems with the rest of the class.

Mathematics: Give the pupils data about average temperatures in a city in one of these places: a hot desert (e.g. Cairo in Egypt), the savannah (e.g. Juba in South Sudan) or the rainforest (e.g. Manaus in Brazil). Ask them to construct line graphs showing monthly temperature changes.

Science: Ask pupils to research the life cycle of one of the creatures they have learned about in this area of study, relating what they discover to environmental as well as biological factors.

Music: Working as a class, create a rainforest storm without using any musical instruments. Start by just tapping your fingers two or three times, slowly but clearly, on the table or desk. Ask pupils to follow your lead so that the sound goes around the room. Increase the speed and number of taps on the next few rounds, finally reaching a crescendo of continual noise to represent the centre of the storm, and then slowly reduce the intensity to a steady patter and the last few drips on the final rounds.

Themes

Biodiversity: Every biome contributes in a different way to the tapestry of life on our planet. Divide the class into small groups and allocate each a biome. They should now consider what makes their biome particularly important. Organise a discussion in which pupils argue the cases for their biomes. Bring the session to a close at a suitable moment, making the point that every biome is a unique ecological network and that they all reinforce each other.

Values and wellbeing: The great diversity found within and across global biomes offers an opportunity to celebrate differences as well as similarities. Plants and creatures work together in extraordinary combinations, cooperating with each other but also competing fiercely for space and dominance. This raises questions about the characteristics of a balanced and harmonious community, and it highlights how both the natural and human worlds are organised.

Progression and assessment

By the end of this area of study, all children should be able to describe a biome and name at least two examples. They will also know that biomes cover very large areas and are the results of different climate conditions. Those who are working at higher levels of attainment will recognise that biomes are linked to latitude. They will also be able to explain some of the other ways in which biomes and climate interrelate. All pupils will be able to talk about some of the plants and animals that inhabit different biomes.

Useful books and websites

Aardema, V. (1981), *Bringing the Rain to Kapiti Plain*. London: Macmillan (also available on YouTube).

Bailey, E. (2015), *One Day on our Blue Planet: In the Savannah*. London: Flying Eye Books.

Bowden, D. and Copeland, P. (2015), *Amazon Adventures: Investigating the South American Rainforest*. Sheffield: Geographical Association.

Smith, M. (2022), *If the World Were 100 Animals*. London: Red Shed.

Arabian Desert video: www.youtube.com/watch?v=gWo5sHandUM

Savannah biome: search for 'Savannah grassland' on YouTube.

17 UK cities, counties and regions

What does the curriculum say?

Pupils should be taught to:

- *name and locate counties and cities of the United Kingdom, geographical regions and their identifying human and physical characteristics, key topographical features (including hills, mountains, coasts and rivers), and land-use patterns; and understand how some of these aspects have changed over time*

- *use maps, atlases, globes and digital/computer mapping to locate countries and describe features studied.*

What do I need to know?

This area of study is designed to deepen pupils' understanding of the UK. It focuses on counties, cities and regions and prepares the way for more-detailed investigations and thematic studies.

Cities

The first towns and cities in the UK are usually regarded as having been founded by the Romans. Some of the towns that they established disappeared, but others, such as London, Exeter, York and Chester, flourished. Most UK cities remained very small for hundreds of years. However, the Industrial Revolution brought great changes. The coal-mining areas of central and northern England saw particularly dramatic growth, as people migrated from the surrounding countryside. Today, the population distribution of the UK still closely mirrors the distribution of the coal measures, apart from the notable exception of London and its satellite towns.

With increasing urbanisation, people are now concerned about the spread of cities and the erosion of the countryside. The areas around many towns are now protected from development and form 'green belts' for planning purposes. Developers have also been encouraged to build on derelict 'brown field' sites within towns and cities. Reducing pollution and improving the quality of city life are high priorities.

Counties

The system of government and administration that we have today dates back to the Normans. They divided Britain into shire counties each centred on a county town, many of which gave their names to the surrounding areas. Thus, the county of Lincolnshire was centred on the city of Lincoln and Derbyshire was centred on Derby. From 1965 onwards, a succession of local government reforms brought many changes, and few county councils can now claim to represent their historic areas. The result is a complicated patchwork of local government with unitary authorities and metropolitan districts.

Despite these changes, many people in the UK today still feel attached to a historic county, even if it technically no longer exists. For example, both Rutland and Middlesex were abolished after 1965 but have retained their identities after long campaigns. Across the UK, clubs, sporting events and other aspects of social and cultural life continue to be organised on a county basis. From a geographical point of view too, historic counties have proved to be an enduring concept, as they are often valuable ways of referring to areas or landscapes with specific characters and features.

Regions

A region is an area that has similar characteristics or historical identity. There is no set size. Physical regions include mountain ranges, river basins and climate zones. Human regions include the hinterland of a town or city, areas that are based on a single industrial activity or the territory that is claimed by a country. Social, historical and environmental factors can all be used to define regions. The regions affected by forest fires or sea-level rises are typical examples.

For the purposes of government and statistical analysis, the UK is often regarded as being divided into 12 standard socio-economic regions. There are nine regions in England, along with Scotland, Wales and Northern Ireland (see **Figure 21**). Working to set boundaries makes it possible to compare different parts of the country using data about health, education, welfare and economic activity, and to evidence change over a period of time.

Misconceptions and research

Discovering that the boundaries of counties and regions are not fixed but change over time can unsettle children, who may think in rigid categories and want definite answers. It is also easy for children to confuse counties and countries. Both refer to territories and the words sound and look extremely similar (there is only one letter's difference). Finally, it is worth noting that administrative districts, whatever their size, are abstract concepts, created by people for government and administration. This makes them hard for children of primary-school age to comprehend.

Interesting facts

- Eighty per cent of the population in the UK lives in towns and cities.
- Since the Second World War, over 30 new towns have been created in the UK to alleviate housing shortages.
- There are 92 historic counties in the UK.

Figure 21: The UK is divided into standard socio-economic regions for statistical purposes

Key questions

1. Why do people want to live in towns and cities?
2. What is the best size for a region?
3. Why do boundaries change over time?

Lesson 1 UK cities

What are the main cities of the UK?

You will need
- access to the internet
- an atlas with maps of the UK cities
- blank outline maps of the UK.

Key vocabulary
- city
- industry
- route
- trade

Getting started
Search for 'London from the air at night' using Google to share with the pupils. Can they recognise any key features, such as the M25, main roads, the central area and large open spaces such as Richmond Park? Are there other places that they can name, such as Heathrow Airport? Does the image show the River Thames? Discuss how cities are very large places where lots of people live close together.

Class activities
City sight-seeing tour: Ask the pupils to imagine that they are taking a friend from abroad on a sight-seeing tour of a city in your area. Challenge them to identify half a dozen or more places that they would want the friend to see. As well as identifying the places, they will need to devise a route linking them together. Ask them to show the route and points along it on a sketch map, working from a street plan that they have downloaded from the internet.

Cities in the UK: Working from a simple atlas map or an image from the internet, ask pupils to compare the numbers of cities in different parts of the UK. Are there more cities in England than all other parts of the UK put together? Can they find an inland area where lots of cities are crowded together? Look for cities that are on the coast. Discuss the reasons for this pattern. The cluster of inland cities grew up as industrial centres in the Industrial Revolution. The cities around the coast developed as a result of sea trade.

Famous buildings: Most cities have famous buildings and historic monuments. Prepare a short quiz to use with the class. Can the pupils work out which city each image comes from? Print off the images and arrange them around a UK map as a class display.

Encourage the pupils to add their own images to develop the display. See that all four countries of the UK are represented. Vary the display by narrowing the focus to statues, bridges, castles or other more-specific themes.

Football teams: Most cities have their own football teams. Give the pupils a blank outline map of England, on which they can mark the cities and name the teams in the Premier League. If they find it difficult to show all the teams, you can restrict them to the top ten or 12 at that particular moment. Alternatively, they can save space by simply numbering the cities on their maps and adding a key.

Intercity journey: Ask pupils to devise two intercity train journeys: from London to Cardiff and from London to Edinburgh. What are the main cities that they would pass through on the way? Ask pupils to show their routes on intercity rail maps, similar in style to the diagrammatic maps displayed in railway stations.

Plenary
Working from an atlas map, challenge the pupils to devise a city 'word chain' in which the last letter of one city becomes the first letter of the next one. For example, London ends in 'n' so it might link to Nottingham, which ends in an 'm' and links to Manchester, etc. Pupils can devise their chains either individually or in pairs. The chains are liable to break as they get longer, so you might suggest that they stop when they have linked five cities and start again. Start the first chain with 'London'.

Lesson 2 UK counties

What are the UK counties and districts?

You will need
- a map of UK counties
- access to the internet
- an electronic or printed map of your county or administrative area.

Key vocabulary
- administrative area
- boundary
- coat of arms
- county
- logo

Getting started

Explain that the UK is divided into counties, some of which are extremely ancient. Schools, policing and many other public services are organised on a county basis. However, over the years, the number of people living in cities has increased, so new administrative areas have had to be created. Today, there is a mixture of ancient counties (some of which are very large) and administrative areas (which are much smaller districts in towns and cities).

Class activities

County map: Ask the pupils to draw sketch maps of your county/area, working from electronic or printed maps. Next, ask them to draw boxes around the edges, leaving generous borders. To complete the maps, ask the pupils to add and name any surrounding counties/areas. They should also mark their own village, town or city as a point of reference, if appropriate.

County features: Using Google Earth or other electronic mapping packages, zoom in on your county/area to locate where you live. Zoom out again slowly until your county/area fills the screen. What can you tell about it from the image on the screen? If possible, obtain extra information working from an atlas map. Are there any hills, mountains or rivers? What are the chief towns and cities? Does your county/area have a coastline? If so, what are the names of the beaches and headlands?

County advert: Working in pairs, ask pupils to design electronic presentations advertising your county/area to visitors. Tell them that they can only use six images each, and that each one needs to show a different feature, e.g. town, countryside, lake, cliff, historic site, sporting events and so on. Get them to share their adverts with each other and to justify their choices of images.

County symbols and logos: Counties and administrative districts have a range of individual symbols and logos, which are used on public buildings, notices and communications. They also have their own coats of arms. Ask pupils to make drawings of one of the symbols or logos that relate to their county or district. Ask them to add notes about the significance of the different elements.

County boundaries: What forms the boundaries between counties? In some instances, the boundaries follow rivers (e.g. the Tamar between Devon and Cornwall); in other instances they follow upland ridges (e.g. the Cheviot Hills between Northumberland and the Scottish Borders); and elsewhere they ring urban areas (e.g. Greater London). Ask pupils to trace the boundary of their own county or district and to look at others around the UK. Discuss what the children think makes the best boundary.

Counties game: Working from a map of the UK, ask pupils to devise some questions for a UK-counties game. For example, they might ask for the name of a very large or very small county, the name of a county starting with a particular letter of the alphabet, the name of a county that is an island, and so on. See that they are clear about all the possible answers themselves. Divide the class into two teams. One team puts their 'best' questions in a bag. The other team tries to answer them. Reverse roles and compare scores. Note: depending on where you live, you might want to restrict the game to your part of the UK.

Plenary

Challenge pupils to plan journeys that involve travelling across the UK from coast to coast, passing through between three and six counties/areas on the way. Ask pupils to draw diagram maps with the names of the counties/areas in order and the names of the sea/ocean at either end.

Lesson 3 Different regions

What are the landscape regions of the UK?

You will need

- photographs of different UK landscapes
- an atlas or electronic map of the UK
- access to the internet.

Key vocabulary

- Giant's Causeway
- Jurassic Coast
- Norfolk Broads
- Pennines
- Thames

Getting started

Compile a set of around a dozen photographs of different UK landscapes to show to the pupils by way of an introduction to this lesson. See that you include hills, coasts and rivers in your selection.

Class activities

River Thames: Using at an atlas or an appropriate map, ask pupils to trace the course of the River Thames. Ask them to make lists of towns and features from the source near Cirencester to the estuary in the North Sea, downstream from London. The pupils can then use this information to create simple pictorial maps. Can they work out how many counties the Thames either runs through or borders? They can also go on a virtual journey down the Thames with Winnie the Pooh (see Useful books and websites, p. 178).

Jurassic Coast: The Jurassic Coast stretches 96 miles from Dorset to Devon and spans a range of geological strata, from chalk in the east to red desert sandstones in the west. There are many fossils embedded in the rocks, including dinosaur bones. There is also a spectacular range of cliffs, caves, beaches and other coastal features. It was designated as a World Heritage Site in 2001. Working in pairs, ask the pupils to select six images of the Jurassic Coast, either on a single theme (e.g. cliffs) or along a route (e.g. the South West Coast Path). Ask them to add text panels in which they say what is special about each image in one or two short sentences. Invite pairs to share their presentations once they are completed.

The Pennines: The Pennines are one of the most significant mountain areas in the UK, separating the Lancashire coast from the lowlands of Yorkshire. Ask pupils to make fact-files about the Pennines. These should list the highest peaks and the main rivers. They could name the counties where the Pennines are found and some of the cities that cluster around their base. You might ask pupils to add information about the landscape, natural environment and industrial history. Finding out the crossing points, such as the Snake Pass, might lead to them to make a cross-section drawing.

The Norfolk Broads: The Norfolk Broads are a special area of lakes and marshes between Norwich and Great Yarmouth. There are over 60 broads (lakes), seven rivers and hundreds of kilometres of navigable waterways. Ask pupils to devise brochures advertising the Broads to visitors. See that they include information about what the Broads are like, how they were created and where they are located.

The Giant's Causeway: With 40,000 hexagonal basalt rocks, the Giant's Causeway in Northern Ireland is one of the most remarkable coastal features in the UK. It is also steeped in legend. Tell the pupils the legend of Finn MacCool and his battle with the fearsome enemies, the Scottish Giants. There are a number of YouTube animations to watch (see Useful books and websites, p. 178) that help to bring the legend to life. Look at a map to find out where the causeway between Ireland and Scotland might have gone.

Plenary

Play a game in which pupils pool their knowledge about the UK. Working collaboratively, can each child in the class think of a different fact or piece of information?

Fieldwork and further investigations

- Walls and fences are one way of establishing the boundaries between different areas. Take pupils to a street near your school where they can see into front gardens from the pavement. Ask them to write down as many pairs of descriptive words that they can think of to describe the environment on the different sides of the boundaries, e.g. concrete/soil, flat/bumpy, public/private and so on. Repeat this exercise in a number of different locations if possible, perhaps along a route that you have planned in advance. What does this activity tell pupils about local land use? Are some ways of managing the land better for plants and wildlife than others?

Cross-curricular links

English: Divide the class into groups and ask them to make up anagrams using the names of counties from different parts of the UK. When each group has come up with around a dozen examples, ask them to select their best three for an anagram game. Going around the class, each group then challenges the others to discover the answers. Time how long it takes for them to solve each puzzle.

Mathematics: Working from a map of the UK, ask pupils to calculate the distances between different UK cities. They should measure the distances using rulers and write down the results. They will then be able to calculate the distances in kilometres, working from the scale bar. What is the longest journey that they can identify?

History: Ask the pupils to find out about the cities founded by the Romans. Ask them to show these cities on UK maps, adding the key roads such as Watling Street, Ermine Street and the Fosse Way.

Themes

Colonialism and social justice: The waves of invaders and settlers who have come to the UK over the centuries have all left their marks on the country today. Finding out about the UK and its counties is a neutral context for exploring how people have mixed together in the past. For example, Britain was a Roman colony and the Romans oppressed local people. However, they also brought new ideas and a long period of prosperity.

Sustainability: Historically, the UK has taken a leading international role in developing national parks and protecting the natural landscape through legislation. Many major cities are now surrounded by 'green belts', which stop them from sprawling into the countryside. Meanwhile, over 500 miles of outstanding coastline have been saved for posterity by the National Trust.

Personal development: As pupils find out about their own district, there will be opportunities to consider what makes it distinctive, which builds their sense of belonging and identity. Local councils, too, often go to considerable trouble to emphasise what is special about their area. This helps to attract business, boosts tourism and highlights leisure and recreational opportunities. Taking pride in the place where they live and valuing its qualities is an affirmative process that contributes to a positive mindset.

Progression and assessment

By the end of this area of study, children will have begun to learn about the key cities of the UK and where they are located. They will also know about how the UK is divided into counties that have distinct geographical and historical characteristics. Some children will be able to name and locate counties and cities on a UK map. All children will know the name of their own region and be aware of some of its key features.

Useful books and websites

Rubbino, S. (2012), *A Walk in London*. London: Walker Books.

Zephaniah, B. (2003), *We Are Britain! Poems by Benjamin Zephaniah*. London: Frances Lincoln.

Country portrait: search for 'Woodlands Junior School project Britain'.

Games: search for 'English counties online games'.

Giant's Causeway animated story: search for 'Giants Causeway Eliade School'.

Photographs: search for 'Images and photos' followed by the name of the city, county or region.

River Thames journey: search for 'Primary homework River Thames a short visual guide'.

18 Europe

What does the curriculum say?

Pupils should be taught to:

- *locate the world's countries, using maps to focus on Europe (including the location of Russia) and North and South America, concentrating on their environmental regions, key physical and human characteristics, countries and major cities*

- *understand geographical similarities and differences through the study of human and physical geography of a region of the United Kingdom, a region in a European country, and a region within North and South America*

- *use maps, atlases, globes and digital/computer mapping to locate countries and describe features studied.*

What do I need to know?

Europe is one of the smallest continents. It is also one of the hardest to identify, as it is joined to Asia on its eastern edge. The division between Europe and Asia was originally established by the Ancient Greeks, and the notion of Europe as a cultural entity is still one of its defining characteristics. In geographical terms, two mountain ranges – the Urals and Caucasus Mountains – form the boundary separating the two continents. This means that western areas of Russia are part of Europe and Moscow is a European capital.

Europe is approximately 4,000 kilometres from east to west and 3,000 kilometres from north to south. The Alps, Carpathians and Scandinavia are the main mountain areas and the Rhine, Danube, Dnieper and Volga are the main rivers. The coastline is deeply indented by the Baltic, Mediterranean and Black Seas, where there are many natural harbours. The climate varies, from the intense cold of the Arctic regions to the heat of the Mediterranean. Western areas have temperate, mid-latitude conditions. Europe is the only continent not to have a desert. Europe is defined by historical and cultural factors as much as by its physical characteristics.

This area of study introduces pupils to Europe and its key characteristics. It focuses especially on Poland and the Tatra Mountains, both of which can be considered as regions. After 2004 and the enlargement of the European Union, many Polish people arrived to work in the UK. Geography lessons provide a natural opportunity to find out more about their country of origin. A comparison of similarities and differences has considerable educational potential. Poland is less densely populated and much more rural than the UK.

Figure 22: Forest and mountain regions in Europe

	Poland	**UK**
Area	313,000 km²	244 km²
Population	39 million	68 million
Largest city	Warsaw: 2 million	London: 10 million
Latitude of capital city	52 degrees north	52 degrees north
Forest areas	31%	12%
Percentage of farm workers	13%	1%

Figure 23: Poland is similar in size and latitude to the UK but is much more rural (statistics from the CIA World Factbook, https://www.cia.gov/the-world-factbook/countries)

It is also instructive to contrast the Tatra Mountains, which lie along the border between southern Poland and Slovakia, with mountain areas such as the Lake District in the UK. Both are major tourist attractions and both are glaciated landscapes with steep rocky mountains, deep valleys and attractive lakes, which are now protected as national parks. The Tatra Mountains are, however, much higher and wilder than those in the Lake District.

They are part of a long mountain range (the Carpathians) that snakes across central Europe, from Poland to Romania. This range was thrown up at the same time as the Alps, when the European and African plates collided around sixty million years ago. The granite peaks of the Tatras are among the highest points in the Carpathians, and are popular for skiing in winter and hiking in summer. Like many mountain areas, they have unpredictable weather. In 2004, a violent windstorm caused massive damage, uprooting thousands of trees, especially on the Slovakian side of the range.

Misconceptions and research

Some pupils may have stereotyped and preconceived images of different countries and areas of Europe. These images, which may be either positive or negative, are liable to act as a filter that will colour their subsequent learning. This area of study provides an opportunity to enlarge pupils' ideas. This is important work because, unless their notions are challenged, there is a danger that existing bias and prejudice will become entrenched as they grow older.

Interesting facts

- Europe's coastline measures 60,000 km, one-and-a-half times the distance around the Earth.
- It is estimated that one in four of the world's population of storks is found in Poland.
- The Tatra Mountains are one of the few areas of Europe where bears and wolves roam freely.

Key questions

1. What makes Europe distinctive?
2. In what ways are Poland and the UK similar and different?
3. Why do many people seem to like mountain landscapes?

Lesson 1 Introducing Europe

What is Europe like?

You will need

- an atlas showing European countries and landscapes
- access to the internet
- a thermometer
- string and scissors
- blank outline maps of Europe.

Key vocabulary

- border
- fjord
- landlocked
- polder

Getting started

Initiate a class discussion in which the pupils pool what they already know about Europe. Some children may have been to mainland Europe on holiday and be aware of differences in language, climate and culture. Some may have lived in mainland Europe or have friends and relatives abroad. Others will know about Europe through sporting events and competitions. Ask the pupils to name any countries or cities that they know. You might also discuss the Brexit referendum. This is a natural opportunity to talk with children about what 'Brexit' means and the effects of the referendum.

Class activities

What is Europe?: As a class, look at a map to see how far Europe extends. The eastern boundary runs along the Ural Mountains to the Caspian Sea – this means that part of Russia lies in Europe, making it the largest European country. Look also at the islands around the edges of Europe: Iceland, Sardinia, Sicily and Crete are all part of Europe, as are the British Isles.

European countries: Working from an atlas map, ask pupils to name two European countries that have: only one land border, two land borders, three borders, and four or more land borders. Which country has the most borders? Now look back to the map to see how many countries are landlocked (have no access to the sea). Discuss how this might affect them.

Country-name ladder: Challenge the pupils to devise a country-name ladder. To do this, they should write the names of different European countries either across or down a page, linking them up so that one letter in each name appears twice. For example, they might write 'Spain' across the page and 'Sweden' down the page, using the letter 'S' twice to link them up. Explain that the pivotal letter could appear in the middle or end of a name. Have fun creating chains of different lengths and shapes.

City temperatures: Ask pupils to find out the temperature outside by looking at a thermometer. Now challenge them to find three European cities that are colder than your area and three that are warmer. Which are the hottest and coldest cities in Europe at the moment? Ask pupils to present the information that they have discovered in charts or on maps.

Different climates: There are a number of different climate regions in Europe, e.g. around the Mediterranean, it is often hot and sunny in the summer but cool and wet in the winter, while Scandinavia has a very cold climate with lots of snow and long winters. The UK lies in between these extremes. Ask pupils to make lists of the clothes that they might need for a holiday on a Greek island in July and a trip to see the Northern Lights in Norway in March.

European landscapes: Working from the internet, ask pupils to download pictures of four different European landscapes to put in their geography books. Examples might include a mountain area such as the Alps or Pyrenees, a river such as the Rhine or Danube, the polders of the Netherlands, the fjords of Scandinavia or a Mediterranean island. Ask them to think about what is distinctive about the photographs that they have chosen and write a sentence or two about each of the different landscapes and where they can be found.

European coasts: For its size, Europe has a remarkably long coastline. Ask pupils to imagine that they are travelling by boat from Istanbul to St Petersburg. They should find out from an atlas map what seas and oceans they would pass through. Can they work out how far they would have travelled by placing a length of string along the route and calculating the distance using the scale bar?

Plenary
Give pupils blank outline maps of Europe and ask them to mark on some of the countries, features and regions about which they have learned during the lesson.

Lesson 2 Focus on Poland

What is Poland like?

You will need
- a recording of some Chopin piano music
- a blank outline map of Poland.

Key vocabulary

- Baltic Sea

- Kraków

- Oder

- Tatra Mountains

- Vistula

- Warsaw

Getting started

Play the pupils some Chopin piano music. The polonaises, waltzes and mazurkas draw on traditional dance tunes and provide a charming and evocative introduction to a lesson on Poland. See whether the pupils can guess the country where the music they have just listened to comes from. What does it make them think of? If any of the children in your class come from Poland, you may find that you will be able to draw on their knowledge in this lesson and the one that follows. Personal experience can be an invaluable resource, but it is important to see that such children are not put in uncomfortable positions or expected to act as class experts when this is not appropriate.

Class activities

Where is Poland?: Find Poland on an atlas map of Europe. Does it lie to the north, east, south or west of the UK? Approximately how far is it to the capital city, Warsaw? How does Poland compare to the UK in terms of size? What are the countries that it neighbours?

Travelling to Poland: Ask pupils to find out about travelling overland from your area to Warsaw by bus and by train. What places would they pass through along the way? How long might it take? What are the advantages and disadvantages of each method of travel? How does overland travel compare with going by air?

River Vistula: The River Vistula is approximately 1,050 km long. Ask pupils to draw lines 10.5 cm long in their books to represent the Vistula, marking the Carpathian Mountains at one end, the Baltic Sea at the other and Warsaw in the middle. Next, ask them to make similar diagrams of the River Rhine (1,230 km long), which flows from the Alps to the North Sea through Frankfurt, Cologne and Rotterdam. It is instructive to add the River Thames, which, at 350 km, is very much shorter than the chief rivers of mainland Europe. Pupils might like to add other rivers of their choice for comparison, using the same scale (1 cm for 100 km).

Traditional dishes: Put some potatoes, beetroot, cabbage and mushrooms on a display table. These are some of the ingredients used in traditional Polish dishes. Ask pupils to research one of these recipes: *bigos* are made from meat and sauerkraut (pickled cabbage); *pierogi* (dumplings) can be stuffed with cottage cheese, mince or cabbage; *barszcz* is a beetroot soup, known in some places as 'borscht'. Potato pancakes are another popular dish. Discuss how these dishes make use of ingredients that grow well in Poland, where the summers are warm but rather wet.

Plants and wildlife: Poland has extensive forests and an exciting range of wildlife. The Bialowieza National Park is one of the oldest nature reserves in Europe. It contains a large area of ancient forest and is famous as the home of the world's largest population of European bison. In the north-east, there are more than 2,000 lakes in the Great Masurian Lake District, which were created in the past by glaciers. These attract a vast array of birds, including storks and cormorants. There are wild bears in the Tatra Mountains. Ask pupils to make labelled drawings of some of the different creatures that can be found in Poland.

Plenary

Ask pupils to draw their own maps of Poland or give them blank outlines to complete. These should show the main cities, such as Warsaw, Łódź, Kraków (the former capital) and Wrocław, as well the Tatra Mountains, River Vistula and River Oder. Depending on the space available, pupils could name surrounding countries, the Baltic Sea and other features of interest. See that they add north points and enclose their maps with ruled lines.

Lesson 3 The Tatra Mountains

What are the Tatra Mountains like?

You will need
- a photograph of the Tatra mountains and lakes
- access to the internet
- art materials.

Key vocabulary
- altitude
- beech trees
- Carpathian Mountains
- glacier
- lichen
- ridge

- Tatra Mountains
- U-shaped valley

Getting started

Find out whether any pupils in the class have visited mountain areas, perhaps on skiing or walking holidays. What do they remember about the mountains? Talk about the mountain landscape, vegetation, weather and wildlife. Did they visit any places that seemed remote? Now tell them that in this lesson they are going to find out about the Tatra Mountains, a famous mountain region between southern Poland and Slovakia.

Class activities

Tatra Mountains brochure: Ask pupils to design leaflets advertising the Polish part of the Tatra Mountains. This will need to indicate where they are (the nearest city is Kraków), what they are like, what people can do there and the weather that they can expect. Encourage pupils to say what is special about the area. There is plenty of information readily available on the internet.

Plants and wildlife: Ask pupils to make diagrams showing how the plants and wildlife change according to altitude in the Tatra Mountains. Start by drawing a vertical line down the side of the page, 25 cm long. Tell the pupils that each centimetre represents 100 metres. Now ask them to mark the heights shown in **Figure 24**, and make drawings of the different plants and animals that might be found there. Discuss what causes these changes in vegetation and animal life.

Altitude	Plant life	Animal life
Below 1,300 metres	Beech trees	Brown bears
1 300–1,800 metres	Pine trees	Deer and wolves
1,800–2,300 metres	Grass	Chamois
Above 23,000	Lichens and bane rock	Eagles

Figure 24: How plants and animals change according to altitude in the Tatra Mountains

Traditional houses: Find out about the traditional buildings of the Tatra Mountain region. Wood is the chief building material. The houses can be tall, with steep pitched roofs covered in wooden tiles. Side gables are common. Share pictures with the class (search 'Tatra Mountain wooden houses' on the internet) and ask pupils to make drawings of traditional houses in their geography books.

Shaped by ice: Unlike other parts of the Carpathian mountain range, the Tatras were covered by glaciers in the last Ice Age. The action of the ice eroded the rock and sculpted the landscape that we see today. Project a photograph of the lakes and the mountains onto the interactive whiteboard. As a class, discuss the features that pupils can see – ridges, rock faces, boulders, valleys and lakes. Can they see how each valley is shaped like a 'U', with steep sides and a flat bottom? Try to imagine the whole area filled with ice, with just the mountain peaks showing.

Tatra Mountains paintings: There are many paintings of the dramatic landscapes of the Tatra Mountains (available through Google Images). Ask pupils to download paintings of their choice. Using this as a reference, they should now make their own pictures of the Tatra Mountains. Alternatively, they could try to copy the paintings that they have selected to produce their own versions of famous originals.

Plenary
Discuss how the Tatra Mountains are similar to and different from the Lake District (the region of the UK studied in Chapter 14, pp. 140–148). Think about physical features, economic factors, cultural and social issues, and the environmental dimension. Compile a class list on the interactive whiteboard or ask pupils to make up tables of their own.

Fieldwork and further investigations

* Many places have specialist shops that sell Polish goods. If you can arrange to take your class to visit one of these, they will be able to see a range of typical products, look at the labels and consider their geographical significance. Alternatively, you may find that a person of Polish heritage is willing to come to your school and answer questions about life in Poland. Ensure that the pupils prepare their questions before any visit. That way, you can avoid repetition and ensure that you cover a range of geography topics, from landscape, weather, and economic and social life to possible changes and future developments.

Cross-curricular links

English: Ask pupils to imagine that they are on holiday in Poland and visiting the Tatra Mountains. Ask them to write postcards to friends, telling where they have been and what they have been doing.

Mathematics: Ask pupils to make tables of facts and figures comparing Poland and the UK. These might include the name and length of the longest river, name and height of the highest mountain, name and population of the capital city, total population, land area and length of coastline.

Science: Set up a display table contrasting the hard granite rocks that make up the Tatra Mountains with softer rocks like limestone and sandstone. Extend the activity by finding out about the Mohs scale of mineral hardness.

History: Over the last 600 years, Poland has varied between being the largest country in Europe to being completely absorbed by its neighbours. There are a number of YouTube videos showing how the borders have been constantly changing (see Useful books and websites, p. 189). Show one of these to the class and discuss why they think that Poland might have been much more vulnerable to invasion than, say, Britain or Spain.

Themes

Climate change: Mountains have fierce and unpredictable weather, and the plants and creatures that live there are often at the edges of their biological ranges. In 2004, a terrible windstorm hit the Tatras, uprooting tens of thousands of trees, especially on the southern (Slovakian) side. Find out more about how natural disasters like this are putting pressure on vulnerable mountain environments, both in Europe and in other parts of the world. Discuss with the pupils whether this is linked to climate change.

Personal development: Learning about Poland and the Tatra Mountains helps pupils to engage with other people and cultures. This is part of a long-term process of personal development that is founded on notions of inclusion and international understanding.

Values and wellbeing: Discuss the ways in which the UK is linked to mainland Europe. You might want to touch on aspects of geography, history, religion and so on. Explain how ideas about democracy originated in Ancient Greece and have now been adopted in many parts of the world. Is there a sense in which British values are similar to but different from those of our European neighbours?

Progression and assessment

By the end of this area of study, all children will have begun to form an image of Europe and be aware of some of its countries, cities and physical features. They will also have a more detailed knowledge of a European region (Poland and the Tatra Mountains). Those who are working beyond expectations will be able to make comparisons between Poland and the UK.

Useful books and websites

European Union puzzles and games: search for 'European Union learning corner'.

Flags: search for 'European Union countries flags'.

Polish border changes: search for 'Poland borders territorial changes'.

19 Volcanoes and earthquakes

What does the curriculum say?

Pupils should be taught to:

- *describe and understand key aspects of physical geography, including: climate zones, biomes and vegetation belts, rivers, mountains, volcanoes and earthquakes, and the water cycle*

- *use maps, atlases, globes and digital/computer mapping to locate countries and describe features studied.*

What do I need to know?

The Earth's surface or crust consists of a layer of solid rock, which varies in thickness from 5 km to 100 km. The crust is also broken into a number of huge pieces, called tectonic plates, which slowly move in relation to each other. Some plates are being slowly pulled apart, others are being pushed together or sliding against each other. Volcanoes and earthquakes are commonly found at plate boundaries – around the edge of the Pacific Ocean, there is a particularly striking concentration of volcanoes, called the 'Ring of Fire'. Plate tectonic theory is still evolving and is studied in more depth at secondary phase.

Volcanoes

Volcanoes can be divided into two main types. Shield volcanoes have low sloping sides and emit thin, runny lava. They tend to have frequent but relatively gentle eruptions. Over long periods of time, shield volcanoes can grow to a great height. Mauna Kea and Mauna Loa in Hawaii, for example, rise nearly 9 km above the sea floor. Composite volcanoes are made of alternate layers of lava and ash. They sometimes erupt violently and create what is known as a pyroclastic flow, made of a mixture of hot steam, ash, rock and dust. It was a pyroclastic flow that engulfed Pompeii in AD 79, when it hurtled down the slopes of Mount Vesuvius.

Not all volcanoes are active. Some volcanoes are extinct, which means that they will not erupt again. Dormant volcanoes are ones that have not erupted for a while, but that still may become active again in the future. Distinguishing between those that are dormant and those that are extinct is not always easy.

Earthquakes

Earthquakes are caused by a sudden release of the energy that has built up over many years along fault lines in the Earth's crust. The shaking that results from this can range in intensity from being barely perceptible to being violent and destructive. Indeed, some earthquakes are so powerful that they lift or depress large areas of land by many metres, causing buildings to collapse and whole cities to be devastated. The point on the ground immediately above the origin of an earthquake is called the 'epicentre'. Earthquakes happen at different depths, and shallower earthquakes tend to be more destructive. The Mercalli scale measures the effect of earthquakes on buildings. The Richter scale measures the strength of the largest wave.

When the epicentre of an earthquake is located offshore, the movement of the seabed is sometimes sufficient to cause a tidal wave or tsunami. Tsunamis can be responsible for enormous loss of life for people living in coastal communities, as they can bring flooding far inland in a series of high and powerful waves. In 2004, an earthquake off the coast of Indonesia triggered a tsunami that raced across the Indian Ocean, causing damage as far away as the coast of eastern Africa. Around a quarter of a million people died and many more were made homeless.

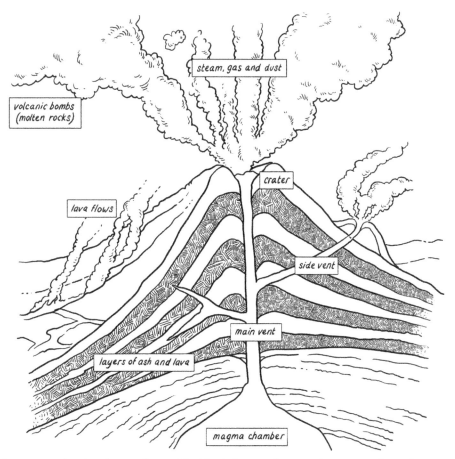

Figure 25: Volcanoes are structured around a vent that leads from underground magma to the surface

Misconceptions and research

Children sometimes become upset when they learn about the terrible damage and suffering that earthquakes and volcanoes can cause. They may also begin to form negative images of the countries and places where these events occur. One way in which to avoid this is to focus on how people cope with these disasters and the way in which they triumph in the face of adversity. Try to avoid images that show people as victims. It is much more instructive to think about how they have empowered themselves.

Interesting facts

- Volcanoes derive their name from Vulcan, the god of fire in Roman mythology.
- Scotland and Northern Ireland have many extinct volcanoes that were formed millions of years ago.
- The most damaging UK earthquake was in the area around Colchester (Essex) in 1884. Some 1,200 buildings needed to be repaired.
- Tsunami is a Japanese word that means 'harbour wave'.

Key questions

1. How are volcanoes created?
2. Why aren't there volcanoes in every country?
3. What causes earthquakes to happen?

Lesson 1 Finding out about volcanoes

What is a volcano like?

You will need
- access to the internet
- art materials
- atlases
- blank maps of the world
- a hard-boiled egg
- junk modelling materials
- modelling clay
- newspaper, kitchen paper and paints.

Key vocabulary

- crater
- crust
- magma
- mantle
- vent
- volcano

Getting started

Ask pupils to suggest a definition of a volcano so that you can judge their initial ideas and misconceptions. Build on what they say to explain that volcanoes occur where hot rocks and gas beneath the ground come to the surface. Use a hard-boiled egg to illustrate the Earth's structure. There are three main divisions: the core (yolk), the mantle (egg white) and the crust (shell). Explain that: the crust of the Earth's surface is as thin, relatively speaking, as the shell of an egg; the mantle is red-hot rock; and the core is made of iron and nickel.

Class activities

Earth model: Show pupils a diagram of the interior of the Earth on the interactive whiteboard (search for 'core, crust, mantle' on Google Images). Next, give pupils some modelling clay in assorted colours. Working in pairs, ask them to create models of the Earth using modelling clay of different colours, ensuring that the crust is as thin as possible. When complete, slice the 'Earth' in half to reveal the layers and create a key to explain what each colour stands for.

Famous volcanoes: Using research online and an atlas, ask pupils to locate some of the world's active volcanoes. Then ask them to mark and label them on blank maps of the world. Pupils could write a fact-file on a given volcano, including information about the size and frequency or last date of eruptions.

Volcano name search: Ask pupils to write down the names of ten different volcanoes from around the world. Then, using a frame 12 squares by 12 squares, ask them to devise a volcano word search. Tell them that they can write the names horizontally, vertically or diagonally. When they are satisfied with what they have devised, they should test it out on other pupils in the class.

Volcano models: Make models to show the structure of a volcano using paper, paint and junk modelling materials. Search for 'volcano model for school project' on the internet to find a range of examples that children can copy. The British Geological Survey website (see Useful books and websites, p. 199) is also helpful.

Name the feature: Give pupils cross-section diagrams of the inside of a volcano and some labels with words describing the different parts, e.g. magma, vent, crater, lava and ash. Ask them to match each label to the appropriate feature.

Plenary
Show pupils a webcam or a piece of footage from current or archived news reports that shows a volcano erupting. You will find a huge selection to choose from on YouTube. Ask pupils to explain what they see happening using relevant vocabulary.

Lesson 2 Mount Etna

What is it like to live near Mount Etna?

You will need
- access to the internet
- maps and atlases.

Key vocabulary
- crops
- fertile
- geothermal energy
- lava
- monitoring centre
- mud flow
- seismometer
- Sicily
- tectonic plate

Getting started
Mount Etna is the most-active volcano in southern Europe and one of the largest volcanoes on Earth. Located on the east coast of Sicily in Italy, it lies at the junction of the African and Eurasian plates. Mount Etna has erupted many times during recorded history. Find out whether any of the pupils have heard of Mount Etna, and locate it on a map.

Class activities
Describe Mount Etna: Show pupils a short video clip of Mount Etna. There are a good number of up-to-date videos on YouTube, as well as some stunning photographs on

Google Images (see Useful books and websites, p. 199). Ask pupils to write brief reports saying what Mount Etna is like and describing what they have seen in the video.

What can people do there?: As a class, make a list of activities that people enjoy doing on the slopes of Mount Etna, such as hiking or skiing. Investigate webcams and Google Earth to get an idea of the scenery and surrounding area.

Living on Mount Etna: More than a quarter of the population of Sicily lives around Mount Etna. Ask pupils to look at maps of Sicily to find out the names of the settlements – Catania is one of the largest. Can pupils find out what crops are grown on the mountain slopes? Ask pupils to write estate agents' reports for a farm that is for sale on the slopes of Mount Etna. They should make them sound as attractive as possible by describing the beautiful views and explaining why the soil is so fertile. They should also include maps of the location.

Advance warning: There is an early warning monitoring centre on Mount Etna that alerts people to any signs of danger. Clues of an imminent eruption include rising temperatures around the top of the mountain, increasing gas levels and many small earthquakes in the area nearby. (Seismometers will measure any barely detectible earthquake activity beneath the ground.) Ask pupils to develop newspaper reports about the impending danger. What is the evidence that a large explosion is likely to happen soon? Ask them to include imaginary interviews with local people and tourists about the risk and how they felt about it in their reports. They could also reassure readers that, in the past, the Italian authorities have used explosives, concrete dams and ditches to divert lava flows away from threatened settlements.

Plenary
Make a list of the positive and negative impacts of a volcanic eruption, and discuss whether people should be allowed to live, play or work near volcanoes like Mount Etna because of how dangerous it is. Have a vote after listing some of the reasons, such as those listed below.

Positive

- The lava and ash can produce very fertile soils.
- Dramatic volcanic scenery and the chance of seeing volcanic displays can attract tourists and bring money into a region.
- Settlements in volcanic regions sometimes benefit from plentiful geothermal energy, as in Iceland.
- Volcanic eruptions bring new rocks and minerals to the surface.

Negative

- Many people can be killed or injured and homes destroyed in an eruption.

- Landscapes can be destroyed and changed forever.

- Ash from volcanic eruptions can travel around the world, affecting climate and disrupting air travel.

- If melting snow or water mixes with volcanic ash it causes mudflows, creating even more danger.

Lesson 3 Investigating earthquakes and tsunamis

Where do earthquakes and tsunamis happen and why?

You will need

- access to the internet
- blank outline world maps
- cream-filled biscuits with two layers
- a plastic tray
- sticky notes
- sand or soil
- small-world play equipment, e.g. Lego®
- paper and glue for papier mâché, or expanded foam and a plastic bottle
- paints.

Key vocabulary

- Earth's crust
- magma
- mantle
- simulation
- tectonic plates
- tsunami

Getting started

Divide the class into small groups and ask them to discuss what they would like to know about earthquakes. Ask each group to think of three or more questions to write out clearly on sticky notes and pin on a display board. Share the questions around the class and use them to focus the work that you decide to undertake in this area of study.

Class activities

Earthquake simulation: Explain to the pupils that you are going to simulate what happens in an earthquake using biscuits. Any biscuit with two biscuit layers and a creamy middle filling will do for this demonstration. Explain that the upper layer of the biscuit represents the Earth's crust, the creamy filling represents the liquid magma beneath the surface and the bottom layer of the biscuit is the lower mantle. Carefully remove the upper layer of the biscuit and then slide it over the creamy filling to simulate the movement of the tectonic plates. Imagine that two plates (biscuits) collide. Snap the top biscuit in half and talk about the sound – this represents the earthquake. Stress how earthquakes happen in the hard crust and not in the softer material underneath.

Earthquake diagram: Remind pupils what happened in the earthquake simulation. The brittle crust travelled slowly across the softer layer below, collided with another part of the crust and snapped. Ask pupils to make series of labelled diagrams showing the crust moving slowly, the collision and then the earthquake.

Famous earthquakes: Divide the class into small groups and ask them to research some famous earthquakes using information from the internet. Ask each group to record their findings in three columns: where the earthquake happened, when it happened and what damage it caused. Pupils may also want to download an image to go with each of the different events that they have identified.

Tsunami simulation: Fill a plastic tray or tank with a few centimetres of water and build up some sand or soil at one end to simulate land. Add small-world play equipment, such as Lego® buildings, miniature figures and trees, to create a village or a city on the 'coast'. Next, agitate the water to create a series of waves and take some 'before' and 'after' photographs to show the impact on your model settlement. This is what happened in Japan in 2011, when an earthquake triggered an enormous tsunami with waves nearly 40 metres high that threatened Fukushima nuclear power station. Two years later, debris from the tsunami was still washing up in the USA on the other side of the Pacific Ocean.

Tsunami disaster: Using a slow-motion film of the tsunami, pupils could add voiceovers to explain what is happening as though it were a news report.

Plenary

Give pupils blank outline maps of the world and ask them to mark and label six or more notable earthquakes and tsunamis as records to put in their geography books.

Fieldwork and further investigations

- Divide the class into groups to produce papier mâché models of a chosen volcano and paint them, labelling the different features. Alternatively, an easier method would be for an adult to squirt expanded foam around a plastic bottle, building up the shape as needed and then leaving it to harden. This can then be painted and labelled by the pupils. Tell the children to base their models on an actual volcano and give it a name. When the models are finished, place them around a world map to show their locations.

Cross-curricular links

English: There is a good deal of specialised vocabulary relating to volcanoes, so you might challenge pupils to compile their own glossaries. Write newspaper reports, fact-files and diary entries about volcanoes. Create a short play entitled 'The day the volcano blew'.

Mathematics: Create an infographic of countries with the most volcanic eruptions since 1950 using these data: Indonesia – 58, Japan – 44, USA – 42, Russia – 33, Chile – 19, Papua New Guinea – 15, Ecuador – 11. How many of these countries border the Pacific Ocean?

Science: The heating and cooling of different materials in a volcanic eruption illustrate the processes of evaporation and condensation, and show how matter can exist in different states. Ask the children to explain this.

History: Devise a timeline of the world's most-significant volcanic eruptions, earthquakes and tsunamis.

Themes

Biodiversity: Volcanic vents deep down on the ocean floor have been important in the evolution of life on Earth. The vents bring hot rocks to the surface, which cool rapidly when they reach the water and deposit the minerals that they carry. These vents support a huge variety of highly unusual creatures that are able to survive without sunlight. Scientists are studying them to find out how life has continually adapted to environmental challenges.

Climate change: In the past, volcanoes have played a very important part in creating the atmosphere on Earth. Although volcanoes continue to release carbon dioxide into the atmosphere, human activity is now contributing around one hundred times more. You might explain to pupils that, while eruptions are part of a natural cycle, rapid climate change is a sign that the balance has been lost.

Sustainability: Find out how people use materials and construct buildings to withstand earthquakes in some parts of the world, such as Japan.

Values and wellbeing: Investigate how different groups of people around the world have the resilience and tenacity to rebuild their lives after devastating events, and how collaboration and support between and within communities help people to recover and prosper again.

Progression and assessment

By the end of this area of study, children will have learned about some famous volcanoes and earthquakes. They will have begun to understand in simple terms what causes volcanoes, earthquakes and tsunamis. Those who are working at higher achievement levels will be able to explain their distribution and how this links to the structure of the Earth, using simple geographical vocabulary.

Useful books and websites

Cut-out volcano models: search for 'BGS cut out volcano models free'.

Earthquake simulations: search for 'Plate tectonics and biscuits'.

Mount Etna erupting: search for 'Mount Etna webcam' on YouTube.

Tsunami simulation: search for 'How earthquakes trigger tsunamis'.

Volcano models: search for 'Woodlands School volcanoes'.

20 Celebrating our world

What does the curriculum say?

Pupils should extend their knowledge and understanding beyond the local area to include the United Kingdom and Europe, North and South America. This will include the location and characteristics of a range of the world's most significant human and physical features. They should develop their use of geographical knowledge, understanding and skills to enhance their locational and place knowledge.

What do I need to know?

We live on a remarkable planet. It has taken over 3,000 million years for life to evolve in the abundance and diversity that we find today. During this period, the diversity of plants and creatures has increased enormously. When human beings first emerged a few million years ago, they came into a world that was occupied by as many as fifteen million or more kinds of living organism. This probably represented a point of maximum biodiversity.

Human beings have also been lucky enough to benefit from benign climate conditions. When the ice sheets retreated around twelve thousand years ago, they left behind large swathes of inhabitable land where animals could thrive and crops could be cultivated. Farming and settled communities became established, initially along riverbanks in the Middle East. The surpluses that came from agriculture then created the conditions in which the cities and urban cultures that we know today could start to be established.

It has taken people thousands of years to explore and map the world. Early trading links between different cultures and civilisations alerted historical communities to places far beyond their immediate travel experience, but their knowledge was partial and incomplete. The Ancient Greeks, for example, never ventured much beyond Europe and neighbouring regions of Africa and Asia. It appears that the Vikings started to settle in Greenland in the tenth century, but it wasn't until 1492 that Christopher Columbus landed in the Bahamas (which he called the West Indies). Meanwhile, Captain Cook reached the coast of Australia only in 1770 and the Antarctic ice shelf wasn't sighted until around 1820. For Europeans, Central Africa remained 'blank on the map' well into the Victorian period, when expeditions led by Speake, Stanley and Livingstone ventured inland and recorded the source of the River Nile.

This area of study focuses on the extraordinary beauty and wonders of the world that we are fortunate enough to inhabit. It seeks to celebrate our planet and to give children an opportunity to find out more about its richness and diversity. The first lesson introduces the notion of exploration by looking at famous world journeys. It has a strong Eurocentric focus because it seeks to explain how Europeans developed their knowledge of the world map. The second lesson uses islands as a way of highlighting geographical wonders, while the third lesson has a direct focus on world wonders, both natural and built by humans.

Figure 26: The seven wonders of the ancient world: (a) Great Pyramid of Giza (b) Hanging Gardens of Babylon (c) Statue of Zeus at Olympia (d) Temple of Artemis at Ephesus (e) Mausoleum at Halicarnassus (f) Colossus of Rhodes (g) Lighthouse of Alexandria

Misconceptions and research

The links between motivation, engagement and learning have been long acknowledged by teachers and widely researched by educationalists. At a time when mounting environmental concerns are coming to dominate everyday life, it is more important than ever to promote a sense of hope and a vision for the future. Celebrating the world in all its diversity is part of a hopeful mindset and an essential counterpart to doom-and-gloom scenarios.

Interesting facts

- Planets like the Earth, which are potentially habitable, have been called 'Goldilocks planets' after the girl in the fairytale who chooses items that are 'just right'.
- Living organisms appear to have evolved on Earth by creating the conditions in which they themselves can survive.
- The natural world is full of geometrical patterns and mathematical sequences. For example, the seeds in a sunflower head are arranged in a precise Fibonacci sequence (a series of numbers found by adding up the two numbers before it).

Key questions

1. What inspired people to explore unknown lands and oceans?
2. What is it that we most value about the Earth?
3. Are there any habitable planets in the universe apart from the Earth?

Lesson 1 World journeys

How did people explore the world?

You will need
- access to the internet
- information and picture books about famous explorers
- sheets of A2 and A4 paper.

Key vocabulary
- explorer
- Nile
- Silk Road
- South Pole
- West Indies

Getting started
As a class, discuss what it might be like to be an explorer. What clothes and equipment would the pupils need? How would they know where to go without a map or guide? Would they be frightened, setting out into the unknown? What hardships might lie ahead? Why do they think that people might decide to take the risks of leaving the security of their homeland in the first place?

Class activities
Poster display: Ask pupils to investigate different world journeys and voyages of exploration for a poster display. Give them a prescribed framework to follow: each of the posters should be A2 in size, with a clear heading at the top naming the explorer or the expedition; each poster needs to include an A4-size map, with small panels and drawings around the edges saying what happened on the journey; there also has to be a short summary panel at the end that says why the journey was significant. Additional information could include an image of the explorer and, if relevant, the ship in which they sailed. Allow pupils to work individually or in pairs on this project. They could select one of the ten examples from the list below or choose a journey that they have identified

Celebrating our world

themselves. The internet is liable to be a particularly useful source of information for this work, but reference and picture books will also be valuable.

- **Eric the Red:** A Norwegian Viking, Eric the Red is remembered in legend as having founded the first Viking settlement in Greenland, thus beginning the European colonisation of North America.

- **Marco Polo:** Polo was a Venetian merchant traveller who set out on a series of adventures in 1271 and who reached China along the Silk Road. His chronicles spread knowledge of Central Asia across Europe, inspired other travellers and influenced world map-making.

- **Ibn Battuta:** One of the greatest travellers of all time, Battuta set out from Tangier in Morocco in 1325 on a pilgrimage to Mecca, but didn't return home for nearly 30 years. His travels took him across North Africa, the Middle East and many parts of South Asia.

- **Christopher Columbus:** Columbus was an Italian sailor from Genoa who set out to cross the Atlantic in 1492 to find a new route to China. He landed in the islands of the Caribbean, which he called the 'West Indies'.

- **Ferdinand Magellan:** The first sailor to lead a voyage around the world, Magellan sailed around South America into the Pacific Ocean (which he named), but he didn't actually return to his home in Portugal, dying in the Philippines in 1521.

- **James Cook:** Cook was a captain in the British Royal Navy who sailed thousands of miles across uncharted waters. He mapped places as far apart as Newfoundland (North America), Hawaii and New Zealand and was the first European to reach the eastern coast of Australia.

- **David Livingstone:** This Scottish missionary became obsessed with finding the source of the River Nile but failed in his quest. He helped to end the East Africa slave trade but facilitated the colonial exploitation of Africa.

- **John Hanning Speke:** A British Army officer who led several expeditions to Africa, Speke became the first European to reach the source of the River Nile, which he called Lake Victoria.

- **Roald Amundsen:** This Norwegian explorer led the expedition to Antarctica and became the first European to reach the South Pole in 1911.

- **Sir Ernest Henry Shackleton:** Shackleton was the British polar explorer who led several expeditions to Antarctica and became trapped in the ice in 1914, but who famously brought all his crew back to safety.

203

Plenary

Arrange for the pupils to visit another class to give a talk about what they have found out about famous world journeys. Aim to keep the presentations quite short – three minutes would be ideal. Alternatively, you could display the posters in the corridor and invite other classes to join a 'gallery walk' in which they find out about world journeys, just as visitors to a museum or gallery tour different exhibits.

Lesson 2 Remarkable islands

What makes a place special?

You will need

- access to the internet

- paper for posters and art materials.

Key vocabulary

- environmental issues

- human features

- location

- physical features

- settlements

- weather chart

Getting started

Start by projecting a picture of a coral island onto the interactive whiteboard. Discuss with the class about what makes islands special and why we are attracted to them. Next, show them some images of different types of island around the world. This will broaden their concept of what an island is and whet their appetites for the rest of the lesson. If the pupils are philosophically inclined, you might also discuss whether there is a minimum and maximum size for an island. When do islands become so small that they are no more than offshore rocks or so large that they are classified as being a mainland in their own right?

Class activities

Island investigation: Ask the pupils to investigate an island of their choice that is in some way remarkable (some ideas are listed below; see **Figure 27**). They might work individually or in pairs or small groups. The aim is to devise portraits to share with the rest of the class. Each could take the form of a poster, electronic presentation or oral report with supporting visual material. The study could include the following:

- **Maps:** Ask the pupils to draw detailed maps of their island that show its key physical and human features. Physical features include mountains, hills, rivers and coasts, as well as rocks, soil and weather. Human features include settlements, roads, farms and quarries, as well as beliefs, customs, religions, languages and traditional food.

- **Location:** The pupils might well need to locate their islands in relation to other places using small-scale maps, diagrams or some other device.

- **Background information:** It is often helpful to include background information that describes islands' key features and explains how they have evolved.

- **Weather chart:** A chart, table or diagram is a useful way to show typical weather and seasonal patterns during a 12-month period.

- **Fact-file:** Ask pupils to make up fact-files that give details of physical features, such as the highest point, names of any settlements, details of economic life, language, religion and customs, and also identify any environmental issues.

- **Photographs:** Encourage the pupils to include some photographs of their islands. These should show something of geographical significance, e.g. a harbour or a range of wildlife.

- **Environmental issues:** Investigate current issues and problems, such as pollution and loss of plants and creatures, that affect the island at the moment or that have affected it in the past.

Galapagos Islands – remarkable for wildlife	**Reunion** – a volcanic island in the Indian Ocean
Easter Island – home to strange stone statues	**Andaman islands** – home to ancient peoples
Surtsey – a new island off the coast of Iceland	**Zanzibar** – a tropical spice island
The Maldives – home to beautiful coral islands	**St Lucia** – home to unusual pitons
Elephant Island – named after elephant seals	**Skomer** – in western Wales and famous for puffins

Figure 27: Examples of islands to research

Plenary

Pupils present their island portraits to the rest of the class, making it clear the ways in which each island is remarkable and geographically interesting.

Lesson 3 World wonders

What are the wonders of the ancient and modern world?

You will need
- access to the internet
- PowerPoint
- blank outline maps of the UK.

Key vocabulary
- ancient world
- canyon
- civilisation
- landscape

Getting started

There are two key ideas in this lesson: the first is the notion of 'wonders', which can be either natural or built; the second is the idea of a list that follows but updates the 'seven wonders' identified by the Ancient Greeks. There can, of course, be no definitive list, as the selection process is necessarily subjective. Ensure that the pupils understand this before they begin this lesson. For example, you might ask them to name the most famous or interesting building in Britain. The pupils will have a range of different ideas. Compile their answers on the board and make the point that there is no right answer. Judgements vary from person to person.

Class activities

Seven wonders of the ancient world: Ask pupils to find out about the seven wonders of the ancient world. These date back to the first and second centuries BC and served as a kind of travel guide to the Greek Empire at that time. Only one of the ancient 'wonders' still remains: the Great Pyramids at Giza. Pupils will find some wonderfully evocative images of the 'wonders' on the internet, dating from different periods, as well as maps showing their locations.

Seven wonders of the modern world: Using the format of the seven ancient wonders, ask the pupils to identify seven modern wonders. Encourage them to select examples from different parts of the world that reflect different cultures and civilisations. They could download images from the internet, mark their chosen examples on a map or make notes and drawings to show their ideas.

Seven natural wonders: What natural wonders would the pupils identify around the world? There are many remarkable geological features, such as canyons, cliffs, waterfalls, mountains, lakes and volcanoes, to choose from. There are also many extraordinary landscapes, ranging from Monument Valley in Utah (USA) to the limestone scenery of Guilin in China. As a class, compile a PowerPoint presentation that brings together the different examples that the pupils have selected.

Seven UK wonders: Think about remarkable buildings and landscapes around the UK. Ask pupils to name and locate their seven chosen wonders on blank outline maps. You might extend this idea by focusing on a specific theme, such as ruins, monuments, buildings, statues, coastlines or landscapes.

World Heritage Sites: Around the world, some places have been designated as World Heritage Sites, either for their cultural or for their environmental significance. There are 26 such sites in the UK. Find out what they are and why they have been listed. You might find it convenient to ask each pupil to investigate a different site. Alternatively, they might just investigate the sites that are closest to where you live. Do the pupils agree that these sites are special? Can they think of any that have been left out?

Local wonders: Talk about the places that the pupils value in your own area. Can they come up with a list of local wonders? These don't have to be major buildings or special landscape areas; they might simply be interesting decorations or patterns, unusual doors, an attractive garden or a special tree.

Plenary

Talk about the range of sites that the pupils have identified and studied in this lesson. Are they all equally special or are there some places that the whole class agrees are more exceptional than others? Consider the way in which people's ideas about special places are liable to change over time. Do adults and children always have the same ideas?

Fieldwork and further investigations

- Ask pupils to identify features and examples of local 'wonders' in your school building and school grounds. What is it that makes these things a little bit special? Discuss whether places are always the same or whether they change at different times of the day and according to the season or weather conditions. What places do they most value in the summer and which do they most value in the winter?

Cross-curricular links

English: Ask pupils to make up a poem celebrating the world in which we live. This could focus on everyday places, people and events. Alternatively, it could take a global view and highlight the pattern of the seasons and/or the journey of the Earth through space.

Mathematics: People seem to have a natural sense of harmony and balance, and many of the world's most famous buildings are symmetrical in shape. Show the pupils some images of Greek temples and other classical structures that exemplify this idea, and get them to develop their own symmetrical patterns as part of their work in geometry.

History: Develop the lesson on voyages of exploration as a joint history/geography project, in which pupils learn more about how Europeans developed their knowledge of the world and then used this to develop colonial empires.

Religious education: Developing a sense of wonder relates directly to spiritual awareness. Finding out about special places also encourages pupils to think about what they value and why they value it.

Themes

Colonialism and social justice: There are statues celebrating famous explorers in many parts of the UK. It is now recognised that their achievements are part of a colonial legacy that many people find deeply uncomfortable. The monument to Captain Cook near Whitby, for example, declares that he spread the benefits of Christian civilisation to 'pagan and savage tribes'. What does this tell us about how people viewed the world at that time? Which people from the past do pupils think that we should celebrate today and why?

Sustainability: Stewardship is a notion that is widely used by those who are involved in environmental education. However, people will only care for the environment if they value and treasure it. The activities in this area of study are designed to deepen children's engagement and commitment.

Values and wellbeing: Finding out about the remarkable monuments and structures that people have erected around the world helps pupils to develop an appreciation of other cultures and sets our own achievements in context.

Progression and assessment

This area of study is largely concerned with consolidating children's learning and helping them to develop their sense of wonder at the diversity and beauty of the world around them. The enthusiasm that children exhibit for different places and their growing appreciation of their surroundings will be one indicator of achievement. Finding out about famous journeys provides an opportunity to revisit world map knowledge, as does the focused study of a specific 'remarkable' island. The confidence with which children talk about places and the skill with which they navigate the UK and world maps will demonstrate the progress that they are making in developing a locational framework. Those who are working beyond expectations will be able to name and locate a dozen or more countries by the time that they reach the end of Year 4.

Useful books and websites

Grill, W. (2014), *Shackleton's Journey.* London: Flying Eye Books.

Humphreys, A. (2022), *The Girl Who Rowed the Ocean.* London: Lightening Books.

McCann, J. (2021), *If the World Were 100 People.* London: Red Shed.

Wills, D. (2013), *Tiny Islands: Sixty Remarkable Little Worlds Around Britain.* London: AA Publishing.

World wonders: search for 'World wonders' and 'World wonders art' using Google Images.

Part 3
Upper Key Stage 2

21 Spinning in space

What do I need to know?

The Earth spins on its axis as it travels around the Sun and journeys through space. It takes 24 hours for the Earth to rotate. Places that face towards the Sun experience daylight. Places that face away from the Sun experience night. The basic pattern of day and night is created by this process.

The fact that we measure time by the Sun means that, at any one moment, some places will be in daylight and others will be in darkness. Starting from Greenwich in London, for example, places to the east will be later in the day and places to the west will be earlier. This creates the need for time zones. In theory, the clock needs to be adjusted one hour for every 15 degrees of longitude travelled. In practice, countries adopt the time zone that best suits their needs. Thus, China has a single time zone, even though it spans more than 50 degrees of longitude.

Cartographers face a seemingly impossible task. They have to translate the features of the Earth, a three-dimensional object, onto a flat map where they can only operate in two dimensions. A grid allows the cartographer to do this while acknowledging the distortions that result. Depending on the grid or projection selected, the shape of the continents and oceans will appear to vary – there is no perfect solution.

Using grids to reference, locate and explain aspects of geography applies throughout upper Key Stage 2, as children learn to develop and sharpen their skills in procedural thinking – for example, building from being able to read and use four- to six-figure grid references, learning to apply map-reading skills to the geography of the UK, especially using OS maps, and also applying their developing map skills to global geographies.

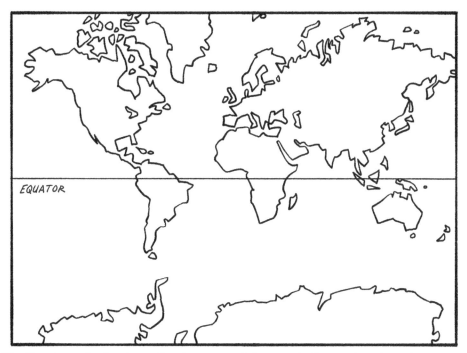

Figure 28: **The Mercator projection shows direction accurately but greatly distorts the polar regions**

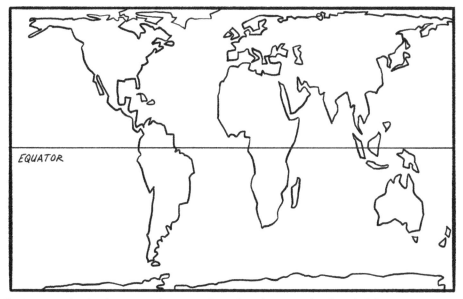

Figure 29: **The Peters projection is accurate in terms of area but elongates the shapes of the continents**

Misconceptions and research

Children often have ambiguous ideas about the globe. They may appear to accept that the Earth is a sphere but still retain elements of earlier 'flat Earth' theories. Thus, when asked in experiments which way a stone would fall in different parts of the world, they may continue to say that it will fall 'downwards' rather than 'towards the centre of Earth'. As their ideas mature during the primary years, their understanding becomes increasingly sophisticated.

Interesting facts

- The first known map of the world was made around 2,600 years ago in Babylon (within modern Iraq).
- Until around the sixteenth century, most European maps were orientated towards the east, the direction of sunrise.
- Some experts believe that the Earth collided with another planet early in its history. This knocked it off its axis and the debris created the Moon.

Key questions

1. Does the world map always have to have north at the top?
2. Why is it impossible for a place to have a latitude of more than 90 degrees and a longitude of more than 180 degrees?
3. What causes day and night?

Lesson 1 The world map

How accurate is the world map?

You will need
- an inflatable or fixed globe
- an atlas
- some satsumas or tangerines.

Key vocabulary
- human geography
- map projection
- north point
- physical geography

Getting started

Using a globe as a visual prompt, discuss how the Earth has three dimensions: height, width and depth. Maps of the world have to represent these three dimensions on flat (two-dimensional) pieces of paper. This inevitably involves some distortions. The system of latitude and longitude provides a grid that enables map-makers to take a systematic approaches.

Class activities

Map projections: Conduct a simple experiment to illustrate the difficulties of mapping the Earth in two dimensions. Give each pupil a satsuma to represent the Earth. Ask them to peel the skin carefully so that it can be laid out flat on the table in front of them. Explain that map-makers unfold the Earth's surface in much the same way when they devise map projections. However, it isn't very convenient to have a map that consists of lots of different pieces. Using a grid allows them to squash some places and stretch others so that the Earth can be represented on a sheet of paper.

Size and shape: Look at how map projections distort the sizes and shapes of continents. One simple test is to compare the size of Greenland and South America on a world map. Greenland is less than an eighth of the size of South America but is sometimes drawn much bigger than this. Antarctica is another challenge for map-makers. It is usually shown as little more than a thin line at the bottom of the page when it is actually more or less circular!

Which way up?: By convention, maps are nearly always drawn with north at the top. However, there isn't really a right or wrong way up to the Earth, which simply spins in space. Try asking the pupils to turn the map they are looking at upside down. Antarctica is now at the top, along with Australia and Argentina. Can they find the UK? How does this make them feel?

Different themes: Maps can be used to portray information on a wide range of themes and topics. The world map, for example, often shows countries (human geography) or landscape features (physical geography). Working from an atlas, ask pupils to list the different types of world map that they can discover. Decide whether each one is focused on human or physical geography, or whether it conveys information about both.

Plenary

Discuss with the pupils the relative advantages of a globe and an atlas. Which do they think is most useful, or is it necessary to have both in order to understand the Earth in different ways? If they could have only one, which would they choose?

Lesson 2 Day and night

What causes day and night?

You will need

- access to the internet
- an inflatable globe
- drawing paper
- a torch.

Key vocabulary

- axis
- day
- night
- spin

Getting started

Talk with the children about the differences between day and night. How do places look different in the dark? Do pupils sometimes go to bed when it is light? What do they like about the dark? Does it frighten them at all? Explain that in this lesson they are going to learn about what causes day and night.

Class activities

Light and dark: Demonstrate how the Earth spins on its axis. Begin by getting the children to identify where they live on an inflatable globe. Now give one of the children a torch and ask them to shine the light (representing sunlight) directly onto the UK. Spin the globe very slowly so that the light starts to fall more obliquely, until it eventually no longer reaches the UK at all. What has happened? Go on spinning the globe so that the light starts to reach the UK again. Explain that it takes 24 hours for the Earth to rotate and that this creates day and night.

Daylight hours: Get the children to make a block graph showing daylight hours in the UK throughout the year, using these figures: January – 8, February – 9, March – 11, April – 13, May – 15, June – 16, July – 16, August – 16, September – 14, October – 11, November – 10, December – 8. Depending on what pupils have learned earlier, you may want to remind them how to make a graph. You could also focus on seasonal change by just using the data for January, April, July and October.

Long summer days: Why are the days so long in summer and so short in winter? To answer this question, you will need to use the globe once again. Hold it up in front of the class and identify the location of the UK. Now tilt the globe so that it is angled towards the children. This is what happens in summer, when the Sun is high in the sky and brings plenty of daylight. Now tilt the globe away from the children. This is what happens in winter, when the Sun is low in the sky and the nights are long.

Midnight Sun: Explain to the children that places near the North Pole have continual sunlight in mid-summer and perpetual darkness in mid-winter. Show them some time-lapse images of the midnight Sun from Google Images on the interactive whiteboard. How would it feel to live in a place where it never got dark? What are the benefits as well as the drawbacks of the night?

Plenary
Discuss with the children what would happen if the Earth didn't spin. Half the world would be in continual sunlight and get extremely hot. The other half would be in continual darkness and get very cold. Now think about how life would be different if the Earth's axis were vertical. There would be no seasons and all the places would have fixed amounts of daylight. Make the point that the spinning of the Earth and the tilt of the Earth are key features of our planet.

Lesson 3 Time zones

What are time zones?

You will need
- a globe (or other spherical object like a football)
- an atlas
- coloured counters
- dice
- sheets of card.

Key vocabulary
- Greenwich/prime meridian
- International Date Line
- time zone

Getting started
Using a globe (or other spherical object like a football), demonstrate to the pupils that, if the UK is angled directly towards the Sun, places on the other side of the Earth are bound to be in darkness. Now consider the reverse scenario, in which the UK is in darkness and other places have daylight. Use the ensuing discussion to establish why we

need time zones. Also point out that, by convention, time is measured from the prime meridian, which passes through Greenwich.

Class activities

Different times: Find out what time it is in other parts of the world at a given time in the UK. Select a place that lies either to the east or west and give the time there. Find out what the time will be in other named places around the world. Use webcams to 'visit' places ahead and behind UK time and discuss what is happening there.

World time diagram: Ask each pupil to draw a circle at the centre of the page, in which they write '12.00 noon Greenwich time'. Arrange a dozen small circles around the edge where the numbers would appear on a clock. Complete the diagram by writing the names of a dozen cities around the world in the circles, together with the local times (am or pm), adding an arrow from the centre for each one. You might ask the pupils to see that each city is in a different time zone. You might also give the diagram a theme, e.g. they might only decide to include cities from the Commonwealth, tropics or Northern Hemisphere.

Time travel: As a class, find out how long it takes to fly from the UK to other places around the world. How will each flight be affected by changes in time? Notice that flights that follow a line of longitude, e.g. London to Ghana, do not cross any time zones, while flights of a similar distance that stay at broadly the same latitude, e.g. London to New York, cross four or five time zones.

World time zones: Look at the world time-zone map in an atlas or download one from the internet. Using this map, invite pupils to devise some quiz questions for others to answer. For example, which country is divided into the most time zones? Which time zone is used by the most countries? Which continent has no time zones at all?

Time-zone game: Give the pupils sheets of card and ask them to divide each into 12 squares for a board game. Ask the pupils to number each square. They should then write the name of a city or country underneath that is ahead of London by that number of hours. For example, they might write 'Paris' in the first square because it is one hour ahead of London, and 'Istanbul' in the second square because it is two hours ahead of London. Working in pairs, pupils play the 'Time-zone game' by throwing either a single or two dice and putting a counter on the square of the number that they have thrown each time. The winner is the person who covers all the squares first.

Plenary

Devise a simple world map as a class display. Ask pupils to add clocks showing the times at different places. Add the prime meridian and International Date Line.

Fieldwork and further investigations

- Explain to the pupils how to calculate six-figure grid references using Ordnance Survey maps. Working from a map, they need to imagine that each grid square has been divided into ten subdivisions, both horizontally and vertically. The four-figure reference gives the coordinates for the bottom left-hand corner of the square. The six-figure reference is more precise, as it specifies the location within the square using tenths. The first three numbers give the horizontal location, known as the 'easting'. The second three numbers give the vertical location, known as the 'northing'. Practise using six-figure references in coordinate quizzes organised by the pupils or that you have prepared in advance.

- Set up a display board where pupils display different versions of the world map from magazines, newspapers or the internet. See how map-makers use a variety of map projections. Which versions do pupils think are the best and why?

- On a sunny day, take a magnetic compass and large inflatable globe outside with you into the playground. Find the UK on the globe and ensure that it is uppermost. Now, using the compass to help you, align the globe so that the axis points north–south in reality. You should now be able to see the way in which the Sun moves across the Earth and the divide between day and night. If you conduct this exercise at different times of the day, you should be able to note the changes.

Cross-curricular links

English: Ask the pupils to imagine that they are on a space station orbiting the Earth. Ask them to devise a short transcript of the conversation that they might have with an operator at mission control. The NASA website hosts a range of images that may help them to generate ideas, as well as a live stream from the International Space Station (see Useful books and websites, p. 220).

Mathematics: Reinforce the pupils' understanding of the 24-hour clock by getting them to use it to represent times at different places worldwide. Investigate actual flight times for specific journeys from London to major cities in different parts of the world. Pupils could record what they discover in a table using the following headings: departure time, arrival time, journey time and time difference.

Computing: Satellites have revolutionised modern communication networks and, among other things, underpin the services provided by computers and mobile phones. Ask pupils to discuss in groups the benefits that we get from electronic communication. How would it affect our lives if these virtual networks suddenly became disabled?

Science: This area of study relates directly to the work in Key Stage 2 science on Earth and space. Describing the movement of the Earth relative to the Sun and exploring how the Earth's rotation causes day and night are scientific matters. Finding out how these processes affect people's lives and how places have different seasonal patterns introduces a geographical perspective.

Themes

Colonialism and social justice: The decision to measure longitude from the meridian going through Greenwich was taken at an international conference held in Washington DC, USA, in 1884. By that time, most maps and charts had already adopted this convention, reflecting Britain's position as the world's foremost maritime country and imperial power at that time. Prior to that, other countries had adopted different systems. The French, for example, wanted the prime meridian to pass through Paris and the Germans through Berlin.

The Space Race was a competition between the USA and Soviet Union to see who could conquer space first. It developed in the aftermath of the Second World War and culminated with a joint mission in 1975. Finding out more about this fascinating story captures children's imagination. However, it also reveals how the desire for power and control drives other activities.

Sustainability: Regarding the Earth as a planetary system introduces children to holistic thinking and emphases the unity of the planet on which we live. The astronaut Neil Armstrong famously described the Earth from the Moon as looking like a 'tiny pea, pretty and blue' (New Mexico Museum of Space History). What do children think about the fragile beauty of our world? In what ways are they aware of it?

Progression and assessment

By the end of this area of study, all children should be able to explain what causes day and night and how the way in which people live their lives varies according to the conditions around them. Pupils will also understand the significance of longitude in relation to time zones. The ability to criticise different map projections indicates a higher level of achievement, but all children should be able to compare the relative merits of globes and world atlas maps and talk about how they might affect the ways in which we interpret the world.

Useful books and websites

Richardson, P. and Richardson. T. (2016), *The Everyday Guide to Primary Geography: Maps*. Sheffield: Geographical Association.

NASA Eyes on the Earth: https://eyes.nasa.gov/apps/earth

RSPB website: www.rspb.org.uk

The Solar System: https://science.nasa.gov/solar-system/planets/

22 World countries and capitals

What do I need to know?

There are over 200 countries in the world. They vary in size from the very large (e.g. Canada and the Russian Federation) to the very small (e.g. Monaco and Vatican City). Some form a compact square or rectangular shape. Others are long and thin. There are a number of island nations, which are scattered over a large sea area. One country, Lesotho, is entirely surrounded by another.

Figure 30: Europe is divided into around 50 countries, all of different shapes and sizes

What makes a country? There is no set definition. Many countries are bound together by a common heritage, language or culture, but every country has minorities and different groups. It is tempting to think that a country makes its own laws and defends its own borders, but again this is only partially true. Laws are made at regional and international as well as national levels, and many borders are disputed. The simplest and perhaps most effective way of identifying a country is to refer to the symbols that mark its identity. Of these, the national flag and national anthem are the most notable and iconic. It is also true that most countries have a capital city, which is the seat of national government.

Theoretically, the capital should be the largest city in the country and centrally placed geographically. However, historical forces may result in the capital being displaced or pushed to one side. Berlin, for example, is in the extreme east of Germany, and Vienna is on the edge of Austria. Some countries have deliberately relocated their capital to more central locations for political reasons: Brasilia (Brazil), Ankara (Turkey), Dodoma (Tanzania) and Astana (Kazakhstan) are all examples. In each of these cases, the new capital is considerably smaller than the previous centre of government. Meanwhile, in the Netherlands, South Africa and Israel, the functions of the capitals are split between different cities.

Learning about world countries and capitals is a good way to build children's knowledge of the world map and introduce them to some of the complexities of human geography. There are plenty of opportunities to make meaningful comparisons and to reveal hidden patterns. Since the 1950s, the number of countries around the world has increased around four-fold, as territories fragment. At same time, there is an increasing need for countries to work together, both to promote their livelihoods and to combat global environmental and security problems. Such issues open up a discussion about some of the most pressing problems facing the modern world and give children the chance to begin to engage with them constructively.

Misconceptions and research

A country is a largely abstract concept in the sense that it cannot be seen directly and it is difficult to envisage in its totality. Helping children to appreciate the diverse elements that combine to create a country – landscape, people and culture – will deepen their understanding. It will also help to challenge any stereotypes that they may already have acquired. Research shows that children sometimes develop an attitude towards a country and its people before they acquire any factual information about it.

Interesting facts

- Monaco is the most crowded country in the world.
- South Africa has 11 official languages.
- The border of Morocco is disputed along almost its entire length.

Key questions

1. What are the differences between a region and a country?
2. Is there an ideal size for a country?
3. Why is the capital sometimes not the biggest city?
4. If we didn't have countries, what difference would it make?

Lesson 1 World countries

What are the different countries of the world?

You will need
- an atlas or electronic world countries map.

Key vocabulary
- border
- country
- index
- landlocked
- location

Getting started

As a class, discuss how the world is divided into countries of different shapes and sizes. What countries have pupils heard of and why? Make a class list. Which countries have the children visited? Do any pupils have friends or relatives who live in different countries? Discuss the ways in which countries are different from each other.

Class activities

Country quest: Working from a world atlas map, ask pupils to find countries of different shapes and sizes. You could structure this activity by giving them the challenge of finding three countries that are very large, three that are very small, three that are divided into islands, three that are landlocked, three that have more than five borders and so on.

Country location: Focus on the locations of different countries by making links to latitude and longitude. How many countries are on the equator? How many lie within the Arctic Circle or on the Tropic of Capricorn? Are there more countries at 40 degrees north or 40 degrees south? Which line of longitude links the UK and Ghana? Give pupils the challenge of making up their own set of surprising or interesting facts about the locations (latitudes and longitudes) of countries.

Country borders: Explore electronic or printed maps to find countries that have straight borders that obviously follow lines of latitude or longitude. The borders between Canada/the USA, Egypt/Libya and Mauritania/Mali are very clear examples. Discuss how these borders might have come about. You might also discover that some countries have disputed borders, which are sometimes shown with dotted lines, e.g. India and Pakistan dispute Kashmir, while Morocco has hardly any agreed borders at all.

Atlas index: Make up a list of ten or 12 countries scattered across different continents and hemispheres. Ask pupils to look each of them up in the index of their atlas to discover the page reference. Then ask them to turn to that page to find a neighbouring country with the same reference. They should check in the index to see whether they are correct. Talk about the purpose of the index. Who needs to use it and when?

Imaginary country: Invite pupils to make up their own imaginary countries. They might devise a list or table with key facts such as the name of the capital city, highest mountain and longest river. They could say something about the climate, national festivals, religion, local food, crops and industries. Are there any environmental problems? What flag does their country have? Can they say a few words in the national language? Extend the activity by asking pupils to draw maps of their countries. Not only will this engage them creatively, but it will also help them to focus more strongly on key human and physical features.

Plenary
Make up a set of enquiry questions or puzzles that pupils can answer using an atlas map. Here are some examples: Find a country beginning with 'B'. Can you name a country that has no land borders? How many countries lie on the prime meridian? Write each question or puzzle on a separate piece of paper, fold it and put in a bag before the lesson. Play a game by going around the class and inviting a child to select a question and read it out. The rest of the class then have to look at their atlases to find the answer.

Lesson 2 World cities

What are the world's main cities?

You will need
- an atlas
- access to the internet
- blank outline maps of the world.

Key vocabulary
- capital
- country
- monument

Getting started
Remind pupils that every country has a capital city where laws are made. The capital will also be a major centre for trade and industry, with many important buildings. It will have good transport links, making it readily accessible to other places. There will be many sporting and cultural events. The capital city sets the pace of life for the rest of the country.

Class activities

Largest cities: Give pupils blank outline maps of the world and a list of the world's ten largest cities (you could project this onto the interactive whiteboard). Using an atlas map to help them, ask pupils to mark and label each city on their map. Are there any patterns that emerge? How many of the cities are in Asia? How many are in the Northern Hemisphere? In which continents are there no extremely large cities at all?

Capital-city word search: Make up a word search containing the names of a dozen or more capital cities as a puzzle for the pupils to complete. You could devise the word search yourself or generate one electronically using an online website. Ask pupils to make up city word searches of their own. You could ring the changes by restricting them to cities in Europe or cities in North and South America, to add to the challenge.

Capitals and countries: Play a class game matching capitals and countries. Before the lesson, identify around 20 major capital cities across the world. Call out the name of each city in turn. The pupils have to use their atlases to find the country to which it belongs.

Famous cities: Ask the pupils each to select a capital city of their choice. Now get them to find out more about it using atlases, books and the internet. Does it have any famous monuments? When was it founded or created? How many people live there? Is it on a river or sea? Is it famous for food/music/festivals or other cultural events? The pupils could devise a set of interesting facts to use in 'Guess the city' quizzes. Alternatively, they might create simple portraits of their cities as electronic presentations to share with the rest of the class.

City weather report: Ask pupils to collect data about the weather in a city of their choice over a period of a week. They could include information about the temperature, wind direction, rain, cloud and sunshine. Ask them to write a weather report or diary. How has the weather in their chosen city been similar to or different from the weather in the UK?

Plenary

Unannounced, simply ask the pupils to write down as many cities as they can think of in a five-minute period. Present this as a fun activity, and not as a test. Alternatively, give pupils blank world maps where they can mark the cities that they know.

Lesson 3 Nations working together

How can different countries work together?

You will need
- access to the internet
- data about the aims and growth of the European Union (EU).

Key vocabulary
- Commonwealth
- European Union (EU)
- United Nations (UN)

Getting started
Discuss how being part of a country gives people a sense of belonging and identity; however, it can also lead to rivalry and conflict. Tell the pupils that in this lesson they will find out more about how countries cooperate with each other. This is important when countries are linked more closely than ever by trade, travel and environmental issues.

Class activities
The European Union: The EU is one of the largest trading blocks in the world, with a population of around 500 million people. As well as economic growth, the EU aims to promote human rights, environmental protection and political cooperation. Ask pupils to find out how the EU has grown over time. When and why did the UK decide to leave? This is a natural opportunity to use histograms to show changes in the number of EU countries at different times in the past. The same information can also be displayed cartographically. Discuss the advantages and disadvantages of each mode of representation.

The Commonwealth: The Commonwealth has 53 member states, most of which were formerly members of the British Empire. It covers almost a quarter of the world's land area and spans every inhabited continent. Commonwealth countries have no legal obligations to each other but are united by shared history, language, culture and values. Make a class book about the Commonwealth, with each pupil responsible for half a page of drawings, maps and writing about a different country.

United Nations: The UN was set up after the Second World War to promote peace and friendship between nations and to help to improve social, economic and environmental conditions. Divide the class into groups and ask them to say what they would put in their own charter of human rights. Look at a simplified version of the actual charter (see Useful books and websites, p. 229). Are there any surprises? Discuss any differences in priorities. Which three rights do the pupils think are most important?

Environmental issues: Imagine that an oil tanker has run aground, spilling large quantities of oil into the North Sea. Organise a role-play, with three or four pupils representing each of the countries affected. Here are some positive suggestions to start off the discussion:

- The UK will send ships to help collect oil that has spilt into the sea.
- France will give money to compensate fishermen for their loss of trade.

- Germany will try to reduce the amount of oil that it imports in future.

- Norway will establish new reserves for sea birds.

- Denmark will make more wind turbines to generate clean energy.

- The Netherlands will tow the damaged tanker back to port.

- Belgium will help to clean up beaches.

Choose a 'representative' from each country to say why they can't actually fulfil their promise or need another country to act first. If you organise the classroom so that pupils sit facing each other in a square, in groups behind their countries' flags, it will help to stimulate the debate and show why international cooperation is so difficult to achieve. It is also valuable to project a map of the North Sea onto the whiteboard so that the pupils can point out how the pollution appears to be spreading.

Plenary
As a class, discuss how pupils think that countries might best work together in the interests of peace and the environment, as valuable new resources such as oil and metal ore are found in the Arctic. Discuss the impact of Brexit in relation to these issues.

Fieldwork and further investigations

- Share with the pupils some of the amazing NASA images of cities at night, which can be readily accessed via a Google search for 'Cities at night from space'. Talk about the shapes and structures of different cities and the features that the pupils can see. Next, switch to a night image of the UK and neighbouring cities. What places can the pupils see? Use an atlas to name some of the other places shown in the image.

Cross-curricular links

English: Show pupils the famous cartoon entitled 'Cooperation is better than conflict', which is readily accessed via a Google search. Ask pupils to write at least three captions to go with the different pictures, explaining the argument.

Mathematics: Around the world, more and more people are living in cities. Give pupils some basic data about city populations now and in the past to turn into a block graph. Discuss with them possible future trends. Will there ever be a time when cities stop growing larger?

History: Look at historical maps of the world to see how country boundaries have changed. It is particularly instructive to compare the modern political map of Europe with a map of countries in 1914. Can the children name some of the countries that have emerged? Discuss how some countries that appear to be 'new' actually have an extremely long history. Poland, for example, once ruled much of Eastern Europe. It 'disappeared' in the eighteenth century, when it was completely absorbed by its neighbours, but has now reappeared and shifted westwards.

Themes

Colonialism and social justice: Maps and map-making were an essential part of colonialism. As well as delineating the key features of different territories, they established their boundaries and provided details of land ownership. The influence of the colonial past is still evident today. One particularly obvious clue is the straight-line borders found in Africa and the Middle East. These were popular with colonial administrators, who completely ignored local circumstances and traditions.

Sustainability: Around the world, cities are growing larger. Have a discussion with pupils about whether they think that living in the city or countryside is more sustainable. Cities bring people together, reducing the need for private transport and making it easier to provide public services. People who live in the countryside are closer to nature and have better opportunities to grow their own food.

Values and wellbeing: Finding out how nations can cooperate with each other raises questions about underlying values. The EU, Commonwealth and UN all have formal statements about their beliefs and principles. The importance of democracy and justice is clearly affirmed; so too are peace and friendship. These are noble aspirations, even if they are difficult to apply in practice. Discuss with the children what they would do to promote world peace. Be alert to any stereotypes that emerge in the discussion. General statements about what 'they' do, how 'they' live or what 'they' believe are liable to be oversimplified and misleading.

Progression and assessment

By the end of this area of study, all children should be able to name a range of countries around the world and their capital cities. Those who are working beyond expectations will have a basic understanding of how countries vary in terms of size, shape and location. They will also be able to describe and explain some of the international agreements that seek to improve living conditions.

Useful books and websites

Scoffham, S. (ed) (2023), *World in Maps* (3rd edn). London: Collins.

Countries quizzes: search for 'World countries quiz'.

Charter of Human Rights: search for 'Amnesty International Charter of Human Rights simplified'.

Photos of cities at night: search for 'Cities at night from space' on Google Images.

United Nations: search for 'United Nations – explained: CBC News' on YouTube.

World population: search for 'If the world were 100 people'.

23 North America

What do I need to know?

North America is the third largest continent after Asia and Africa. It lies between the Pacific and Atlantic Oceans. North America includes the Greenland ice sheet and the islands of northern Canada. It also incorporates the Caribbean. North America is joined to South America by a narrow strip of land.

North America has a great diversity of landscapes. The Rocky Mountains are one of the main geographical features. The highest peaks are over 6,000 metres high, and the mountain ranges extend 5,000 km from Alaska to Mexico. The Great Plains, the Great Lakes and the Mississippi river lie to the east of the Rockies. There are deserts in Mexico and the southern United States. Many northern areas are covered by forests and tundra. The Caribbean islands form a distinct region in the south.

Canada, the USA and Mexico are by far the largest countries in North America, but there are also many much smaller nations and island states. Across the continent there is a mixture of peoples. From the sixteenth century onwards, the native population was overwhelmed by European colonisation, which followed the voyages of exploration. The historical influence of Spain, France and England is reflected in the languages spoken in North America today. Over ten million enslaved people were also brought from Africa and forced to work on the sugar and cotton plantations, forming a distinctive ethnic group.

North America has some of the world's largest cities, including Mexico City, Los Angeles and New York. Conurbations are a feature along the east and west coasts of the USA. By contrast, there are vast open areas, especially in the Rocky Mountains, northern Canada and Greenland. Farming, industry and economic activity have had a considerable impact on

Figure 31: North America has a great diversity of landscapes, including vast mountain and forest regions

the natural environment. As a major polluter and world power, the USA has a particularly important role to play in mitigating global climate change.

Misconceptions and research

Children sometimes think that North America and the United States of America (USA or US) are the same place. You need to make it clear that North America is a continent and that the USA is a country within it. The term 'America' can also cause confusion, as it is used more generally to denote the Americas and Oceania. In geographical terms, North and South America are separate continents, even though they are sometimes grouped together as 'the Americas'.

Interesting facts

- The name 'America' is derived from Amerigo Vespucci, the Italian explorer who mapped the Caribbean Islands and Brazil.
- Canada has the world's longest coastline – nearly one-fifth of the total.
- Commonly known as the world's smallest volcano, Cuexcomate in Mexico is only 13 metres tall.

Key questions

1. What are the most significant landscapes and regions in North America?
2. Why is the USA the most powerful country in North America, even though it is not the largest?

Lesson 1 Introducing North America

What is North America like?

You will need
- an atlas
- access to the internet
- sheets of A3 paper.

Key vocabulary
- prairie
- Rocky Mountains
- tundra
- names of key countries and cities in North America

Getting started
The pupils will have gleaned many images of North America from books, advertising and the media. Some may even have travelled to North America – especially Disneyland. Ask pupils to write down three things that they associate with North America, reminding them that North America includes Canada, Mexico and the Caribbean, and not just the USA. Compile a list of their images. Are there some images that seem particularly common or widespread? Take note of any obvious gaps in the pupils' knowledge that you can usefully address in your teaching.

Class activities

North America map: Working from an atlas, ask the pupils to draw their own outline maps of North America. They could use these maps to show the countries, places and geographical features that were mentioned in the class discussion at the start of the lesson.

North America fact-file: Ask pupils to develop their knowledge of North America by compiling fact-files about the continent using the following headings: largest countries, largest cities, longest river, highest mountain, main environments/regions, environmental issues. Most of this information will be available from an atlas, but the pupils could also do simple internet searches to support their research.

North America A to Z: Working from an atlas, challenge the pupils to compile a list of North American countries and cities from A to Z, with one example for each letter of the alphabet (apart from X and Z, which are very difficult to include).

North America display board: Set up a North America display board compiled and monitored by the pupils. They could contribute news items, photographs from magazines, brochures, weather information and so forth. If any pupils have family or relatives living in North America, they may want to contribute personal information. Others might want to add photographs taken while on holiday in North America.

North America environments: Ask the pupils each to draw six circles or boxes on an A3 sheet of paper. Ask them to make drawings of different North American environments in each one, adding the name of each place and what it is like in a sentence beneath. There are many different environments to choose from: mountain, desert, swamp, forest, tropical beach, city centre, prairie, coral reef, ice cap and so forth.

Plenary

Ask pupils to return to the maps of North America that they devised at the start of the lesson. Ask them to add some of the new knowledge that they have acquired during the lesson.

Lesson 2 Focus on the Caribbean

What is special about the Caribbean?

You will need

- an atlas
- access to the internet
- a range of brightly coloured fabric remnants
- glue and sheets of bright blue paper.

Key vocabulary
- Caribbean
- coral reef
- hurricane
- Tropic of Cancer

Getting started
Ask the pupils to imagine that they are going on holiday to the Caribbean. How long do they think that the flight will take? What will the weather be like? What will they see when they arrive? What places might they be able to visit? What local food might they be able to experience?

Class activities
Caribbean islands: Working from an atlas, pupils should find and list six or more Caribbean island countries. Which is the biggest? Which island is divided into two? Which belong to the USA? What are the names of the smallest island countries that you can find?

Caribbean weather: As a class, find out about the temperatures and weather conditions today in three different Caribbean locations. Are they warmer or colder than where you are? Discuss how the position of the Caribbean, just south of the Tropic of Cancer, will influence its climate.

Hurricanes: The Caribbean lies in the path of hurricanes that track their ways from the Atlantic Ocean towards Central America and the USA. Look at some satellite images of hurricanes to see how the cloud and wind spiral around the centre. If possible, use the internet to find out about a named hurricane and the damage that it caused. Is there a map that shows the route that it took?

Caribbean cruise: Ask pupils to plan week-long Caribbean cruises involving at least four stops. Ask them to show the routes on maps and add annotations (labels with brief descriptions) about the places and features along the way.

Coral reef collage: The Caribbean is rich in sea, plant and animal life. In particular, the region is famous for its coral reefs, which are rich in biodiversity and a significant attraction for tourists. Ask pupils to create coral reef collages by adding small pieces of cloth to a bright blue 'underwater' background. Look at photographs of coral reefs to help to give an idea of the range of plants and creatures that are found around a reef.

Plenary
Consolidate pupils' knowledge about the Caribbean region by challenging them to devise an acrostic structured around the letters in 'the Caribbean'.

Lesson 3 Jamaica: A Caribbean island

What is Jamaica like?

You will need

- access to the internet
- a file of photographs of different aspects of Jamaica
- a map of Jamaica from an atlas or the internet.

Key vocabulary

- aluminium
- image
- Jamaica
- season
- tropical climate

Getting started

Explain that the pupils are going to learn about the Caribbean island of Jamaica. Many of the pupils will have heard of Jamaica, due to its historical links with the UK. Some may have members of their immediate family or more distant relatives who live in Jamaica. Establish that Jamaica is a relatively small tropical island, and that it has high mountains and strong historical links with the UK.

Class activities

Links with Jamaica: Compile a set of ten or a dozen photographs showing how the UK is linked to Jamaica. Show pictures of tourism and products such as sugar, coffee and bananas. Remember to include pictures of people. Benjamin Zephaniah (poet), Bob Marley (musician), Usain Bolt (runner) and Naomi Campbell (model) all have links to Jamaica. So too does the King, in his role as head of state. Finally, you might include an aluminium can, as Jamaica is a world producer of bauxite – the ore from which aluminium is made.

Jamaica map: Give the pupils the opportunity to practise their map-work skills by drawing maps of Jamaica. As well as the outline of the coast, they should show the main mountain areas, Kingston and Montego Bay. Remind the pupils to add titles, scales, keys and north points. See that their maps are enclosed in boxes or rectangles and ask them to add drawings of the Jamaican flag, if time permits.

Jamaica climate: Jamaica has a tropical climate. It is hot throughout the year (around 30 degrees Celsius/centigrade). There are only two seasons – a wet season and a dry season. In the capital, Kingston, the driest weather occurs from December to March. The wettest months are May, June and September. Total rainfall is around 800 mm, which is about the same as in many parts of lowland England. Ask pupils to draw or download temperature and rainfall graphs. Ask them what clothes they might need in December or in June.

Positive or negative images?: Using downloads from the internet and other sources, set up a class display of photographs about Jamaica. When the display is completed, discuss each photograph with the class. Does it show a positive or a negative image? Is there a balance in the photographs between landscapes/scenery, people and the natural environment? Do the photographs show people of different ages and backgrounds? Decide what photographs (if any) need to be added to the display to create a more balanced impression.

Making comparisons: Ask pupils to make comparisons between Jamaica and Northern Ireland – countries that are roughly similar in size. What are the similarities and differences in terms of physical features (mountains, rivers, coasts, weather) and human features (population, largest cities, industry, farming)? How are both countries attempting to protect wildlife? The simplest way to make a comparison is to draw up a chart with two columns. It is surprising how many comparisons it is possible to make.

Plenary
Ask pupils to devise a 'Did you know?' quiz with 12 questions about different aspects of the physical, human and environmental geography of Jamaica.

Fieldwork and further investigations

- If possible, arrange for a parent, friend or relative who is associated with your school to come and talk to the children about what their life was like when they lived in Jamaica. Ask pupils to write down their questions in advance of the visit so that they know what they are going to ask. See that the answers are kept reasonably brief so that the children have plenty of time to participate.

- Take the pupils outside and establish from which compass direction the wind is blowing. Back in the classroom, look at a world atlas map to find where the wind might have originated. The Caribbean lies directly south-west of the British Isles, and winds from that direction often carry warm and moist tropical air to our shores.

Cross-curricular links

English: Extend any work that you do on hurricanes by asking the pupils to write their own 'eye-witness' reports. There are plenty of examples on the internet, particularly of Hurricane Katrina, which destroyed the city of New Orleans in the USA in 2004.

Mathematics: Ask pupils each to create a grid 24 squares wide and 12 squares deep. Give them an outline map of Jamaica and ask them to translate the shape as accurately as they can onto the grid that they have created. They should add the key settlements and other features, such as the mountains and railways. They could also calculate distances, as each grid square on their map will be exactly 10 km across.

History: Find out about Christopher Columbus and his famous journey across the Atlantic Ocean to the Caribbean. What was he searching for? What were the lasting impacts of his discovery?

Music: Introduce the children to the music of Bob Marley, Desmond Dekker, Boney M, UB40 and other Jamaican artists. Teach them to sing some of the songs that appeal to them.

Themes

Colonialism and social justice: Nearly 150 years ago, Chief Seattle, the leader of the Suquamish and Duwamish Native American tribes, sent a message to the government in Washington DC, USA, who wanted to buy his people's land. He believed that all life on Earth – and the Earth itself – is sacred. Pupils can read this inspiring message in *Brother Eagle, Sister Sky* by Susan Jeffers (1993). For another story about how indigenous people struggled for human rights in North America, you could watch the excellent YouTube film about Luther Standing Bear (see Useful books and websites, p. 238).

Biodiversity: Find out more about the threats to wildlife in the Caribbean. Some of the key problems are: deforestation to create farmland; industrial pollution, e.g. from mining bauxite; shortages of water, caused by the demand from tourists; overfishing; invasive species; and the impacts of climate change and tourism on coral reefs. Think about each of these in turn and try to put them in rank order. Can they be dealt with separately? How do they link to poverty?

Values and wellbeing: Communities from Jamaica and other parts of the Caribbean are part of the social fabric of modern Britain. Find out more about the famous Jamaicans mentioned in the previous lesson and add your own examples to this list. Ask the pupils to write short pieces about the ways in which links with Jamaica have brought cultural, social, sporting and other benefits to the UK.

Progression and assessment

By the end of this area of study, all children should have an outline knowledge of the key physical and human features of North America and be able to locate and describe the

Caribbean. Those who are working beyond expectations will be able to make meaningful geographical comparisons between Jamaica and a region of the UK, such as Northern Ireland. The ability to generate significant enquiry questions will be further evidence of achievement.

Useful books and websites

Jeffers, S. (1993), *Brother Eagle, Sister Sky*. London: Puffin (also available on YouTube).

Smith, D. J. (2009), *If America Were a Village: A Book About the People of the United States*. Toronto: Kids Can Press.

Chief Standing Bear: A hero of Native American civil rights: www.youtube.com/watch?v=LzkYCeO-gYE

First Nations in Canada: www.rcaanc-cirnac.gc.ca/eng/1307460755710/1536862806124

Photos of Jamaica: search Google Images.

The meaning of 'indigenous': search for 'Indigenous – explained: CBC Kids News' on YouTube.

24 South America

What do I need to know?

South America is an isolated continent bounded by the Pacific and the Atlantic Oceans. It is joined by a narrow strip of land, or isthmus, to the continent of North America, which is nearly 50 per cent larger. The equator crosses northern regions but most of the land lies in the Southern Hemisphere. The boundary between North and South America is generally said to be the Panama Canal.

There are 12 sovereign states in South America: Argentina, Bolivia, Brazil, Chile, Colombia, Ecuador, Guyana, Paraguay, Peru, Suriname, Uruguay and Venezuela. There are two non-sovereign states located within the continent: French Guiana, an overseas department of France, and the Falkland Islands, a British overseas territory. Panama, Trinidad and Tobago, and the ABC islands in the Caribbean may also be considered part of South America.

South America occupies an area of approximately 18 million square kilometres. Brazil is the largest country and covers nearly half the continent, while Chile is 4,000 km long but less than a couple of hundred kilometres wide on average. With 215 million people, Brazil makes up more than half of the continent's population, followed by Colombia, Argentina, Venezuela and Peru. The largest city in South America is São Paulo. Most of the population lives near the coast. The interior and the far south are sparsely populated.

The Andes, which run down the western edge of the continent, are the dominant physical feature and the world's longest chain of mountains. The largest rainforest area in the world is found in the Amazon basin, and the Atacama Desert in Chile is the driest hot desert on Earth. There are a number of great rivers, such as the Amazon, Orinoco and Paraná, all of which drain into the Atlantic Ocean. In terms of physical geography, South America is

Figure 32: Brazil borders every country in South America apart from Chile and Ecuador

often described as a huge bowl because of its flat interior, which is almost ringed by high mountains.

South America is famed for the ancient cultures of people such as the Incas, who have left glimpses of the past through artefacts and architecture. The continent has a long history of colonialism. Interactions with other people and cultures, especially from Portugal, Spain and the continent of Africa, have left their mark. Today, most South Americans are likely to speak Portuguese or Spanish.

Misconceptions and research

Children may think that South America is just part of North America or even a country by itself, rather than a continent with many countries and cultures. They are likely to have heard of the Amazon rainforest and may believe that all of the continent is like this rather than diverse in climate, flora and fauna. Even the Amazon rainforest has large cities where people live and work, and this often surprises some children.

Interesting facts

- There are around 200 potentially active volcanoes in the Andes.
- The Amazon carries more freshwater than any other river – ten of the 20 largest rivers in the world are found in the Amazonian basin.
- Potatoes were brought to England from the Andes by the Spanish in around 1550.

Key questions

1. What are the key features of South America?
2. What different regions are there?
3. What environmental issues affect the continent?

Lesson 1 Introducing South America

What is South America like?

You will need
- an atlas and inflatable globe
- access to the internet
- blank outline maps of South America.

Key vocabulary
- continent
- country
- equator
- rainforest
- region
- pampas
- South America
- tropics

Getting started
Find out what pupils already know about South America. Can they locate it on a globe? Can they describe its position using words like 'ocean', 'tropic', 'equator' and 'hemisphere'? Use an inflatable globe to play a game of 'globe tossing'. Throw the globe

to an individual pupil and ask them to say something that they know about South America and its features when they catch it.

Class activities

South American countries game: A quick internet search using the key words 'South American countries game' will lead you to some geography games in which pupils can click and drag country names to the correct places on a map. These games are fun and help to develop and reinforce core knowledge.

Countries map: Give pupils blank outlines of South America with country borders marked, and challenge them to name each one correctly using an atlas. Can they also mark in some capital cities?

Key features: Ask the pupils to research and find some of the key features of South America, and then mark them on map outlines. You could include some 'must haves', such as the Andes, Lake Titicaca, the Amazon rainforest, the River Amazon, Angel Falls, Machu Picchu, the Atacama Desert, the Argentine Pampas and Patagonia. Pupils could extend their research using digital maps. There are a number of free programs where they can add text labels, icons and images (see Useful books and websites, pp. 247–248).

Feature facts: Ask pupils to choose five significant features of South America and write brief descriptions about each one, giving its location and saying why they think that it is significant. They could also research images as illustrations.

Map display: In advance of the lesson, generate a list of questions highlighting different aspects of South America, such as rivers, trade, climate and terrain. Divide the class into small groups and ask each one to select a category. Ask each group to produce a map with factual information for the category. Compile the maps as a class display, showing different facets of the continent.

Dreaming of South America: Ask pupils to select a place in South America and say why they would like to go there. Put their words into thought bubbles, along with their photographs, and add to a world map.

Plenary

Ask pupils to work in groups and write down all the things that they know about South America. Get each group to paste their ideas into a word-cloud app such as Tagxedo (www.tagxedo.com). Some of these have templates shaped as continents into which words can be pasted.

Lesson 2 Learning about Lima

What is Lima like?

You will need
- an atlas
- access to the internet
- travel brochures on Peru (optional)
- large pieces of paper.

Key vocabulary
- city
- Lima
- Peru
- population
- urban

Getting started

Ask the pupils to find Peru on an atlas map and ask them to comment on its size. This is one of the largest countries in South America. Ask how many times bigger than Great Britain they think that it is. (It's four times bigger in area but has about half the population.) Show and discuss some of the different regions of the country, using Google Earth or other available aerial imagery. Ask pupils to find out the name and location of the capital city. The answer is Lima, and it is one of the largest cities in the Americas. The city and its outskirts (known as Metro Lima) cover an area slightly larger than the Lake District. Ask pupils which they think covers the greater area: Metro Lima, Peru or the Lake District. Explain that in this lesson they are going to find out about Lima and compare it with the Lake District (or some other region that you have studied in the UK).

Class activities

Lima maps: Working in pairs, ask the pupils to create two digital maps at different scales to show the location and layout of Lima. Discuss why maps of different scales are useful and how far you might 'zoom in' to show a helpful view of the place being studied. Ask pupils to print out their maps for their geography books.

Tourist poster: Is Lima a popular place with tourists? What kind of attractions are there? Using internet research (and brochures from a local travel agent if you can source them), ask pupils to select some key attractions within the city. Devise a poster giving the location and a brief description of each attraction. Other useful sources are Street Map and Google.

Take one picture: Is there one picture that best defines Lima? Search online to find some images of Lima and ask pupils to come up with suggestions for the best images, from which the class select a shortlist. Discuss why one picture ought to be chosen over another. Are there pictures that show the best and the worst of the city? How and why are they different?

Environmental concerns: All cities have environmental issues, such as: How do they cope with a large population? How do they source fresh drinking water and where does the city's waste go to? Pupils could use keyword searches of reputable media and newspaper sources. Ask them to prioritise some of the key issues and, if they can't find out how these are being solved, suggest some ideas that might help.

Research questions: Working in small groups, give each group a research heading and ask them to brainstorm some useful enquiry questions on a large shared sheet of paper. Give each group time to walk around and look at the questions that other groups have come up with and add to them. The groups should then go back to their own bases and select the best questions to research. Ask each group to produce a short fact-file about Lima and the Lake District using their chosen headings. For example, this might include references to longitude and latitude, the location of each region within the country, and information about surrounding features, such as mountains and coasts.

Plenary
Use the work produced for a display, class assembly or mini exhibition. Start a question wall of additional enquiry questions that have not been answered and use this as prompts for fieldwork. Have a class vote on a pair of defining pictures for Lima.

Lesson 3 Lake Titicaca

What is Lake Titicaca like?

You will need
- atlases and internet access.

Key vocabulary
- Andes
- Lake Titicaca
- reeds
- Uros people

Getting started
Give the pupils the following statements about Lake Titicaca one at a time, and ask them to say whether they think that they are true or false.

Lake Titicaca is:

- nearly 4,000 metres above sea level
- one of the highest navigable lakes in the world
- the largest lake in South America
- nearly four times as large as the entire Lake District National Park
- one of the oldest lakes in the world
- split between Peru and Bolivia
- in the Andes mountains
- in an earthquake zone
- dotted with islands that people have made from reeds.

All of the above statements are true. Now discuss and generate some key questions about Lake Titicaca that the pupils want to investigate.

Class activities

Lake Titicaca map: Ask the pupils to draw maps of Lake Titicaca. As well as showing the country borders, they should mark some of the roads and settlements around the shore. See too that they add scales and north points and enclose their maps with ruled lines.

Getting there: Discuss some of the ways of getting to Lake Titicaca from different starting points in South America and using different methods of transport.

Floating islands: Using information from the internet, ask pupils to find out about the Uros people (who live on the floating islands made of reeds). Ask them to write short descriptions of their traditional way of life, illustrated by drawings or pictures of a reed village.

Diary entry: Ask pupils to imagine that they have been to visit one of the Uros islands for a week, to help a local family with the tourist trade. Ask them to describe the location, landscape, daily activities and weather, and explain how it might feel living on an island made of reeds.

Infographic: Ask pupils to collect numerical facts about Lake Titicaca and some of its people, settlements and related geography, to create highly visual infographics using different kinds of graphs and charts. As a prompt, you might ask the pupils to collect data about the longitude and latitude, size, height, climate, local population and so on.

Sustainability: Thousands of people depend on Lake Titicaca for water, food and tourism. However, the lake is becoming increasingly polluted, as it faces the challenge of increased urban development on its shores. As well as contamination from heavy metals such as cadmium, arsenic and lead waste, overgrazing of livestock is also depositing nutrients that encourage harmful algae blooms, reducing water clarity and oxygen. Using a 'mantle of the expert' approach, pupils could research one or more of the problems and make recommendations about what can be done. Remind them that they need to consider the different interest groups – tourists, town planners, those seeking a new life in growing urban developments and indigenous peoples like the Uros people.

Plenary

As a class, discuss what the pupils have learned about Lake Titicaca and what they think is most interesting.

Fieldwork and further investigations

- Lake Titicaca provides a unique habitat for plants and creatures. Arrange a fieldwork trip to your nearest pond or lake so that children can investigate an aquatic environment for themselves. What different life forms can they discover? Now think about some of the ways in which people use the area and make use of the water. Where would be a good place for a new pond in your area? Ask the pupils to draw maps and notes about their proposals.

Cross-curricular links

English: Using *Mia's Story* (see Useful books and websites, pp. 247–248) as a prompt, ask pupils to devise their own accounts of contrasting environments in South America.

Mathematics: Ask pupils to draw climate graphs showing monthly temperature and rainfall for Lake Titicaca, using the data in **Figure 33**. How do these figures compare with those for the UK?

	Jan	Feb	Mar	Apr	May	Jun	Jul	Aug	Sep	Oct	Nov	Dec
Temperature	8°C	10°C	13°C	16°C	20°C	23°C	26°C	26°C	24°C	17°C	11°C	6°C
Rainfall	200 mm	120 mm	140 mm	90 mm	50 mm	40 mm	20 mm	30 mm	30 mm	100 mm	200 mm	130 mm

Figure 33: Monthly temperatures and rainfall for Lake Titicaca (source: www.holiday-weather.com/lake_titicaca/averages/)

History: Lake Titicaca has been the cradle of many ancient South American civilisations, including the Inca. Get the children to find out more about the Inca and their achievements, such as the network of roads and bridges that they built across the Andes. Archaeological remains are a feature of the region. As the children find out about these, they will be drawn into finding out more about Inca myths, legends and religion.

Music: South America has its own distinctive musical genres, including the tango, salsa and samba. The haunting pipe music of the high Andes represents an entirely different style. Select some suitable examples to play to the pupils to give them a sense of the vitality and diversity of the continent. A good place to start if you want to access resources from the internet is www.singup.org.

Themes

Colonialism and social justice: There are probably well over a million indigenous people living in the Amazon, many of whom are threatened as farming and industry encroach on the rainforest. One of the most well-known groups is the Yanomami, who are fighting for their survival. Pupils can find out more about their ways of life and relationships with nature from a wide range of teaching materials, stories and videos available online. Campaign groups, such as Survival International, are another source of information.

Sustainability: Studying the Amazon rainforest highlights conservation sustainability issues, because of both its huge size and the threats that it faces. The forest is vitally important as the richest and most diverse ecological treasure trove in the world. It is also important meteorologically, creating its own weather systems and helping to regulate the world's climate. Scientists warn that, if too many trees are cleared, it could trigger a feedback loop in which reduced rainfall causes trees to die, leading to even drier conditions and irreversible change.

Values and wellbeing: The sheer diversity of people and cultures in South America raises questions about how different communities can live in harmony with each other and what it means to live well. It is also an opportunity to explore the way in which indigenous people relate to nature and regard the environment as sacred.

Progression and assessment

By the end of this unit, children will be able to locate South America on a globe and on a 2D map, and locate and describe some of its significant features. They will be able to talk about one or more of the continent's large cities and some of the issues that it faces as it grows. Children will also be able to make some comparisons between a region in South America, such as the urban sprawl of Lima or Lake Titicaca, and a region in the UK.

Useful books and websites

Ballin, B. and Whittle, J. (2014), *Back2Front: The Americas.* Glasgow: Wildgoose.

Bowden, D. and Copeland, P. (2015), *Amazon Adventures: Investigating the South American Rainforest* (Geography Plus series). Sheffield: Geographical Association.

Foreman, M. (2007), *Mia's Story*. London: Walker Books.

Humphreys, A. (2014), *The Boy who Biked the World. Part Two: Riding the Americas.* Much Wenlock, Shropshire: Eye Books.

Digital maps: go to www.arcgis.com, www.scribblemaps.com or www.quikmaps.com

25 Food and farming

What do I need to know?

People first started farming around 12,000 years ago in the area that we now call the Middle East. Before then, they gathered food from the land and hunted wild animals in hunter-gather societies. The shift to settled agriculture brought about profound changes. It enabled people to store food and gave them greater security when the weather was harsh. It also meant that people started to own land and claim it as their own. As farming practices became more effective, it was no longer necessary for everybody to be engaged in food production. In fertile areas, the first towns and cities began to develop, and powerful leaders emerged.

Agriculture has seen profound changes over the centuries. In medieval times, the development of deep ploughs pulled by teams of oxen or horses helped to control weeds and improve water conservation in the soil. From the seventeenth century onwards, the crop-rotation system that had been developed in England improved soil fertility and reduced the prevalence of pests and diseases. The use of tractors and other machinery powered by fossil fuels transformed practices in the twentieth century, greatly reducing the need for agricultural labour. In the 1960s, new high-yielding varieties of wheat and rice were introduced around the world in what is known as the 'green revolution'. More recently, genetically modified crops have further extended the impact of technology on food production and processing.

These developments in agriculture have come at a cost. Intensive farming is leading to soil degradation and the loss of biodiversity. The pollution of rivers and ground water from insecticides and fertilisers is another problem. As agriculture becomes increasingly industrialised, large companies have sought to exercise control over new varieties of seeds.

There are also concerns about the loss of genetic diversity and overdependence on a very limited number of food crops.

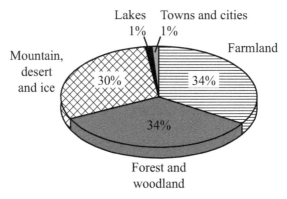

Figure 34: Only about a third of the Earth's land can be used for farming

There have also been major changes in food distribution associated with globalisation. One way in which this is evident to both children and the general public is in retailing. Many small shops in villages and towns, and suburban side streets, have been replaced by out-of-town supermarkets and internet shopping. The effect that this is having on traditional town centres is a matter of increasing social and economic interest.

Geographers study many different aspects of food and food production. The interaction between the climate, soil, agriculture and settlement is a fascinating area of study. Patterns of trade and trade routes are another dimension to consider. More recently, the contribution that agriculture is making to carbon emissions has come to the fore in the climate-change debate. It has also been recognised that environmentally friendly practices can considerably enhance wildlife and biodiversity. As a result, a wide range of eco-friendly practices known as 'regenerative agriculture' is attracting considerable interest.

Misconceptions and research

Many children have very little idea of where their food comes from and are uncertain as to how it reaches the local supermarket or shops. This is partly because there are few direct ways in which to see the links and connections between what they eat and the soil where is it grown. One way in which to illustrate this relationship is by planting food crops like tomatoes or strawberries in the school garden. It is also a memorable experience when it comes to picking what has grown!

Interesting facts

- Ants work together to harvest the sap from plants, making them 'farmers' just like humans.
- In the UK, we eat over five billion bananas a year – on average, that's 100 bananas per person.
- There are approximately thirty million sheep and 140 million chickens in the UK.

Key questions

1. Why do we make different choices about what we eat?
2. Why does some of our food come from abroad?
3. Does it matter how our food is produced?

Lesson 1 Food in our lives

How does food feature in our lives?

You will need
- paper plates
- modelling materials, such as modelling clay.

Key vocabulary
- allergy
- biodegradable
- carbon footprint
- diet
- ocean gyre
- recycling
- soya
- vegan
- vegetarian

Getting started
Ask the children whether they have ever grown any food that they have eaten. Now make a list on the interactive whiteboard of some of the food that children have eaten

recently. Draw a simple diagram tracing how a few selected items are linked to the soil. It is easiest to do this for unprocessed food. Milk, for example, links cows to grass and soil in a simple sequence.

Class activities

A balanced diet: Most children know that too much sugary food is bad for them. Fruit and vegetables make an important contribution to a balanced diet, so its important to eat enough of them. Children can find out more about a balanced diet from the NHS 'five a day' campaign. They could also investigate the 'Harvard healthy eating plate'. Now, using paper plates and modelling materials, such as modelling clay, get pupils to make a model of a meal that they would recommend. Ask them to write a few sentences about what they have chosen and its benefits for themselves and the environment.

Food choices: Initiate a discussion about food choices but remember that this can be a sensitive topic that raises personal issues, which some children may want to keep to themselves. Begin by finding out whether there are any children in your class who are vegetarian or vegan. Discuss why they have made this choice. When did they make it? Are there any children in the class with food allergies? What problems do they have if they eat certain foods? Broaden the discussion to include questions about how food is produced. You might also talk about how animal husbandry is linked to environmental destruction. The forests of South America, for example, are being cleared to create land to rear cattle and to grow soya for animal feed.

Food packaging: Much of the food that we eat is packaged or wrapped. Ask the children to collect some of the plastic and other packaging from their home shopping to bring to school, avoiding anything that is dirty or sharp. Sort the packaging into materials that can be recycled and those that will not biodegrade. Discuss what happens to waste once it has been collected from homes and schools. How could the amount of packaging be reduced, and are there opportunities to use more environmentally friendly materials? You could develop this activity into a wider project on plastic and plastic pollution. There are some excellent children's books on this topic, as well as information on the internet about how plastic has accumulated in ocean gyres (see Useful books and websites, p. 258).

Supermarket visit: Arrange a visit to a local supermarket. Before you go, divide the children into small groups to devise a set of questions that they want to ask. They might ask about where the food comes from, whether any of it is local, the opportunities to reduce the amount of packaging (including plastic wrappers), how they choose which goods to put on promotion, how they are reducing their carbon footprint and whether they are experiencing any difficulties due to climate change. If the children have done some work on the Amazon, they might want to ask about the supermarket's policy towards palm oil. They might also ask questions about fair trade and how the supermarket is supporting environmentally friendly farming.

Plenary

Working individually, ask the children to write down one thing that they have learned from this lesson. Compare results around the class.

Lesson 2 Farming

Where does our food come from?

You will need

- blank outline maps of the UK
- a selection of food labels
- a world map and mapping pins
- atlases
- dice.

Key vocabulary

- crops
- food miles
- import
- plantation
- plan view
- season
- symbol
- trade
- tropics

Getting started

Talk with the children about the food that they have eaten recently. Where do they think that it came from? Some will have come from the UK but a considerable proportion will likely have come from overseas. Can the pupils explain why we need to import food? Do they think that it is transported by air, ship, lorry or train?

Class activities

UK farming: Farmers use the land in different ways across the UK:

- In the hilly areas of Wales, the Lake District and Scotland, many farmers keep sheep.
- In eastern Scotland, Northern Ireland and eastern and south-eastern England, farmers often grow crops such as wheat.
- In South West England and the Midlands, many farmers keep cows.

Share this information with the children, making the point that it is highly generalised. Now give the children blank outline maps of the UK and ask them to draw symbols showing the different types of farming in the correct places. Talk about how the climate and nature of the physical landscape influence what farmers do.

Food from abroad: Make a display of food labels from tins and packages that indicate the countries of origin. As well as looking at any wrappers from the food that they eat during the day, pupils could bring items from home to add to the display. Use mapping pins to identify the countries of origin on a world map. As the display develops, talk about any patterns that emerge. Do some countries seem to supply a lot of our food? Is there any obvious reason for this?

Food miles: Ask the pupils each to draw a plate in the middle of the page showing a meal that they really like. It is best to use a plan view so that each item stands out clearly. Now ask them to annotate their drawings by naming each item and suggesting a possible country of origin. Can the pupils find out how far the foods travelled to get to their plates? Use a food-miles calculator to find out the answer (see Useful books and websites, p. 258). Can the children think of methods of reducing the food miles for the meals that they have chosen?

Banana trade: Bananas are one of the most popular fruits sold in the UK. They are grown all over the tropics but most of the bananas sold in the UK come from plantations in Central and South America and the Caribbean. Get the children to devise diagrams showing how bananas reach UK supermarkets. They will each need five large circles linked with arrows to show the bananas: (1) growing in bunches, (2) put into boxes, (3) transported by ship, (4) carried by lorry and (5) on sale on a shelf.

Plenary
Discuss what might happen if the UK could no longer import food from abroad. How would it affect (a) you personally and (b) the way in which land is farmed?

Lesson 3 Sustainable farming

Should farming be more sustainable?

You will need
- a few bars of organic and non-organic chocolate
- examples of Fairtrade products for a display table
- jam jars and soil from the school grounds.

Key vocabulary
- additive
- Fairtrade
- fertiliser
- free-range
- organic
- pesticide
- pollinator
- water supplies

Getting started

Modern farming methods depend on fertiliser, pesticides and other chemicals to increase yields and kill weeds and pests. However, these are expensive to buy and cause problems for plants, people and wildlife. If farmers use too much fertiliser, it damages the soil and contaminates water supplies. Insecticides do not simply kill pests; they upset the balance of nature and can harm human health. Talk about these issues with the children as an introduction to this lesson on sustainable farming.

Class activities

Pollinators: A pollinator is a creature that fertilisers flowers by carrying pollen from one plant to another. The most common pollinators are bees, flies, wasps and other small insects. Together with the children, compile a class list of foods that depend on pollinators. This will include just about all the fruit and vegetables that the pupils can think of. Now ask the children to research 'bee-friendly' flowers. They could make drawings of these for a class display. If you have a school garden, the children will be able to grow bee-friendly flowers for themselves.

Free-range animals: Some farm animals are kept outdoors and allowed to move around freely, but others are kept indoors, often in very cramped conditions. Battery chicken farming is a particularly emotive issue, and has been associated with serious outbreaks of disease. Discuss this with the children and, working in groups, ask them to draw up a charter of animal rights. The United Nations Charter of the Rights of the Child might provide a useful model.

Organically grown: Many pupils will be aware that some food is organically grown. This means that it will have been produced in a way that respects the environment, using only certain approved pesticides and fertilisers. Organic food also doesn't usually contain additives. Conduct a simple experiment in which pupils compare the taste of small pieces of organic and non-organic chocolate. This is likely to be a very popular activity!

Can the pupils tell any difference in the taste? Do they think that it is worth paying extra for an organic product?

Soil experiment: All the food that we eat comes either directly or indirectly from the soil. Conduct a simple experiment to find out about the soil in your area. You need to fill a jam jar about a third full of soil, add water to the top, shake the jar and let it settle. Talk about the different layers that appear when the soil has separated and ask the pupils to bring samples from their own gardens at home for comparison. Talk about the differences between healthy and degraded soil. It was poor farming practices that caused the Dust Bowl disaster, which turned farmland to desert in the USA in the 1930s. You will find lots of images on the internet.

Fairtrade: Fairtrade is an organisation that guarantees farmers a reasonable wage for their labour and promotes practices that protect the environment. Many shops in the UK stock coffee, sugar and bananas that are grown under Fairtrade agreements. Show the children a video about the benefits of Fairtrade (search for 'Fairtrade' on YouTube) and discuss it with them. Remember to consider the drawbacks. Fairtrade products are more expensive to buy than other goods, and farmers who are left out of Fairtrade agreements may find their lives even harder than before. Finish the activity by setting up a display table with examples of Fairtrade products and information about them.

Plenary

Organise a class debate on the advantages and disadvantages of sustainable food and farming:

- It is better for wildlife.
- It keeps the soil healthy.
- It is more nutritious.

- It is more expensive.
- It can be less attractive.
- It decays quickly.

If the children each roll a die, you could make the debate more lively by allocating them one of these six roles according to the number that they have thrown.

Fieldwork and further investigations

- See whether you can arrange to visit a farm in the area where you live. Alternatively, invite a local farmer to come and talk to the pupils about their work. What crops are grown on the farm? Is there a reason why the land is used in this way? Are there any animals or fruit trees? If so, what are they and what do they produce? Find out about the equipment used on the farm and some of the challenges of looking after the land. If possible, get a map of the farm showing the different fields and how they are used, so that pupils can draw their own maps when they write their accounts of their farm visit.

Cross-curricular links

English: Martin Luther King once famously said, 'Before you've finished eating breakfast in the morning, you've depended on half the world.' Ask the pupils to write short prose passages or haikus explaining what they think that he meant by this.

Mathematics: Get the children to compile databanks about UK farming. This might include the total number of farms, the numbers of different farm animals, the amount of farmland, the percentage given over to different crops and so forth.

History: Find out about farming in Ancient Egypt, the crops that were grown and the seasonal sequence. There are wall paintings that show the land being tilled and the tools that were used at the time. From a geographical point of view, the flooding of the Nile is an excellent example of human–physical interaction.

Music: Listen to the songs by the folk singer Woody Guthrie about the dust storms that hit the American Midwest in the 1930s. What caused this terrible disaster and how was it eventually dealt with?

Technology: Find out about how scientists are developing genetically modified (GM) seeds to increase crop yields. What are the benefits of GM crops and why are some people worried about them?

Themes

Colonialism: The plantations that were established in colonial times still supply food for the UK today. This is one of the reasons why Fairtrade agreements focus chiefly on products that were once grown using slave labour.

Biodiversity: There are many ways in which farmers can enhance biodiversity. As well as setting aside land for nature, they can plant trees and hedges, reduce their dependence on chemicals and make use of natural fertilisers. See whether you can locate a farm that is adopting regenerative practices in your area as a case study, or find out about a local rewilding project.

Progression and assessment

By the end of the area of study, all children should know that the food that they eat comes from plants and animals. Children who have a more advanced understanding will have begun to appreciate the importance of maintaining biodiversity and nurturing soils. They will also have engaged with two key principles – patterns and interconnections – that apply to other areas of geography and aspects of learning.

Useful books and websites

Parsons, S. and Foley, M. (2012), *Food for Thought: Investigating Where Our Food Comes From.* Sheffield: Geographical Association.

Paul, M. (2017), *One Plastic Bag.* Minneapolis: Millbrook Press.

Factory farming: search for 'Number of farm animals in the world'.

Food miles calculator: www.foodmiles.com

Plastic in ocean gyres: search for 'Plastic gyres'.

Regenerative agriculture: search for 'What is regenerative agriculture?' on YouTube.

Soil experiments: search for 'Soil experiments' on YouTube.

26 Natural resources

What do I need to know?

A natural resource is defined as anything that people use that comes from nature. Some natural resources, like oil, gas and metal ores, are limited, which means that they will eventually run out. Others, such as food crops and wood, are renewable, which means that they can be replaced. Wind and sunshine are both examples of renewable resources. Soil, too, is regarded as a renewable resource. However, if soil is damaged or overused, it becomes degraded and may blow away or become unable to support plant life.

People depend on the Earth's resources in order to survive. Air, water and food are our most fundamental needs. Oil, gas and coal provide us with energy for heating and machines, along with the Sun, wind, waves, tides and rivers. Meanwhile, minerals supply the raw materials needed in manufacturing and industry. We build houses for shelter out of bricks, wood, steel, glass and concrete.

Natural resources are distributed unevenly between countries and regions. In the eighteenth and nineteenth centuries, the Industrial Revolution was fuelled by the discovery of large quantities of coal in the UK. Since the middle of the twentieth century, the Middle East has played a key role in world economic affairs, due to its huge reserves of oil. Countries such as the USA, Canada and Australia that export surplus wheat are in a strong economic position, particularly as food security becomes a matter of growing concern. A few countries are unusually rich in minerals. South Africa, for example, is famous for diamonds and Brazil has huge deposits of iron ore.

This area of study introduces pupils to natural resources by highlighting minerals, energy and water. Although we all use these resources on a daily basis, we often take them for granted. Learning that resources are unevenly distributed geographically is one of the starting points for understanding the power dynamics of the modern world. The increasing demand for natural resources also raises important questions about sustainability. Finding ways in which to live in harmony with the planet that supports us is becoming ever more urgent as we move towards the middle years of the twenty-first century.

Figure 35: Eventually the world will run out of new supplies of gold and other natural resources.

Misconceptions and research

Children tend to take it for granted that we have ready access to electricity, water and natural resources. One of the key ideas that underpins this area of study is the notion of sustainability. We depend on the Earth's resources in all manner of unexpected ways. This means that we need to be aware that those natural resources that are finite need to be used as sparingly as possible.

Interesting facts

- One in eight people in the world lacks access to clean water.
- Oil is made from the remains of sea creatures that lived millions of years ago.
- The word 'gold' comes from the Old English word *geolu*, meaning 'yellow'.

Key questions

(1)   Are the countries with the most natural resources always the richest?

(2)   Which natural resources are most important?

(3)   Will natural resources ever run out?

Lesson 1 Minerals

How are minerals important in our lives?

You will need

- access to the internet
- blank world maps
- magnets
- rocks for a class display.

Key vocabulary

- Earth's crust
- indigenous people
- iron
- minerals
- mobile phone
- rare earth

Getting started

Set up a display table with different types of rocks. You could start this off with some rocks of your own and invite the children to add some of their own as well. Explain that rocks are made of different minerals. Some rocks also contain fossils, which were once laid down at the bottom of a lake or sea.

Class activities

Made of iron: Give the children magnets so that they can discover whether any of the things in and around the classroom are made of iron. They will discover that some items that appear to be made of iron are actually made from alloys or plastic. Talk about how iron has been important in human history, most notably in the Iron Age and the Industrial Revolution. Pupils may be surprised to learn that most of the Earth's inner core and around five per cent of the Earth's crust are composed of iron.

Minerals in our bodies: Talk about how very small quantities of minerals are important for human health. These include calcium, sodium, iron, copper, zinc and cobalt. Are there any foods that are particularly mineral-rich? What happens if we don't eat enough minerals?

Minerals in our lives: We depend on minerals in lots of unexpected ways. **Figure 36** shows some examples of how they are used in everyday life.

Mineral	Use	Mineral	Use
Gold	Coins	Lithium	Batteries
Silver	Tableware	Aluminium	Cans
Diamonds	Jewellery	Silica (sand)	Glass
Copper	Wires	Gypsum	Plaster
Graphite	Pencil leads	Kaolin (clay)	Crockery
Zinc	Sunscreen	Halite (salt)	Cooking

Figure 36: How minerals are used in everyday life

Ask the children to select some of the minerals that particularly interest them. Get them to find out more about them and how they are used for a small illustrated class book or wall display.

Inside your phone: There are literally dozens of precious minerals inside every mobile phone, computer and electronic device. These include gold, cobalt and other rare earth metals, and they are likely to have come from every continent on Earth apart from Antarctica, where mining is not permitted. For an excellent video about this, search for 'Where does your phone come from?' on YouTube. Talk about why it is important to recycle old phones and how you can do this.

Gold worldwide: Gold has been prized by people all over the world for thousands of years. It is very attractive, bends easily and resists corrosion. However, it is rare and difficult to extract. Give the children blank outline maps of the world and ask them to identify and label the top ten gold-producing countries. In rank order, these are, at the time of writing: China, Russia, Australia, Canada, the USA, Ghana, Peru, Mexico, Indonesia and South Africa. Tip: you may find that it helps if you add the country outlines beforehand. Are these also the world's largest countries?

Mining in the Amazon: Ask the children to find out about the impact of mining on the Amazon rainforest. They will find plenty of information about damage to the natural environment and pollution of waterways. The threats to indigenous people are another issue. Pupils might also focus on the activities of campaigners such as Chico Mendes. Get them to present their findings as short PowerPoint presentations.

Plenary

Ask the children what has surprised them most about the things that they have learned in this lesson. What impact do they think that the lesson will have (if any) on the way in which they live their lives?

Lesson 2 Energy

What are the main sources of energy?

You will need

- access to the internet
- graph paper
- long strips of paper or card.

Key vocabulary

- biomass
- gas field
- hydroelectric
- nuclear power
- solar farm
- tidal lagoon
- turbine

Getting started

Ask the children to reflect on the different ways in which they have used energy since they got up this morning. Challenge them to think about things that are not immediately obvious. When we turn on a tap, for example, the water that we use will have been pumped out of the ground; when we throw away rubbish, it will eventually be collected by a vehicle that is powered by an engine.

Class activities

Oil in our lives: Oil is a particularly versatile resource. It can be used for driving engines and cars, making electricity or to heat ovens and boilers. It can be turned into products such as plastic, washing powder and car tyres. It is also one of the materials used in fertiliser. Discuss with the pupils how oil is essential to our lives. Ask them to write short reports about how our lives would change if we suddenly had no supplies of oil.

Oil worldwide: Most of the world's oil comes from just a few countries. Get the children to draw bar graphs showing oil production using these figures for a million barrels a day in 2022: USA – 17, Saudi Arabia – 12, Russia – 11, Canada – 6, Iraq – 5, China – 4, UAE – 4, Iran – 4. You may want to use graph paper for this activity and obtain more recent figures and information from the internet.

Making electricity: Although renewable energy is becoming much more important, a significant proportion of the electricity used in the UK is still generated using gas. Give the pupils long strips of paper or card and ask them to show how electricity is generated as a sequence diagram:

(1)   Gas is found in underground gas fields.

(2)   It is brought to power stations along pipes.

(3)   The gas is burned to heat water.

(4)   This makes steam, which drives turbines.

(5)   The electricity goes along cables suspended from pylons to substations.

(6)   It is used in factories, farms and houses.

Wind farms: Ask the children to find out about wind farms in their area. A simple internet search for 'Wind farms near me' is a good way in which to start this research. Ask pupils to devise short written descriptions of wind farms that interest them, and to draw maps of the locations. What makes pupils think that this was a good site? Can they identify any other places in your area or region that might be suitable for a new wind farm?

Tidal power: Tidal lagoons generate energy as sea levels rise and fall. Show the class a map from Google Images of tidal ranges around the UK. Which places or regions appear to have the most potential for harnessing this type of energy? Now find out about the Swansea Bay tidal lagoon, which was eventually abandoned in 2022 (see Useful books and websites, p. 268).

UK energy: Compare the different ways in which electricity is generated in the UK. Using the whiteboard, look at the interactive maps produced by Carbon Brief for oil, gas, hydro, wind, solar, biomass, nuclear and coal capacity (see Useful books and websites, p. 268). Can the children explain the reasons for the different patterns and distributions? Why is it important to have a range of different energy sources? Are there any that pupils think should be enhanced or phased out?

Plenary

Working as a class, get the children to think of one advantage and one disadvantage of each different method of generating energy.

Lesson 3 Water

How is water important in our lives?

You will need
- access to a computer
- access to the internet
- kitchen paper and chunky wax crayons
- local maps and atlases.

Key vocabulary
- drought
- flood
- hydrant
- reservoir
- water conservation

Getting started
Ask pupils to start thinking about water and its significance. Where are the nearest taps? Do any of the pupils have water bottles? Is there a fountain in the playground? What is the first thing that they check when they are looking after a pet?

Class activities
Water survey: Ask pupils to make a survey of the number of times that they use water for drinking, washing, flushing the toilet and other activities during the day. Record the results on a tally chart before transferring them to the computer to generate a graph. Why is water so important in our lives? Could we cut down on the amount of water that we use?

Saving water: Discuss different ways in which water is being saved in your school. Examples might include toilets that have reduced flushes, taps that turn off automatically and water butts that save rainwater from the roof. Ask pupils to write reports noting the positive measures that have already been taken and suggesting ways in which water conservation could be improved.

Water in the street: Carry out a survey in the streets around your school to find some of the covers, gratings, markers and other clues relating to the water supply system. For example, each house usually has a water stopcock and meter, which is often set into the pavement outside; yellow fire-hydrant markers displaying a large letter 'H' indicate the locations of nearby fire hydrants; signs marked 'SV' tell maintenance engineers where to find safety valves to adjust water pressure and problems in water pipes. Meanwhile, gutter pipes and street drains all help to remove rainwater or take it away when it has been used. Pupils can make rubbings of the metal traps and gratings that they discover, using kitchen paper and chunky wax crayons, for a classroom display. They might think about what happens to the water that flows into drains. Look at maps to locate your nearest river, which will carry this water down to the sea.

Reservoirs: Look at a rainfall map of the UK in an atlas map or project a map of UK rainfall onto the whiteboard. Which are the wettest and which are the driest regions of the UK? Explain that we need to store the water that falls in wet areas so that it can be piped to people in towns where there is much less rain. Use the internet to find out about reservoirs in your area and other parts of the UK. Some of the largest are Kielder Water in North East England, Rutland Water in the Midlands and Llyn Celyn and Lake Vyrnwy in Wales. The pupils could prepare their own information sheets about a reservoir that they have chosen. See that they include maps and information about wildlife, as well as the amount of water that the reservoir supplies.

Droughts and floods: Some parts of the world suffer from almost continual droughts and water shortages. Others have too much rain, resulting in floods. Set up a news board where pupils can display reports of droughts and floods around the UK and other parts of the world. You might develop this activity by researching some of the most notable examples. UK examples include floods in South Yorkshire (2019) and in Shrewsbury and along the River Severn (2020). Worldwide, the long-term droughts in Australia, California (USA) and East Africa contrast with devastating flooding in Pakistan (2022).

Plenary
Working in pairs or small groups, ask the pupils to come up with their own lists of 'watery facts'. Have fun turning these into a rap or some other musical form.

Fieldwork and further investigations

- Locate a quiet street near your school where the pupils can study different houses and their surroundings. Ask them to make lists of the different materials that they can see. They might find clay bricks, slates or Perspex™ roofs, paving stones, metal fences/gates, concrete posts, tarmac roads, gravel paths, glass windows and so on. Ask them to make simple field sketches or take photographs. On returning to school, pupils can print and mount the photographs in the centre of large sheets of paper and add notes about natural resources around the edge.

Cross-curricular links

English: Get the children to write adventure stories involving a search for fabulous gold treasure. Encourage them to think of the landscapes and natural hazards that they might encounter. Do they need maps to show where the characters go?

Science: What materials can be recycled? Paper, glass, plastic and aluminium can all be used again to make new items. Food waste can be turned into compost to create new soil. Ask the pupils to investigate what happens in one of these processes and draw labelled diagrams.

Music: Water is often celebrated in music. Handel's *Water Music* and Shubert's *Trout Quintet* are two classical examples. 'Old Man River' and 'Singing in the Rain' are just two of many songs with a watery theme.

Themes

Colonialism and social justice: Patterns of trade around the world are still significantly linked to colonialism. Inequalities of power mean that rich countries often have a stranglehold over raw materials, and globalisation means that they can switch production from one country to another, seeking out places with the lowest labour costs. One example is the clothing industry in Bangladesh, which supplies many UK outlets but has a reputation for exploitation and child workers.

Sustainability: Explore the differences between renewable and non-renewable resources. Revisit the conversations from earlier activities about the resources that we use on a daily basis. Key headings might include: water, electricity, food, transport, clothing and electronic devices. Taking each in turn, ask pupils to report on ways in which they could continue to use these resources with minimal or zero environmental impact.

Personal development: Helping pupils to become more aware of the resources that they use and their impact on others is one way of developing responsible behaviour. Finding out about how pupils can reduce their resource use also opens up a discussion about the type of person that they want to be, and how they can make positive contributions to society.

Progression and assessment

By the end of this area of study, all children will have learned about the resources that they use and where they come from. They will also be aware of environmental considerations and know that people need to conserve resources and use them wisely. Those who are working at higher levels of achievement will have begun to understand the multiple links and connections between people in different parts of the world and how the decisions that they make may impact others, both locally and overseas.

Useful books and websites

Fuges, C. (2006), *The Terrible Greedy Fossifoo*. London: Simon and Schuster.

Parsons, S. and Foley, M. (2012), *Food for Thought: Investigating Where Our Food Comes From*. Sheffield: Geographical Association.

Minerals and metals (British Geological Survey): search for 'Critical minerals classroom activities KS2'.

Regenerative agriculture: search for 'What is regenerative agriculture?' on YouTube.

Sustainable energy projects (short video clips): www.ashden.org

Tidal lagoons: search for 'Tidal lagoons Swansea Bay' on YouTube.

UK power capacity: search for 'Carbon Brief how the UK generates its electricity'.

WaterAid: www.wateraid.org/uk

Energy teaching resources: search for 'Energy teaching resources KS2' and go to STEM learning.

27 Trade and economic activity

What do I need to know?

Economic activity is one of the dynamics that underpins the modern world. In the past, many people depended on their own resources to support themselves and make a living. Over the centuries, the benefits of trade have become increasingly apparent, as successful trading centres have flourished and grown into important towns and cities. In recent times, the volume of trade has increased enormously, giving rise to a single, globalised world economy. Geographers are interested not only in the way in which different regions and areas specialise in particular types of economic activity, but also in trade routes and connections between centres of production.

Economic activity is traditionally divided into three main categories (see **Figure 37**): primary activity, secondary activity and tertiary activity.

- Primary activity involves acquiring raw materials. For example, coal and metal ore are dug out of mines, trees are cut down to obtain wood, and oil and gas are extracted from underground wells. Fishing and farming are also a key part of primary production.
- Secondary activity involves turning raw materials into goods that people value. For example, the wheat that farmers cultivate is turned into bread in bakeries, and mineral ore is turned into metal and used in factories. Building and construction are also considered part of the secondary sector.
- Tertiary activity refers to the services that support primary and secondary activity. This sector covers a wide range of activities, including healthcare and education.

Generally speaking, countries where the economy is less developed have a relatively high proportion of their workforce engaged in primary activity. The most developed economies, on the other hand, have a strong bias towards tertiary activity.

Within the UK, some regions have specific economic focuses. In the mountains of Wales and Scotland, for example, farming and forestry are important activities. The West Midlands has a particularly high concentration of manufacturing industries. Meanwhile, South East England, the Severn Valley and the central lowlands of Scotland are noted for electronics and service industries. However, this pattern is constantly changing, as new economic forces come to shape our working lives.

Primary activity	Secondary activity	Tertiary activity
Farming Fishing Forestry Mining	Making goods Processing materials Generating electricity Building roads/railways Building houses	Education Financial services Healthcare Shop and office work Driving vehicles Entertainment Advertising

Figure 37: Economic activity can be divided into three main categories

On a global scale, there are also clear patterns. In very general terms, many of the countries in Africa and South America provide the raw materials for the USA, Japan, China and Europe. However, the prices that they receive are often very low. This imbalance in the terms of trade is one of the reasons for massive global inequalities of wealth. There are also some very worrying questions about whether it is possible to sustain economic growth on a finite planet. Ultimately, people may have to find new ways of living that do not depend on ever-increasing levels of consumption.

Misconceptions and research

Children often do not recognise factory buildings and have very little idea of industrial processes. They also have little or no direct experience of farms and are often unaware of where their food comes from before it reaches their local shops. Farm and factory visits can play a valuable part in enlarging their understanding.

Interesting facts

- Shanghai Port is the largest and busiest port in the world.
- Despite legislation to promote equality, women in the UK are still paid less than men for doing the same job.
- China trades more goods than any other country in the world.

Key questions

(1) What is the difference between work and leisure?
(2) Which type of work is most important – primary, secondary or tertiary?

(3) Why are countries that supply raw materials often paid very low prices for their goods?

(4) Is economic prosperity the only way in which to measure development?

Lesson 1 Shops

Are all shops the same?

You will need
- a large-scale map or plan of a local shopping area
- an atlas or electronic map.

Key vocabulary
- country
- season
- shopping centre
- survey

Getting started
Talk about the shops in your local area. What are the shops nearest to your school and what can you buy there? Where is your nearest supermarket? Are there any new shops in your area or have any closed recently?

Class activities
Shop visit: Arrange a visit to a local shop so that the pupils can learn more about what it does and how it is organised. See that they have a range of questions ready to ask before the visit. They might find out how many staff work in the shop, what hours they are employed and whether they need any special training. Where do the goods in the shop come from? Are there plenty of customers? Is there a lot of competition?

New shop: If you were to set up a new shop in your area, what would it sell and where would it be? Begin by carrying out a survey of ten children in your class to find out what type of shop they think is missing. Using this information, decide on what you would like to sell. Next, using information from a large-scale plan or map, decide on a suitable local location. Pupils could present their proposals to the rest of the class to see whether other children agree with them.

Delivery routes: Using an atlas, ask pupils to work out the route that a lorry loaded with washing machines might take from Turkey to the UK. Draw a map or diagram to show the countries and cities that it would pass through.

Grapes all year round: Supermarkets usually have the same fruit and vegetables on their shelves throughout the year, even if they are not in season. They do this by obtaining supplies from different countries around the world. **Figure 38** details how one supermarket obtains its grapes:

Months	Countries
February–March	South Africa
March–May	South Africa and Chile
June–July	South Africa and India

Months	Countries
August–September	Greece
October–November	Spain and Italy
December–January	Spain and Brazil

Figure 38: How one supermarket obtains its grape supply year round

You can show this information visually. Get the children to draw large dials divided into 12 segments in their books and ask them to add the names of the months in the segments. Now ask them to draw rings around the outsides where they can write the names of the countries where the grapes come from. Complete the activity by seeing whether the children can find the countries on a world map.

Plenary

As a class, discuss the benefits that shops bring to the local community in terms of services, employment and community cohesion. What are the advantages and disadvantages of shopping online?

Lesson 2 Work

What are the different types of work?

You will need

- back copies of local newspapers
- A4-size outline maps of the school and grounds
- blank sheets of A4 paper and glue.

Key vocabulary

- primary activity
- secondary activity
- tertiary activity

Getting started

As a class, discuss the differences between work and leisure. Consider different types of job and draw out the distinction between manual labour and desk jobs. What jobs require very specific skills and long periods of training? What jobs do children think that they would like to do when they grow up?

Class activities

Types of work: Discuss with the class how jobs can be sorted into three different categories: primary, secondary and tertiary. Ask pupils to think of the different jobs that they know of and make a class list. Think about each job in turn. Which category does each belong to?

Newspaper survey: Look at the jobs pages in back copies of your local newspaper. Ask the pupils to take a sample page or issue and classify the jobs advertised into primary, secondary and tertiary. Which category appears most frequently? Can the pupils explain this?

Areas in school: As a class, look at a plan of your school that shows the classrooms, corridors, playground and other spaces. Think about how each space is used. Can the pupils find any areas that are used for primary activities, such as growing food? Are there any workshops, kitchens or places where things are made, representing secondary activities? Tertiary activities, such as learning, eating, keeping fit, playing, and moving about, will almost certainly dominate. Give the pupils blank copies of the school plan and ask them to devise a colour code and key to show how different areas are used.

The pencil industry: Think about the different types of work in the pencil industry:

- Raw materials (graphite and wood) are extracted or grown and gathered (primary activity).

- The pencils are made from strips of wood and lengths of graphite (secondary activity).

- The pencils are delivered to shops by lorry and sold to customers (tertiary activity).

Ask the pupils to fold blank sheets of A4 into three horizontal strips (leaving tabs at the bottom edges for gluing). Now ask them to make drawings and notes to show the three different stages. Finally, fold and glue the paper to make open trapezium models.

Plenary

Discuss with the pupils the type of work that they would like to do when they grow up. Make a class survey and find out what proportion have opted for jobs in each category: primary, secondary and tertiary occupations.

Lesson 3 Trade

How are we are linked to other people through trade?

You will need

- a bag of sugar

- access to the internet

- blank outline maps of Europe showing country boundaries

- an atlas with thematic maps of shipping routes.

Key vocabulary

- barter

- Fairtrade

- goods

- shipping route

- trading bloc

Getting started

As a class, discuss why trade developed. Primitive systems of bartering enabled people to exchange individual items. The transfer of goods and services for money developed into the economic system that we have today. Pupils may have direct experience of swapping toys and other items with each other. Ask them to recall some of the deals that they have made in the past. Hint: Trade and development are complex matters that rarely have simple answers. Encourage the pupils to adopt critical stances as they explore the issues. Fairtrade is not *always* best, and it is not *always* better to buy local as opposed to imported goods.

Class activities

A bag of sugar: Bring a bag of sugar into the class and place it in a prominent position. Explain to the pupils that they are going to find out where the money goes when they buy a bag of sugar from the shops. There are four different roles: farmer, shipper, factory manager and shop manager, so you may need to have two or three groups in each role. Follow the role-play activities in Session 6 in 'Find your way through trade' on the Oxfam website (see Useful books and websites, p. 277). Pupils have to decide how much money each of the four people should get. They are shocked – often outraged – to discover that the farmer gets just 2p for every £1 spent.

Trading games: Organisations such as Oxfam, Save the Children, Christian Aid and CAFOD have all devised trading games to illustrate how producers in poor countries are exploited by trade deals that reward those further along the supply chain. A good example is the paper-bag game available on the Christian Aid website (see Useful books and websites, p. 277). This game explores global issues relating to poverty, unfairness and inequality in a way that children can readily understand. Play one of these games with the children and discuss the possible solutions to present injustices.

Fairtrade: Fairtrade is an organisation that seeks to change the way in which trade works through better prices, decent working conditions and fairer deals for farmers. Pupils may have seen the Fairtrade logo on goods in the shops. Ask them to investigate some Fairtrade products and the stories behind them for short presentations. Invite them to consider the disadvantages as well as the advantages of Fairtrade. Complex issues are usually not clear-cut. Do they think that Fairtrade really does makes a difference, and would they be willing to pay a premium for their goods?

Trade blocs: A trade bloc is a group of countries that agrees to cooperate on trade so that goods can move freely within their borders. The EU is the most important trading bloc in Europe. Ask the pupils to find out more about the aims of the EU. Ask them to show the countries that belong to the EU on blank outline maps of Europe that show country boundaries.

Shipping routes: Look in an atlas to find a map of world shipping routes. Ask pupils to list six or more important routes, saying which countries or regions they link. If time permits, ask pupils to say a few words about what goods might be traded along these routes.

Plenary

Discuss with the class how their lives would be affected if we suddenly stopped trading. What shortages would they experience first? What would be the consequences? Who would be likely to lose their jobs?

Fieldwork and further investigations

- Make a visit to your local high street or nearby shopping centre. Record the name of each shop and note down what it sells using the following codes: (N) newspapers (e.g. newsagents), (F) food, (C) clothes, (D) drinks and meals, (H) household goods, (M) money services, (E) empty and (O) other. Use this information to create a bar chart showing the range of shops in your survey. Is there a pattern and are there any obvious gaps? If possible, make a copy of a large-scale map of the area that you have surveyed. Colour the plan outlines using a different colour for each category. Does the map reveal any additional information about the distribution and range of shops?

Cross-curricular links

English: Ask pupils to imagine that they have been asked by the school governors to draft a job description for a new class teacher in your school. As a class, make a list of essential qualifications, desirable experience and personal qualities. Next, draft a job description using the same headings for a builder who is constructing a new classroom. Discuss differences that emerge.

Mathematics: As a class, create a pie chart to show the values of the commodities traded internationally using the following statistics: oil – 20 per cent, electrical goods – 20 per cent, machinery – 20 per cent, vehicles – ten per cent, plastics – five per cent, other – 25 per cent.

History: Find out about some historical trade routes. One of the most famous is the Silk Road, linking Europe to China across Central Asia.

Themes

Colonialism and social justice: At the start of the twentieth century, European empires dominated the rest of the world, especially Africa, South Asia and the Caribbean. The patterns of trade and politics that date from that time are still evident today. Countries such as Nigeria, India, Jamaica, Australia, Canada and New Zealand retain strong ties with Britain. Meanwhile, France has special connections with West Africa, and the Dutch with Indonesia. You could explore this by getting children to investigate the colonial 'shadow' in a country of their choice.

Sustainability: There is a sequence to the production of non-renewable resources. In the early stages of production, they are often relatively cheap and easy to produce, but in due course they become harder to find and more expensive to access. 'Peak production' occurs in the middle of this process and marks a high point, after which a long period of irreversible decline sets in. It is believed that 'peak oil' has already been reached.

Values and wellbeing: Finding out about global inequalities and how they are perpetuated through trade lays the foundations for a deeper understanding of the modern world. Challenging and confronting gross inequalities is closely linked to developing a respect for democracy and a respect for other people – two fundamental values.

Progression and assessment

By the end of this area of study, pupils will have begun to understand about different types of work, why trade evolved and how it affects their lives. They will also have a growing awareness of global inequalities and how some people in poor nations get paid very little for their produce. Those children who are able to talk about and suggest possible ways of addressing these problems will be moving towards a higher level of achievement.

Useful books and websites

Milway, K. S. (2008), *One Hen: How One Small Loan Made a Big Difference.* London: Kids Can Press (also available on YouTube).

Banana trade teaching resources: search for 'Go bananas Oxfam'.

Fairtrade explained: search for 'Explore Fairtrade Oxfam'.

Interactive game on how people may struggle to earn a living: search for 'Christian Aid paper bag game'.

Teaching resources from the BBC: search for 'BBC Bitesize human geography KS2'.

Trade game: search for 'Find your way through trade Oxfam'.

28 Climate change

What do I need to know?

Climate change is one of the most pressing issues facing humanity at the current time. It is a complex problem because there is no direct link between cause and effect. Pollution that occurs in one part of the world impacts people elsewhere who are distant in both time and space. This means that future generations are set to suffer the consequences of activities undertaken by their ancestors. The poor are especially vulnerable because they lack the resources to protect themselves.

History

It has taken nearly two centuries for scientists to agree that people are causing climate change. The first key discovery came in the 1820s, when Joseph Fourier calculated that the atmosphere was keeping the Earth surprisingly warm, thereby identifying the greenhouse effect. Some 40 years later, John Tyndall showed that water vapour and carbon dioxide do indeed absorb heat. Further research into the nature and causes of climate change in the twentieth century eventually led scientists to conclude that human activity was having a discernible impact on global climate. We now know, despite intensive lobbying from the oil, gas and coal industries, that this is the main cause of the changes that we are witnessing today.

Greenhouse gases

The gases that cause the 'greenhouse effect' include carbon dioxide, nitrous oxide and methane. These act together with other compounds to trap heat from the Sun and stop it radiating back into space. Without these gases, global temperatures would be around 30 degrees centigrade lower than they are at present, and the Earth would not be habitable. However, fossil fuels have been burned so extensively over the last couple of hundred years that this has affected the balance in the atmosphere and enhanced the greenhouse effect.

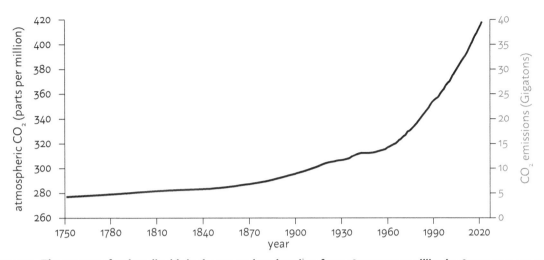

Figure 39: **The amount of carbon dioxide in the atmosphere has risen from 280 parts per million in 1800 to over 400 parts per million today**

There is a hidden risk that, if global temperatures rise by more 1.5 degrees centigrade above pre-industrial levels, there is an ever-greater danger of triggering runaway feedback effects.

Searching for solutions

It is tempting to think that climate change is a technical problem that can be fixed by technology and innovation alone. However, because it has been caused by human action, any lasting solution will depend on changes in human behaviour. This means that it is a moral issue every bit as much as a scientific challenge. Geography has an important part to play in helping us to understand climate change and search for solutions. It highlights links and connections, focuses on change and helps to reveal patterns that would otherwise go unnoticed.

Misconceptions and research

Children sometimes become anxious when they start learning about climate change and what is happening to the planet. However, research suggests that classroom studies can replace unfounded fear with knowledge. Giving children the opportunity to do something positive to make a difference, however small, is also empowering. The key principle is to focus on hope and steer away from gloom-and-doom scenarios.

Interesting facts

- The Earth is now warmer than it has been for thousands of years.
- Scientists calculate past temperatures by studying ice cores from Antarctica and Greenland.
- Global warming is uneven – the Arctic is one area that is warming very fast.

Key questions

(1) What causes climate change?

(2) What can governments do about climate change?

(3) How might climate change affect us locally?

Lesson 1 World climate

Does the world's climate always stay the same?

You will need
- access to the internet
- graph paper
- a map showing climate change.

Key vocabulary
- atmosphere
- carbon dioxide
- climate change
- greenhouse effect
- ice age
- snowball Earth

Getting started

Talk with the children about the difference between weather and climate. The weather varies from day to day and across the seasons. Climate is the long-term weather pattern in a region, calculated from thousands of individual weather readings. There are over a dozen major climate zones around the world. That is one of the reasons why climate change takes many forms and it is has taken scientists a long time to establish that it is happening.

Class activities

Warm and cold periods: Over geological time, there have been huge variations in the Earth's climate. Long warm periods have alternated with periods of extreme cold. At one time, the entire planet was covered in ice. This is known as snowball Earth, when even the equator was ice-bound. At other times, the Earth has sweltered. Around 90 million years ago, for example, there were warm forests at the South Pole and creatures resembling crocodiles lived in the Arctic. Draw a simple graph on the interactive whiteboard to show a repeated pattern of warm and cold periods. There are plenty of images available on the internet that provide references.

Ice age: The last ice age ended around 12,000 years ago. As the ice sheet melted, sea levels rose by more than 100 metres, flooding low-lying areas all over the world. Get the children to search for maps on Google Images showing the extent of the ice sheet. Look especially at the UK. Can you tell whether your school was once beneath the ice? Try to imagine what the climate would have been like at that time.

Greenhouse effect: Talk with the children about how gardeners use greenhouses to keep plants warm. Now explain that so-called 'greenhouse gases' have a similar effect on a global scale. Get the children each to draw two simple diagrams. The first one should show heat from the Sun hitting the Earth's surface, passing through the atmosphere and bouncing back into space. The second diagram should show the same process but with a layer of greenhouse gases in the upper atmosphere. These trap some of the heat as it bounces back, keeping the air warm. The American space agency NASA has produced a useful video for children illustrating what happens (see Useful Books and Website, p. 286).

Carbon dioxide: Carbon dioxide is a key greenhouse gas and it is created by burning fossil fuels such as coal, gas and oil. Here are the data for carbon dioxide levels in the atmosphere (parts per million) over the last 200 years: 1800 – 280, 1850 – 285, 1900 – 295, 1950 – 310, 2000 – 360, 2020 – 415. Get the children to use this information to draw their own graphs to show increases in carbon dioxide levels. Why do they think that this has happened?

Global warming: Look at maps showing global temperature changes over the last 50 years. You can find examples on the internet or in modern school atlases (see Useful books and websites, p. 286). Get the children to look at the maps carefully and write short reports about what they show. They might say what is happening in different continents or at different latitudes, or focus on specific countries and regions such as India, Alaska and the Amazon.

Plenary
Working in groups, ask the children to identify three things that they have learned from this lesson. What has surprised them the most? What are the things about which they would like to learn more?

Lesson 2 Climate emergencies

How is climate change affecting people, plants and creatures?

You will need
- access to the internet
- blank outline world maps.

Key vocabulary
- Arctic
- biome
- climate emergency
- coral reef
- drought
- Overshoot Day
- tropics
- wildfire

Getting started
Climate change is having an increasing impact on both the physical and human environments currently. Compile a list with the children of some of the things that they know about, such as wildfires and floods. Expand the list to include the ways in which people, and especially young people, are responding to the current emergency. This will set the scene for the activities suggested in this lesson.

Classroom activities
In the news: Climate-change emergencies are often in the news these days, as floods, storms, droughts and wildfires affect different parts of the world in unexpected ways. Ask the children to find out about some recent events, perhaps working in groups and reporting back to the rest of the class. Tell them to include suggestions for mitigating or solving each problem, as well as the impact that it has had on people and wildlife.

Melting ice: The Arctic ice cap is an important influence on climate in the Northern Hemisphere, regulating temperatures and weather patterns. As temperatures rise, the amount of ice is quickly diminishing. Children can see this for themselves by researching comparison images (see Useful books and websites, p. 286). They might also explore what this means in human terms. *Melt* (Ele Fountain, 2023) is an urgent story of adventure and survival in a warming climate.

Disrupted wildlife: Climate change is causing problems for plants and animals, disrupting carefully balanced patterns in which young creatures are reared when food supplies are plentiful. Some species are benefitting from greater warmth, but other less-adaptable species are threatened. Show the children some of the excellent videos available on YouTube, searching for 'animals affected by climate change', and discuss what they have learned from them.

Coral reefs on the brink: Coral reefs are an important biome. They are sometimes described as the rainforests of the seas because they support such a huge diversity of plants and creatures. Ask the children to compile fact-files with six or more key facts about why coral reefs matter and the dangers facing them today. You could extend this activity by getting pupils to mark some key coral areas on a blank outline world map and adding lines for the equator and Tropics of Cancer and Capricorn.

Earth Overshoot Day: Earth Overshoot Day is the day each year when the demand that we collectively make for resources and the amount of pollution that we create exceed Earth's capacity. It is getting earlier and earlier each year. Ask the children to draw dials with 12 labelled segments, one for each month. They should then mark overshoot dates using the following data: 1970 – 29 December, 1990 – 3 November, 1990 – 11 October, 2000 – 23 September, 2010 – 8 August, 2023 – 2 August.

Plenary
Discuss with the children what they would say to somebody who knew nothing about the fact that we are witnessing a climate emergency. Draw up a list of the points that they think are most relevant.

Lesson 3 Climate action

How can we respond to climate change?

You will need
- access to the internet
- sticky notes.

Key vocabulary
- carbon footprint
- coral reef
- greenhouse gas
- net zero
- questionnaire

Getting started
Introduce the lesson by discussing the things that pupils might do in response to the climate emergency. Write down all their ideas on the interactive whiteboard, noting the benefit of each one. Emphasise that all actions, however small, make a difference. Climate change is a global problem that we will never solve individually but one for which everyone has some responsibility.

Classroom activities

Carbon footprints: Invite the children to complete a carbon-footprint questionnaire. You will find several different versions online if you search for 'Children's carbon footprint calculator'. Some of these ask questions that are more suitable for grown-ups, while the 'LoveToKnow' questionnaire is well pitched but designed for American youngsters. Talk with the children about whether they agree with the findings and whether they feel prompted to make any changes as a result.

Difficult choices: Discuss how we all have to make difficult choices about how we live our lives. When it comes to climate change, although we may decide to take action to reduce our carbon footprints, we may still end up doing other things that are environmentally damaging. Now give the children sticky notes where they can write down some 'I can do... about climate change but...' statements to put on the wall. Stress once again the value of making *some* changes – perhaps one a year – rather than none at all. This is an honest way in which to recognise the complexities of behaviour change.

Greta Thunberg: Tell the children that they have been asked to devise pieces about Greta Thunberg for a blog or website. Ask them each to write a description of her childhood, devise some bullet points about what she has achieved and include at least two photographs. How effective do they think that Greta has been in raising climate-change awareness, and do they agree with her campaign for school climate-change strikes?

Net zero: The UK has adopted legally binding targets to achieve net zero by 2050. Put simply, this means cutting greenhouse-gas emissions as much as possible, so that any remaining emissions can be reabsorbed – for instance, by oceans and forests. What might net zero mean in practice? Divide the children into groups, giving each group one of the following headings to consider: (a) travel, (b) food, (c) clothes, (d) water, (e) energy or (g) housing. Ask them to report on their conclusions to the rest of the class.

Climate-change fund: Tuvalu is a Pacific Ocean island nation made up of coral reefs and atolls, which could disappear completely as sea levels rise. In 2022, it was agreed at an international conference (COP 27) to establish a fund for countries suffering from a problem that they didn't cause. Find out what other countries are at risk as sea levels rise. Discuss how much money and help children think that they should be given.

Plenary

Has your school declared a climate emergency? If so, find out what was agreed and the action that has resulted. If not, work with the children to devise a declaration. It will need an opening that describes the problem, a set of actions that could realistically be undertaken or targets to be achieved, and some indicators to show what has happened.

Fieldwork and further investigations

- As they undertake this area of study, pupils will identify some of the things that they can do in and around the school that could help to reduce its carbon footprint. These might include monitoring energy use, thinking about and changing the way in which they travel to school, setting up a school garden or reducing food waste. Discuss how their ideas have changed as a result of the work that they have done in this area of study. What do they now think are priorities and what can they do to put them into action? Making links with outside organisations that promote climate change is a natural next step.

Cross-curricular links

English: Set up a debate about climate change in which pupils argue for and against mobilising all available resources to deal with climate change and the problems that it is creating.

Science: Convection currents are one of the key dynamics underpinning the science of climate change. To demonstrate how convection currents operate, provide the pupils with some cubes of frozen coloured water and get them to observe and record what happens when they place their cubes in cold water. The circulation that is established on a very small scale is replicated on a continental scale in ocean currents, illustrating both cycles and interconnections.

Design and technology: There are many ingenious proposals to harness technology in order to address climate change. One idea is to build massive solar farms in the Sahara Desert to generate electricity for countries in Europe. Another is to inject millions of tonnes of sulphur into the high atmosphere to deflect sunlight. Pupils could investigate these and other options, commenting on their feasibility.

RE: What responsibility do those who are burning fossil fuels today have to the people of the future? Climate change raises important questions about intergenerational equity, which children can explore through discussion.

Themes

Colonialism and social justice: Attempts to reach international agreement on climate change are hampered by inequalities between nations. The small island states especially have banded together in order to get their voices heard. Despite this, post-colonial power relations are all too evident in current negotiations.

Biodiversity: Climate change is not a problem that can be viewed in isolation. It links to many other issues, including biodiversity. This is illustrated in a positive way by trees, which both remove carbon dioxide from the air and provide food and shelter for creatures.

Values and wellbeing: Learning about and investigating climate-change issues challenges children to consider how they want to live their lives and what sort of people they want to be when they grow up.

Progression and assessment

By the end of this unit, children will have learned about how climate change is affecting their lives and identified some of the actions that they could take to mitigate its impact. They will have considered their responsibilities to others and reflected on their own values and principles. At a deeper level, they will have begun to identify multiple links and connections. Recognising that there are no simple ways of addressing climate change is an indicator of more-mature thinking and deeper reflection.

Useful books and websites

MacDibble, B. (2018), *How to Bee.* Pulborough, West Sussex: Old Barn Books.

Fountain, E. (2023), *Melt.* London: Pushkin Press.

Prentice, A. and Reynolds, E. (2021), *Climate Crisis for Beginners.* London: Usborne.

Scoffham, S. (ed) (2023), *Collins Junior Atlas* (6th edn). London: Collins.

Stevens, G. and Rewse, K. (2021), *Climate Action.* London: Little Tiger.

Arctic sea ice: search for 'Arctic sea ice comparison maps' on Google Images.

Climate-change teaching resources: search for 'Stories of climate change Oxfam'.

Greenhouse effect: search for 'Greenhouse effect NASA' on YouTube.

Global warming maps: search for 'Global warming map 2020' on Google Images.

29 Settlement and migration

What do I need to know?

There are nearly eight thousand million people in the world today. Some parts of the world are empty, while others are very congested. About one third of the land is covered by desert and a similar proportion is covered by ice and rock. This means that well over half the world's dry land is more or less uninhabitable and that most people crowd together in what remains. The highest population densities are to be found in lowland regions, where people can grow crops, keep animals and build houses easily. Coastal areas are particularly favoured, partly because of the abundance of fish but also due to trade and commerce. It is no coincidence that many of the world's largest cities are located either on the coast or on navigable rivers.

Since they first evolved, people have always moved around the world in search of better living conditions. Anthropologists think that the first human beings evolved in the Great Rift Valley in Africa, from where they spread to neighbouring areas around 1.5 million years ago. The movement of people out of Central Asia is long-term theme in recorded history. In the last few centuries, large numbers have emigrated to the Americas and Oceania, fuelling the development that has made the USA the world's most powerful country. More recently, Australia has also seen a considerable influx. After the Second World War, for example, around one million Britons went to live there, attracted by the assisted passage scheme.

With few exceptions, migration is fuelled by differentials. Some migrations are voluntary, while others are forced. People move for a range of reasons: political, economic and social. They may also move legally or illegally. It is difficult enough to gather information about international migration, but it is even harder to be certain about the scale of migration within countries. It is estimated, for example, that there are several hundred million migrant workers in China today and that they account for around one-fifth of the population of many Chinese towns and cities, but numbers are very imprecise and the boundaries between categories are necessarily vague.

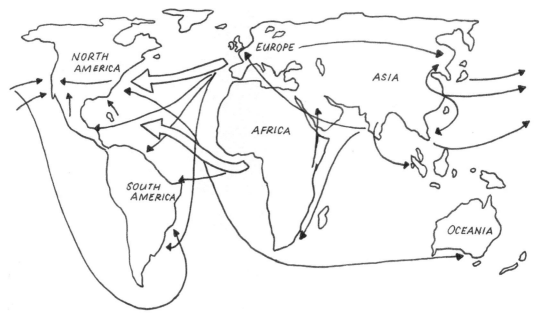

Figure 40: Over the past 300 years, many people have migrated from Europe, Asia and Africa to the Americas and Oceania

People who seek protection outside their countries and successfully apply for asylum are granted refugee status. Many refugees flee conflict rather than direct persecution. They also tend to travel relatively short distances to nearby countries. Despite the impression given in the media, the majority of refugees in the Middle East go to Turkey, Pakistan, Lebanon and Iran rather than to Europe. East and Central Africa is another area where there are currently large numbers of refugees, most of whom have been displaced from neighbouring countries.

Around the world, migration is intersecting with globalisation, conflict and long-term climate change to bring about irreversible social, cultural and economic changes. In the years ahead, it seems likely that the movement of people (either voluntary or forced) will continue to increase, and that growing numbers of women and children will be involved. However, it is also worth noting that there is also a trend for migrants to return home after a period abroad. Circular migration of this kind adds yet another dimension to a very complex picture.

Misconceptions and research

Migration, immigration and changes in population are topics that are never out of the news and that evoke strong feelings in many people. This unit of study aims to build children's understanding by looking beyond contemporary events and helping them to appreciate larger patterns and forces. It will be important to challenge any negative or potentially racist ideas that pupils may express. This is often best done quietly so as to avoid confrontation. Children sometimes unthinkingly repeat what they have heard other people saying. Appealing to the facts and their senses of fairness and humanity are good starting points.

Interesting facts

- More than one-third of the people living in London today were born overseas.
- Migrants sometimes go to live and work abroad for a while but then return to their home countries.
- There are more refugees in the world today, displaced by war and persecution, than ever before.

Key questions

1. Is there a maximum size for cities or will they go on growing ever larger?
2. Does it matter if someone doesn't belong to any particular country and is stateless?

Lesson 1 Settlement patterns

Do settlements have a pattern?

You will need
- access to the internet
- an atlas
- blank world maps.

Key vocabulary
- pattern
- population
- satellite image
- skyline

Getting started

As a class, discuss what we mean by 'pattern'. What patterns can pupils find in the classroom, on their clothes or on the things that they carry with them? Explain that the houses and buildings in towns and cities are arranged in patterns. There is also a pattern of settlement in a country or region. Some areas are crowded, while others will be much emptier.

Class activities

Cities from above: Show the pupils some satellite photographs of cities from above. An internet search using 'cities at night from space' will take you to a number of sites containing stunning images from NASA. The structures and patterns of different settlements are clearly revealed in these night-time photographs. London has a marked radial pattern focused on a core, and Los Angeles is based on a grid; meanwhile, Abu Dhabi (United Arab Emirates) appears to have tentacles that reach out into the desert like some strange creature. Download a few of the images that pupils think are particularly significant for a simple class display. Discuss these different patterns and how they might have come about.

UK at night: Ask the pupils to search the internet for images showing the UK at night from space. They need to find one that shows the whole of the country, orientated north–south if possible, so that the outline is clearly recognisable. Ask them to download or save this image. Then, using an atlas to help them, ask pupils to label some of the key cities, such as London, Newcastle, Birmingham and Glasgow.

World cites: The following cities have populations of over fifteen million people: New York, Mexico City, Karachi, Delhi, Mumbai, Kolkata, Dhaka, Shanghai, Beijing and Tokyo. Share this information with the children and ask them to mark and name the cities on blank world maps. Explain that they may need to use leaders (lines linking the labels to the cities) in some instances. Discuss the pattern that emerges. Which continent is most crowded? Which continents have no extremely large cities?

Bigger and bigger cities: Why are cities growing larger and larger? Discuss with the pupils why they think that people might want to move to a city from the countryside (jobs, facilities, opportunity). Explain that these are called 'pull factors'. Next, think of the forces that might drive them out of the countryside (natural disasters, conflict, lack of opportunity). Explain that these are called 'push factors'. Ask the pupils each to make a drawing of a city skyline in a circle in the centre of a page. They should add a large arrow on one side with the push factors listed inside. They should add a large arrow on the other side with a list of pull factors inside.

1801: 1 million people	1901: 6.5 million people	2001: 7.3 million people
1851: 2.4 million people	1951: 8.2 million people	2023: 9.6 million people

Figure 41: London populate growth since 1801

Plenary

Ask pupils to write a single sentence each, saying one thing that they have learned about settlement patterns from this lesson.

Lesson 2 Migration

Why do people migrate?

You will need

- access to the internet

- access to reference books

- paper and materials to make booklets.

Key vocabulary

- immigrant

- migration

- passage

- trail

- trek

Getting started

Explain that when lots of people decide to move at once it is known as 'migration'. The pupils will know of some historical examples. For example, the Vikings came to the UK as invaders and settlers over a thousand years ago; before that, the Anglo-Saxons came to Britain from mainland Europe, just as other groups of people had in earlier times. Explain that there is nothing new about migration. People have always moved around the world. The main reason why people migrate is to get a better life. However, they may also be seeking freedom, new opportunities and challenges. Sometimes people are forced to migrate – the Atlantic slave trade is a notorious example.

Class activities

Migrations: Ask pupils to investigate some of the different migrations that have shaped the world in which we live today (see examples in the subsequent activities). Divide the class into groups and ask each group to compile a booklet with eight pages about their chosen example. Explain that all the booklets need to include: a map, the reasons for the migration explained, a description of the journey (eyewitness accounts are best) and some images. They may find other material, such as stories, songs, paintings and photographs, which they may decide to include. The hardships and dangers that people endured and the courage that they showed are likely to catch the children's imagination. The internet is a particularly good source of information. Reference books will also be useful.

The Oregon Trail: The Oregon Trail led westward for 2,000 miles from the Missouri river across the Rocky Mountains to the rich farmlands on the west coast of the USA. Over 400,000 settlers, farmers, ranchers, fur traders and miners travelled along the trail in wagons during the nineteenth century. The accounts that they have left are a reminder of the great cold and hardships that they suffered in the mountains.

The Great Trek: The Great Trek occurred in the 1830s and 1840s, as Dutch colonists migrated north from Cape Colony, South Africa, to find freedom in the interior of Africa. It was an arduous and dangerous journey, which involved crossing ravines and rivers and encountering hostility from others.

The Atlantic slave trade: The Atlantic slave trade that flourished from the seventeenth to the nineteenth centuries involved many European nations, especially Britain and France. Altogether, around twelve million Africans were captured and forced to work as slaves in the USA and other parts of the Americas and Oceania. The ships that undertook this awful trade ventured down the west coast of Africa, laden with goods that were then traded for enslaved people. They returned to Europe with cotton from the plantations. The north-east 'trade winds' and mid-latitude westerlies provided a natural source of power.

The Windrush: After the Second World War, immigrants were encouraged to come to Britain from Commonwealth countries to help to solve the labour shortage. Large numbers arrived from the Caribbean, fundamentally changing British society. There are numerous newspaper reports documenting the process. One event that proved particularly famous was the arrival in London in 1948 of a boat called the *Windrush*, with 492 migrants aboard.

Emigration to Australia: Between 1945 and 2007, some 6.5 million people migrated to Australia, encouraged by the government policy of boosting the population by one per cent a year. To begin with, Britons were especially favoured and were able to benefit from an assisted passage scheme, which meant that they only had to pay a fare of £10 (about £380 in value, at the time of writing) for their travel. Altogether, around two million people left the UK and settled in Australia over this period.

Plenary
Display the pupils' booklets in the corridor or some other part of the school where other children can see them and learn about migrations in different parts of the world.

Lesson 3 Refugees

What happens to refugees?

You will need
- a newspaper article about migration or refugees
- an atlas or electronic world map.

Key vocabulary
- inequality
- migration
- refugee
- United Nations (UN)

Getting started
As a class, discuss the ways in which people move house and go to live in different places. Have any pupils moved recently? Did they come a long distance or did they move locally? Explain that sometimes people have to leave their homes in a great hurry to escape danger. This often happens when there is a war or natural disaster.

Class activities
Refugee numbers: There are over sixty million people in the world today who have been forced to flee their homes and are now refugees. Make a bar chart to show the main countries of origin. Either research the latest data to give to the pupils yourself or use the following figures, which are the best available at the time of writing. Syria – 4.5 million, Afghanistan – 2.6 million, Somalia – 1.1 million, South Sudan – 0.7 million, Sudan – 0.6 million. Find these countries in an atlas or electronic world map.

Newspaper reports: Find a recent newspaper article about migration or refugees. Many reports use emotive language and give a biased, rather negative impression. Ask pupils to go through the article in pairs and highlight adjectives and adverbs. Can they spot any similes and metaphors? Ask them to think about the impression that the article is trying to give. Then get them to reread the article and to make a list of verifiable facts. Can they think of a way of recasting the story in a more positive light?

United Nations High Commissioner for Refugees (UNHCR): Find out about the work and activities of the UNHCR. Explore their website in advance of the lesson (see Useful books and websites, p. 296) and select a video that tells the story of a refugee and how they have coped with the challenges that they face. How far did they have to travel?

Refugee story: Introduce the pupils to the story of a refugee family by reading them *The Journey* (see Useful books and websites, p. 296). Discuss what it must be like to leave everything behind and travel to somewhere unfamiliar and strange. Ask pupils to make short picture sequences about the journey that is told in the book. Many of the illustrations used in the book are available on the internet, which makes them easier to share with the class.

World family: According to the video 'If the world were 100 people', if there were just 100 people in the world, one of them would be a refugee and one would be as rich as the other 99. Watch the YouTube video or use information from *If the World Were a Village* by David J. Smith (see Useful books and websites, p. 296). Discuss the problems that inequalities can cause. What might be done to make the world more equal?

Plenary

Ask pupils to work in pairs or small groups to make small presentations about refugees to share with the rest of the class, using visual information as well as the spoken word. Stress from the outset that the emphasis should be on stories of hope, rather than problems and challenges for which there are no obvious solutions.

Fieldwork and further investigations

- As a class, discuss what people need in order to survive. Water, warmth, food, fresh air and waste disposal are some of the most important considerations. Communications and recreation also need to be taken into account. Ask the pupils to design survival capsules for sustainable living. Challenge them to think imaginatively about how their capsules will protect them from extreme conditions and how they can make maximum use of recycling and thus become more or less self-sustaining.

Cross-curricular links

English: Divide the class into pairs and ask each pair to make a list of a dozen essential things that they would take with them if they suddenly had to move out of their homes to other places. Compare the pupils' responses around the class.

Mathematics: Ask pupils to make block graphs showing how the number of people living in London has increased since 1801, using data from the table in **Figure 41** (see p. 290) and a scale of one column centimetre per million people.

History: Create a timeline stretching from 100 BC to the present day, showing some of the main waves of immigration into the UK.

Religious education: One of the themes that runs through religious texts is the mass movement of people searching for home lands: the 'exodus' is the story of tribes of Israel moving around what is now the Middle East. Revisit this story with the class and ask pupils to portray the story in a booklet, along with the other migration stories that they have already researched.

Themes

Colonialism and social justice: In the past, most European settlers simply appropriated the lands that they colonised. What has happened in New Zealand suggests, to some extent, an alternative. There, although land has not been returned, the Maori have retained certain rights, they are widely respected and their culture and values are enshrined in law. One way in which to explore this is through place names. What was known as 'Mount Cook' is now officially called Aoraki and 'New Zealand' is called Aotearoa. Another example of reparation attempts is provided by those for the First Nations in Canada.

Climate change: Climate change is starting to bring disruption to many parts of the world and displacing people who are affected by extreme weather conditions. Sea-level rise is a particular issue for small island states, where coral reefs and fish stocks are also in decline. As well as identifying these countries on a world map, consider what might happen to the people who live there if these problems get worse. What responsibilities do we have towards them?

Personal development: This area of study encourages pupils to take a global perspective and think of the human family as a whole rather than as isolated individuals. It is our common humanity that binds us together and that provides a source of strength when it comes to exploring issues relating to migration and forced displacement.

Values and wellbeing: As a class, prepare and present an assembly for the rest of the school on refugees and the challenges that they face. See that all the children are involved and that values such as compassion and humanity are communicated clearly within a positive and constructive setting.

Progression and assessment

By the end of this area of study, all children will have learned about settlement patterns and the ways in which they are changing. They will have learned that people have migrated from place to place throughout history. They will also have learned how people become refugees and about some of the challenges that they face. Those who are working at higher levels of achievement will have begun to appreciate how human geography can help us to better understand migration issues.

Useful books and websites

Jamieson, V. and Mohamed, O. (2020), *When Stars are Scattered*. London: Faber and Faber.

Sanna, F. (2016), *The Journey*. London: Flying Eye Books.

Scoffham, S. (ed) (2023), *Colllin Junior Atlas* (6th edn). London: Collins.

Smith, D. (2018), *If the World Were a Village*. London: Bloomsbury Educational.

Charter of Human Rights: search for 'Amnesty International Charter of Human Rights simplified'.

United Nations Commissioner for Refugees (UNHCR): www.unhcr.org/uk

See also resources from Oxfam, Save the Children and the Refugee Council.

30 Sustainable living

What does the curriculum say?

A high-quality geography education should inspire in pupils a curiosity and fascination about the world and its people that will remain with them for the rest of their lives. Teaching should equip pupils with knowledge about diverse places, people, resources and natural and human environments, together with a deep understanding of the Earth's key physical and human processes. As pupils progress, their growing knowledge about the world should help them to deepen their understanding of the interaction between physical and human processes, and of the formation and use of landscapes and environments. Geographical knowledge, understanding and skills provide the frameworks and approaches that explain how the Earth's features at different scales are shaped, interconnected and change over time.

What do I need to know?

There is consistent and overwhelming evidence that the planet is under increasing ecological and environmental stress. Most people are now aware of the dangers of climate change and the threats that this poses to human and natural systems. We are witnessing a huge decline in wildlife and biodiversity around the world, epitomised by the clearance of the Amazon rainforest. At the same time, human numbers have increased from around three billion in 1960 to nearly eight billion in 2023. These factors are interacting and reinforcing each other in a surprising and unpredictable manners. Finding ways of living within planetary limits is an increasingly urgent concern and one that seems set to dominate the lives of the children who are currently at school.

Geography provides opportunities for children to explore sustainability in meaningful and purposeful contexts. The purpose of the National Curriculum is for children to develop a 'deep understanding of the Earth's key human and human processes'. It also aspires to develop their understanding of interaction and change over time. These are key concepts that span disciplines and subject areas.

Sustainability

'Sustainability' itself is a term with complex and contested meanings. At the simplest level, it is concerned with notions of interdependence and quality of life. These can be as measured through environmental, economic and social indicators, which operate at a range of scales from the local to the global. Sustainability also involves a concern with the future wellbeing of our planet and its inhabitants. This raises questions about equity and justice, as well as our responsibility to future generations.

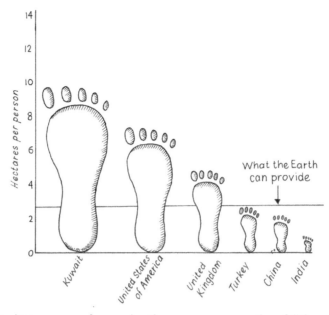

Figure 42: Ecological footprints are a way of comparing the resource consumption of different countries

Thinking about sustainability and how what we do today may have long-term implications involves a great deal of uncertainty. It is difficult to balance the needs of the present against future possibilities and to take into account the values and aspirations of different societies. Sustainability is challenging but it provides a vital lens through which to interpret the geography curriculum. Children will be better equipped to think about life choices and make sound decisions if they have a wide range of information and views at their disposal about how the world works. Learning from other people and cultures is also a reciprocal part of sustainability and helps to avoid taking a stereotypical stance or adopting a charity mentality.

Misconceptions and research

Children may think that climate change is beneficial and that it will bring warmer weather, allowing them more time to be outside and bask in the warmth from the Sun. They don't realise that it actually causes more unpredictable weather, as energy is channelled into complex climate systems. More negatively, they may worry about the state of the planet, as they pick up anxieties from media outlets. Learning about what is happening empowers them to be active decision-makers and provides the basis for grounded optimism and hope.

Interesting facts

- Between 1970 and 2018, average populations of the wildlife species studied by the World Wildlife Fund decreased by 69 per cent.
- After years of debate, scientists are now certain that humans are the dominant cause of the climate change that has happened since the 1950s.
- Unless average global temperature rise is limited to 1.5 degrees, climate change is likely to be the main reason for wildlife loss in coming decades.

Key questions

1. How can we look after ourselves as well as the environment?
2. How are local choices that we make connected to global issues?
3. What kind of future do we want?

Lesson 1 Exploring sustainability

What does sustainability mean?

You will need
- kitchen paper
- a set of photographs showing different examples of sustainability.

Key vocabulary
- campaign group
- carbon footprints
- charity shop
- community
- environment
- food miles
- recycle
- sustainability

Getting started

Divide the class into groups to discuss what they think sustainability means. In their groups, they should agree on and write down five key words or very short phrases. Now challenge each group to make a sentence about or definition of sustainability that uses the words that they have identified. Ask them to write their definition in large letters on a large sheet of paper for a class display and talk about the different views that the groups have expressed. Are there any obvious gaps or omissions? How many of the definitions talk about values and caring?

Class activities

Animals in our lives: Divide the class into groups and ask each group to make a list of creatures that they have seen recently. As well as household pets, they will probably immediately think of birds. Remind them to consider smaller creatures, such as ants, flies, wasps, bees and centipedes. Compare lists around the class, making the point that we share the Earth with lots of other creatures and they all enrich our lives in different ways. Extend the activity to include animal characters from stories and films.

Community links: How does your school contribute to the local community? See whether you can make new links with a local community group and perhaps invite a representative to visit the class to talk about their work. As a follow-up, you might be able to arrange a class visit to their premises. Building community links is part of sustainable living.

Food miles: Explain to the pupils that the distance that food travels to reach our shops and homes is known as 'food miles'. Investigate where the food in the school canteen comes from and map its origins on a world map. Could the same or similar foodstuffs be sourced locally? Discuss the advantages of using local suppliers, but remember that farmers overseas sometimes use less fuel or more-environmentally friendly practices than in the UK.

Carbon footprints: Ask pupils to investigate their 'carbon footprints'. An internet search using the term 'carbon footprint calculator' will take them directly to a number of sites. Select two or more calculators and ask pupils to compare their own results. What does each one tell them about their carbon footprint? How effective do the pupils think that each calculator actually is?

Sustainability photographs: Show the pupils a range of photographs on the interactive whiteboard that relate to sustainability. Examples might include a herd of cows, apple blossom, a shoal of fish, a house made of wood, people riding bicycles, a wind turbine, recycling bins, a water butt and an electric car. Discuss each image with the class. Finish with a photograph of a ploughed field. In what different ways are we connected to the soil?

Plenary

Does living in a more-sustainable way mean that we have to sacrifice the things that we want? Alternatively, does it mean being more thoughtful, consuming less and being better informed? Find out what the pupils think about this dilemma. Do they think that they have any right to tell others how to live their lives?

Lesson 2 Sharing the world's riches

Do we live in a fair world?

You will need

- access to the internet
- a class copy of *If the World Were a Village.*

Key vocabulary

- global
- income
- inequality
- life expectancy
- population
- wealth

Getting started

Ask the pupils whether they can name anyone who is a millionaire. Would they like to be very rich and what would they buy if they had lots of money? How would this affect their lives? Initiate a discussion about whether money always brings happiness. Are there things that we value that simply cannot be bought? Talk about the drawbacks as well as the advantages of having lots of money.

Class activities

Rich and poor: Explain to the pupils that around the world a few people have enormous amounts of money but that lots of people are very poor. Make it clear that there are great differences of wealth in every country, but that some countries are, on average, much richer than others. Working in pairs or small groups, ask pupils to make lists of the things that they think are essential for survival, the things that they would really like to have but can't afford at the moment, and other things that they would buy if they had lots of money. Distinguish between luxuries and essentials as you compare ideas around the class taking care to avoid inequalities between individual children.

Inequalities: Read to the pupils *If the World Were a Village* (see Useful books and websites, p. 306). This book provides statistics on themes ranging from water to life expectancy in a way that primary-school children can readily comprehend. Extend the activity by projecting and discussing some of the images from the book on the interactive whiteboard. Some pupils may well be surprised or shocked by the comparisons. Talk about how inequalities arise and remind them that the data are based on averages. What can we do to ensure that the world becomes fairer for disadvantaged people?

Divided world: Find an image on the NASA website that shows lights on Earth at night from space (see Useful books and websites, p. 306). Ask pupils to work in pairs as geography detectives to say as much as they can about global energy use. Ask them to focus on each continent in turn and to note any patterns that they can see. Do some continents appear to use much more energy (are they more brightly illuminated) than others?

Worldmapper: Worldmapper is a collection of world maps structured around themes. This means that, rather than showing countries and continents according to their geographical areas, Worldmapper shows them according to the sizes of their populations, the income that people receive, how long people live and so on. Ask pupils to explore these maps or look at them as class on the interactive whiteboard (see Useful books and websites, p. 306). Discuss what the maps show and how the UK compares to other countries. It will take pupils a while to get used to seeing this approach, so allow time for them to revisit the site on a regular basis if possible.

Plenary

The Indian leader Mahatma Gandhi once said, 'The world has enough for everyone's need, but not enough for everyone's greed.' Use this famous saying to structure a class discussion. The world now has three times the number of people as there were when Gandhi was alive. Are there still enough resources for everybody in the world today? Will there always be rich and poor people? Is it practical to think that wealth could be shared more evenly?

Lesson 3 Global futures

What kind of future do we want?

You will need

- paper and pens
- atlases and globes
- access to the internet.

Key vocabulary

- choice
- community
- futures
- planning
- sustainable

Getting started

Ask the pupils how they think that the world will change in ten, 50 or 100 years' time and discuss the options that come up. Ask them to focus on different scenarios. What do they think is likely to happen (probable) and what would they like to happen (possible)? Explain that, even though the news can sometimes seem bad, the future is not fixed. The choices that we make really do make a difference.

Class activities

The future we want: Ask pupils to design graphics showing their visions for the future and the world that they want. Ask them to think about how they would tackle some of the issues of which they are aware and what solutions they might come up with. Or, if they have no immediate solutions, which do they think are the most pressing issues to be solved?

Planning for the future: Working in groups, ask pupils to create long-term plans for looking after the school and its grounds, with actions and suggestions that they can take to the governors. Ask pupils to think of useful headings and categories, such as energy and water use, relationships, biodiversity, food and transport. How will what they suggest lead to improvements in the future? Discuss how long-term benefits are often costly in the short term. For example, solar panels are expensive to install and new trees take many years to mature. However, they are both likely to improve the school in the years ahead.

School links: Investigate existing links (or the possibility of creating new links) with other schools in parts of the UK or the wider world, to exchange information about how they are caring for their environment and thinking about the future. You might also swap ideas about their visions for the future. Do they have the same ideas about what they want the world to be like as you do?

Good news stories: Investigate newspapers and the internet for 'good news' stories about how people are improving their lives, both in the UK and in other parts of the world. How are they responding to environmental problems? What new inventions and technologies are being employed? The aid agencies often provide portraits of how individuals benefit from support and intervention. You could use these stories as the basis for a class assembly.

Plenary

Ask pupils to form a line across the classroom and stand somewhere along it according to whether they think that the choices that they make can help to create a better future. One end of the line represents a strong belief that their actions can change things for the better, and the other end represents the belief that the future is fixed and nothing much can be done to change it. Discuss the results and choose individuals to ask why they stood where they did.

Fieldwork and further investigations

- As a class, think about your school and local streets. Are there any places that the pupils particularly value or that they think are special in some way or other? Are there any buildings or features that they think are worth preserving? Investigate whether there are any places locally that have been listed by the local council for their architectural or historical interest. Arrange a fieldwork visit so that pupils can draw and make notes about special places. Link this work to an outline map of the area on returning to school.

Cross-curricular links

English and science: Ask pupils to design and create leaflets on the best tips for energy or water saving, along with accompanying illustrations. Select the best ideas to compile as a class leaflet. Add the school logo and upload the leaflet to the school website, or email it home with the school newsletter.

Mathematics: Using *If the World Were a Village* (see Useful books and websites, p. 306), ask the pupils to convert the data for six key themes into percentages and to present this information either in bar graphs or in pie charts. Ask them to write a sentence or two about each one.

> **Religious education:** Sustainability raises fundamental questions about what we value and treasure. It also challenges us to consider our responsibility to other people around the world and to those who are not yet born but who will inherit the Earth from us in the future. These are issues that pupils can usefully discuss in RE and that relate directly to a sense of global justice.

Themes

Biodiversity: Talk with the children about the global targets for biodiversity that were agreed in 2022 at the COP 15 Convention in Montreal. These include, by 2030:

- effective conservation and management of at least 30 per cent of the world's lands and oceans
- restoring at least 30 per cent of degraded waterways and coasts
- cutting global food waste in half
- halving the risk from dangerous pesticides and chemicals
- targeting invasive alien species
- setting up a fund to pay for projects.

Put the children in groups to discuss what biodiversity targets they would set for themselves and the school community.

Sustainability: The United Nations Sustainable Development Goals (SDGs) set out 17 interrelated goals for a peaceful and prosperous planet. Working in pairs, ask the children to investigate a different goal each. They should then report back to the rest of the class, explaining the goal that they have studied and saying what they think about it. Are there any other goals that need to be added?

Values and wellbeing: As we head into increasingly troubled times, we all have to decide what we think about sustainability and the way in which it impacts on our lives. This challenges us to think about our personal beliefs and values. Fundamentally, if we love the world around us in all its diversity, we want to respect and care for it. This mindset can be developed particularly strongly through practical action and engagement with nature. This is another powerful reason to undertake fieldwork and first-hand investigations as an integral part of the 'life message' that children will take with them from their primary-school years.

Progression and assessment

By the end of this unit, all children will have learned that sustainability involves thinking about quality of life now and in the future and that they can make simple choices that will affect that future. They will all have had opportunities to apply their geographical knowledge to identify how we live in an unequal world, where access to different key resources varies enormously. Those working at a higher level of achievement will have used enquiry and critical-thinking skills to consider how information is portrayed, and will feel confident in suggesting some solutions to everyday issues and problems.

Useful books and websites

Morpurgo, M. (1999), *Kensuke's Kingdom*. London: Heinemann.

Cole, S. (2020), *World Burn Down*. Edinburgh: Barrington Stoke.

Kemp, N. and Scoffham, S. (2022), 'What is sustainability, why is it important and what does it mean for my teaching?', in C. Carden (ed), *Primary Teaching* (2nd edn). London: SAGE, pp. 473–483.

Scoffham, S. and Rawlinson, S. (2022). *Sustainability Education: A Classroom Guide*. London: Bloomsbury Academic.

Smith, D. (2018), *If the World were a Village: A Book about the World's People*. London: Bloomsbury Educational.

WWF Living Planet Report (2022), www.wwf.org.uk/sites/default/files/2023-05/WWF-Living-Planet-Report-2022.pdf

Biodiversity targets: search for 'COP15 global biodiversity framework'.

NASA lights at night: www.earthobservatory.nasa.gov/features/NightLights

Sustainable energy solutions: www.ashden.org

Worldmapper: www.worldmapper.org

Resources

Key mapping programs

Arc GIS: A free mapping program with annotation capability, data search and data-import functions. www.arcgis.com

Google Earth: Digital imagery and 3D views of Earth (ocean and space views also available). https://earth.google.com/web

OS Digimap for Schools: A subscription-based digital mapping program for Great Britain, with additional aerial imagery from the Ordnance Survey, a historical layer and annotation tools. Maps are at different scales, including topographical level, and maps can be printed or saved digitally. www.digimapforschools.edina.ac.uk

Worldmapper: Data about the world, from life expectancy to fuel use, communicated on maps relative to comparative territory size. www.worldmapper.org

Other mapping programs

Bing maps: A free mapping program. www.bing.com/maps

Cloud spotting: An online guide to different cloud types and where they might be found in the sky. www.metoffice.gov.uk/learning/clouds/cloud-spotting-guide

Designing maps: A range of ideas and background reading about different kinds of maps. http://makingmaps.net

Dual maps: A combination of maps and Google Street View imagery to illustrate places. www.dualmaps.com

Earth wind map: Highly visible and updated views of wind patterns around the world, also zoomable. http://earth.nullschool.net

England counties quiz: A mapping quiz to check knowledge of counties in England. http://lizardpoint.com/geography/england-quiz.php

Google Maps: A free mapping program offering Street View. www.google.com/maps

Language of maps: Some helpful ideas about map language for children. http://kidworldcitizen.org/2013/06/02/language-of-maps-kids-should-know

Londonmapper: A social atlas of London. http://london.worldmapper.org

London sounds: A collection of sounds from London of people, places and events. www.soundsurvey.org.uk/index.php

Quikmaps: A free mapping program with some annotation tools. www.quikmaps.com

Scribblemaps: A free mapping program. www.scribblemaps.com

TripGeo: A program that creates animated routes showing Google Street View and Maps together. www.tripgeo.com

Zoom: A short cartoon film exploring the concept of scale and nested hierarchy. www.youtube.com/watch?v=1RPeFJJF73k

Fieldwork techniques

Guidance on:

Fieldwork: https://www.rgs.org/schools/resources-for-schools/local-fieldwork-toolkit www.rgs.org/OurWork/Schools/Fieldwork+and+local+learning/Fieldwork+techniques/Fieldwork+technology/Geotagging.htm

Using a compass: https://www.youtube.com/watch?v=rZdoRfsC-9I

Local area statistics

Place check info: Resource for checking out facts and statuses about local places. www.placecheck.info

Neighbourhood statistics: Data about a neighbourhood from the Office for National Statistics. www.neighbourhood.statistics.gov.ukhttps://www.ons.gov.uk/visualisations/areas

Census data in England and Wales: https://www.ons.gov.uk/census/maps/

Photographs

Piclits: Program for dragging and dropping text from a vocabulary bank to images from around the world. www.piclits.com

Geograph: Photos of the British Isles for schools. http://schools.geograph.org.uk

Word clouds

Tagxedo: A word-cloud program where you can import words into different templates and shapes. www.tagxedo.com

WordArt: A word-cloud program to view most-used words in graphic form. www.wordart.com

Glossary

Aborigines	The first people to inhabit a land or those found living there by colonists.
Aftershock	Small tremors that occur after an earthquake.
Antarctic Circle	The line of latitude south of which places experience continual sunlight in summer (October to February) and continual darkness in winter (March to September).
Aquatic	Relating to water, e.g. an aquatic environment.
Arctic Circle	The line of latitude north of which places experience continual sunlight in summer (March to September) and continual darkness in winter (October to February).
Atlas	A book of maps.
Axis	The imaginary line around which an object spins.
Biome	A community of plants and associated creatures found in a large geographical region.
Capital city	The city that serves as the centre of government for a country.
Catchment	The area or basin from which water flows into a river.
City	With a few exceptions, a very large settlement, which, in the UK, usually has a cathedral.
Climate	A long-term weather pattern established over a period of time (often 30 years).
Coast	Where the land meets the sea.
Commonwealth, the	A group of nations, mostly former British colonies, that works together for their mutual benefit.
Continent	A very large block of land and associated islands.
Country	A territory with its own combination of laws, language, culture and religion.
County	A district in a system of administrative districts found in the UK, which dates back to Norman and Anglo-Saxon times.
Delta	An area of low-lying and often marshy land at the mouth of a river.
Desert	A region, either hot or cold, that is extremely dry and has little or no vegetation.
Earthquake	A violent movement of the Earth's crust caused by forces deep beneath the surface.
Ecosystem	A habitat, viewed with a focus on the relationships between creatures, plants and the environment.
Environment	Our surroundings, varying in scale from the things that surround us to the planet on which we live.
Epicentre	The point on the Earth's surface that is directly above the focus of an earthquake.

Equator	An imaginary line of latitude halfway between the North and South Poles.
Erosion	The processes that wear away the Earth's surface, such as the action of water, ice, wind and Sun.
European Union (EU)	A group of European countries with common economic and social politics.
Fairtrade	Trade agreements that provide reasonable rewards for all those involved and that respect the social welfare of producers.
Fieldwork	Any educational activity undertaken outside the classroom, in the school grounds, local streets or further afield.
Forest	A very large area of trees, either coniferous, deciduous or both.
Fossil fuel	Fuel such as coal, oil and natural gas, created from the remains of trees, plants and animals.
Geographic information system (GIS)	An electronic mapping system that separates and combines different types of data.
Global climate change	Any changes to the climate around the world, but especially the recent rapid changes caused by human activity.
Globe	A model of the Earth often used to show countries or physical features.
Grassland	An extensive area in which grasses predominate.
Habitat	The area that is inhabited by a particular plant, creature or organism.
Hibernation	The process by which animals become dormant and sleep for prolonged periods in order to survive the winter.
Human features	The settlements, roads, factories, farms and other structures that people have built in different parts of the world.
Interdependence	The connections between living things, people, places and processes around the world.
Island	An area of dry land smaller than a continent that is entirely surrounded by water.
Isthmus	A narrow bridge of land connecting two larger areas of land.
Lava	The molten rocks and material that has erupted from a volcano.
Landmark	A distinctive feature, either natural or built, that identifies a route or a region.

Land use	The way in which people use the land, both across geographical areas and over a period of time.
Latitude	A system of measurement for distance in degrees north or south of the equator.
Longitude	A system of measurement for distance in degrees east or west of the prime meridian.
Magma	Molten rocks beneath the Earth's surface.
Map	A drawing that shows the spatial relationship between places.
Map symbol	A stylised drawing used to show features on a map.
Migration	The movement of people or other living things from one part of the world to another.
Mineral	A valuable or useful chemical substance that is formed naturally in the ground, such as gold and iron ore.
Mountain-building	The long-term process by which an area of the Earth's crust is raised up to create mountains.
Mountain range	A group of mountains of roughly similar height arranged in a line.
Natural resources	All the materials that come from the Earth that people find useful.
Net zero	Activities that balance the amount of carbon dioxide that they release into the air with the amount that they remove.
Northern Hemisphere	The area of the Earth that lies to the north of the equator.
Northern Lights	Flickering and twisting lights that appear in the night sky near the North Pole, caused by the interaction of the solar wind and the Earth's magnetic field.
North Pole	The point at the northern end of the Earth's axis.
Ocean	A vast expanse of deep saltwater.
Ordnance Survey	The organisation set up by the government to provide maps of the UK.
Pampas	A grassland biome covering vast areas of South America, especially Argentina.
Physical features	The different elements that make up a landscape, such as mountains, hills, valleys, rivers and coasts.
Place	A space on the Earth's surface of indeterminate size, with personal, cultural and/or geographical meaning.
Pollution	The fumes, noise and waste, created either by people or by natural processes, that damage the environment.
Prime meridian	The line of longitude that goes through Greenwich and from which time is measured.
Region	A geographical area of variable size that has a number of common characteristics.
Relief rainfall	The rainfall that results when air sheds its moisture as it is blown over mountains.
River	The water that flows down a channel from upland to lowland areas.

Savannah	The name for a tropical grassland biome found especially in Africa.
Scale	The amount or ratio by which an area has been shrunk from reality in order to be represented in the available space.
Scale bar	An indication of how distances on a map match distances on the ground.
Season	A period of the year with characteristic weather conditions.
Seismometer	A device that measures and records the vibrations from earthquakes.
Settlement	Any place where people live, such as a hamlet, village, town or city.
Shipping route	The routes that ships take as they move across the sea and ocean.
Southern Hemisphere	The area of the Earth that lies to the south of the equator.
South Pole	The point at the southern end of the Earth's axis.
Sustainability	The ability and ways to live within planetary limits, thereby conserving the environment for future generations.
Taiga	A large region of northern coniferous forest, found especially in Russia and Canada.
Tectonic plates	The sections of the Earth's crust that are carried in different directions by convection currents in the magma underneath.
Temperate climate	A mid-latitude climate where the rainfall and temperatures are not so extreme as in tropical and polar regions.
Trading bloc	A group of countries linked by trade agreements.
Tributary	A stream or river that flows into a larger stream or river.
Tropic of Cancer	The most northerly line of latitude to experience overhead Sun in summer.
Tropic of Capricorn	The most southerly line of latitude to experience overhead Sun in summer.
Tsunami	A long, very powerful wave caused by an earthquake or other disturbance.
Tundra	A cold biome, found especially in the Arctic and high mountain environments, that supports shrubs, mosses and lichens.
United Kingdom	The country made up of England, Scotland, Wales and Northern Ireland.
United Nations (UN)	An organisation that brings together the nations of the world to address common problems, especially war, human rights and economic and social development.
Volcano	An opening in the Earth's crust where red-hot underground rocks and gas break to the surface.
Water cycle	The circulation of water in the atmosphere and on the Earth's surface, triggered by the heat of the Sun.
Weather	The daily combination of temperature, wind, rain and other factors.